PEOPLEMAKING

peoplemaking

by virginia satir

A CONDOR BOOK
SOUVENIR PRESS (E & A) LTD

Peoplemaking by Virginia Satir
Original English language edition

Copyright © 1972 by Science & Behavior Books, Inc.,
Box 11457, Palo Alto, CA 94306, U.S.A.

First published in the U.S.A. by
Science & Behaviour Books Inc.

First British Edition published 1978 by
Souvenir Press (Educational & Academic) Ltd,
43 Great Russell Street, London WC1B 3PA
Reprinted November 1979
Reprinted March 1981
Reprinted June 1982
Reprinted April 1983
Reprinted December 1985
Reissued in paperback 1989
Reprinted 1991
Reprinted 1994
Reprinted 1998

Illustrations by Barry Ives

ISBN 0 285 64872 1

Printed and bound in Great Britain by
The Guernsey Press Co. Ltd, Guernsey, Channel Islands.

To my daughters, Mary and Ruth, and all my family members, including my larger family of all of you all over the world, who helped me to know what family process is all about.

Contents

Foreword

I owe too much of an intellectual and emotional debt to Virginia Satir to make an attempt to be objective in this introduction. I am pleased and excited for you, the anonymous reader, about to embark on a journey that can bring you new understanding and personal growth.

I first met Virginia Satir eleven years ago. She was teaching conjoint family therapy at the Mental Research Institute in Palo Alto. This was the first training program in the country in family therapy. Although my psychiatric training was Orthodox Freudian, her innovative ideas made such an impact on me that I joined her and Don Jackson at the Institute, and in my position as administrative director of the program I had the opportunity to see the effectiveness of her technique. She used one-way mirrors, audio and video tapes, developed games and exercises, and exposed and involved herself in demonstration and simulated family interviews. These techniques have become so widely accepted today that it is easy to lose sight of the creativity that produced them.

I can remember Don Jackson encouraging Virginia to write *Conjoint Family Therapy*. He saw that it would become the basic textbook for family therapy.

After five years, when the family therapy training had achieved a solid foundation, it seemed natural to find Virginia in the forefront of the Growth Potential Movement. There is a center to Virginia that causes her to seek out and assimilate new ideas and techniques. She was the first director of training at Esalen Institute and has played a major role in developing many other growth centers. Almost automatically she incorporated aspects of Sensitivity Awareness, Encounter, and particularly Gestalt psychology. The principles she developed in treating dysfunctional familes now have a broader application as she initiates ways to help all individuals develop their full potential. I remember well a conversation with Fritz Perls shortly before his death when he described Virginia as the most nurturing person he had known.

In reading this book some of you will have a first reaction that it is simple and obvious. In part this is because of the wide dissemination and acceptance of Virginia's ideas. To a greater extent it is because Virginia is like a fine artist or scientist who thoroughly understands the phenomena under study and sees the underlying unifying principles. When an explanation really fits, it comes across with remarkable clarity and familiarity.

Each time you reread this book you will find increasing profundity in its apparent simplicity.

Robert S. Spitzer, M.D.
Publisher

Preface

Seven years ago, I wrote a book called *Conjoint Family Therapy*, which was aimed primarily at professional people who were trying to help families with their pain. Since then I have received many requests for a new book for families that deals with family process. This book is a partial answer to those requests.

Since I don't believe that the last word has been or ever will be spoken about anything, I have continued to experiment with new aspects of *self-worth, communication, system,* and *rules* within the family. I've brought groups of families together in seminars of total living for periods of a week at a time, part of which was a twenty-four-hour continuous contact. What I learned did not invalidate any of the previous family concepts, but greatly embellished them.

All of the ingredients in a family that count are changeable and correctable—individual self-worth, communication, system, and rules—at any point in time. In fact, I would go so far as to say that any piece of behavior at a moment in time is the outcome of the four-way interplay of the person's self-worth and body condition of that moment, his interaction with another, his system, and his place in time and space and situation. If I have to explain his behavior, I have to say something about all these facts, not just one, and then I must also look to see how each part influences the other.

I believe that what is currently going on is the natural consequence of the experience of one's own life. It need bear little or no relationship to either the *awareness* or the *intent* of the individual. Old pains are propagated and made stronger by current interaction about them.

There is hope, then, that anything can change.

Acknowledgments

When I came to thinking about the people who activated and inspired my creativity, I find that there are so many that their individual names would fit a book.

Out of all these people emerge the families and their members who have allowed me free access to their pains and struggles and have therefore brought me to a deeper and more precise understanding of what the human condition is all about. In so doing they have enabled me to write this book.

I wish also to pay tribute to those of my colleagues who have been willing to learn from me and thereby enabled me to learn from them.

I especially want to mention the untiring efforts put forth by Pat Kollings and Peggy Granger with the staff of Science and Behavior Books who gave unsparingly.

1 Introduction

When I was five, I decided that when I grew up I'd be a "children's detective on parents." I didn't quite know what it was I would look for, but even then I realized that there was a lot going on in families that didn't meet the eye. There were a lot of puzzles.

Now, forty-five years later—after working with some three thousand families, ten thousand people—I am finding that there are indeed a lot of puzzles. Family life is something like an iceberg. Most people are aware of only about one-tenth of what is actually going on—the tenth that they can see and hear—and often they think that is all there is. Some suspect that there may be more, but they don't know what it is and have no idea how to find out. Not knowing can set the family on a dangerous course. Just as a sailor's fate depends on knowing about the iceberg *under* the water, so a family's fate depends on understanding the feelings and needs and patterns that lie beneath everyday family events.

Fortunately, through the years I have also found solutions to many of the puzzles, and I would like to share them with you in this book. In the chapters that follow we will be looking at the underside of the iceberg.

In this age of expanding knowledge about the atom, outer space, human genetics, and other wonders of our universe, we are also learning some new things about people's relationships with people. I believe that historians a thousand years from now will point to our time as the beginning of a new era in the development of man, the time when man began to live more comfortably with his humanity.

Over the years I have developed a picture of what the human being living humanly is like. He is a person who understands, values, and develops his body, finding it beautiful and useful; a person who is real and honest to and about himself and others; a person who is willing to take risks, to be creative, to manifest competence, to change when the situation calls for it, and to find ways to accommodate to what is new and different, keeping that part of the old that is still useful and discarding what is not.

When you add all this up, you have a physically healthy, mentally alert, feeling, loving, playful, authentic, creative, productive human being; one who can stand on his own two feet, who can love deeply and fight fairly and effectively, who can be on equally good terms with both his tenderness and his toughness, know the difference between them, and therefore struggle effectively to achieve his goals.

The family is the "factory" where this kind of person is made. You, the adults, are the *people-makers.*

In my years as a family therapist, I have found that four aspects of family life keep popping up in the troubled families who come to me for help. They are—

> the feelings and ideas one has about himself,
> which I call *self-worth;*

> the ways people work out to make meaning
> with one another, which I call *communication;*

> the *rules* people use for how they should feel
> and act, which eventually develop into what
> I call the family system; and

> the way people relate to other people and
> institutions outside the family, which I call
> the *link to society.*

No matter what kind of problem first led a family into my office—whether a nagging wife or an unfaithful husband, a delinquent son or a schizophrenic daughter—I soon found that the prescription was the same. To relieve their family pain, some way had to be found to change those four key factors. In all of these troubled families I noticed that—

self-worth was low;

communication was indirect, vague, and not really honest;

rules were rigid, inhuman, nonnegotiable, and everlasting; and

the linking to society was fearful, placating, and blaming.

Fortunately, I have also had the joy of knowing some untroubled and nurturing families—especially in my more recent workshops to help families develop more fully their potential as human beings. In these vital and nurturing families, I consistently see a different pattern—

self-worth is high;

communication is direct, clear, specific, and honest.

rules are flexible, human, appropriate, and subject to change; and

the linking to society is open and hopeful.

No matter where a surgeon studies medicine, he is prepared to operate on human beings anywhere in the world, because the internal organs and the limbs will be the same. Through my work with families, troubled and nurturing, in the United States, Mexico, and Europe, I have learned that families everywhere have certain working parts in common, too. In all families—

every person has a feeling of worth, positive or negative; the question is,

Which is it?

every person communicates; the question is,

> How, and what happens as a result?

every person follows rules; the question is,

> What kind, and how well do they work
> for him?

every person is linked to society; the question is,

> How, and what are the results?

These things are true whether the family is a *natural* one, where the man and woman who sired and conceived the child continue to care for him until he is grown; a *one-parent* one, where one parent leaves the family by death, divorce, or desertion, and all of the parenting is done by the remaining parent; a *blended* one, where the children are parented by step-, adoptive, or foster parents, not by the persons who brought them into the world; or an *institutional* one, where groups of adults rear groups of children, as in institutions or the modern day commune.

Each of these forms of family has its own special problems in living, and we will return to them later. But bascially, the same forces will be at work in all of them; *self-worth, communication, rules, and linking to society.*

In this book I will talk more about each of these crucial factors, to help you discover how they are operating in your own family and how they can be changed to reduce problems and increase the vitality and joy you can find with one another. Think of my words not as the voice of a so-called expert, but as the accumulated experience of someone who has shared the happiness and sorrow, the hurt and anger and love, of many families.

I am not going to scold anyone in this book. As a

matter of fact, I should probably pin medals on many of you for doing the best you know how with a difficult situation; the very fact that you are reading a book like this tells me that you really care about the well-being of your family. It is my hope, however, that I can give you something more valuable than medals: namely, some new ways to find a better life together as a family.

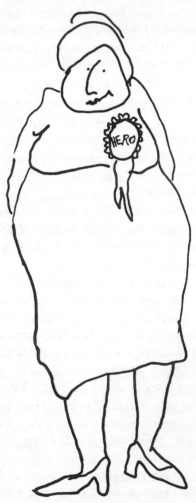

The relationships in a family are extremely complex. To make them a little easier to understand, I will use many *as if*s. These won't add up to the kind of sophisticated model the scholar constructs, but rather they will offer you a variety of ways of looking at your family system, in the hope that you'll find some that have real meaning for you.

As you read, you will come upon suggested experiments or exercises. I hope you will do each one as you come to it, even if at first it seems simple or foolish. Knowing *about* the family system won't change anything. You must learn *how* to make that system work vitally yourself. These experiments are positive, concrete steps your family can take to become less troubled and more nurturing. The more members of your family who take part in them, the more effective they will be. You will begin to *feel* your system working and sense whether it is leading to trouble or growth.

Perhaps you might wonder how to get the rest of your family members to participate in these exercises with you. This might be especially true if ruptures are already occurring in your family.

My suggestion is that you become thoroughly familiar with what you are asking so you will be able to more clearly present your request. If you feel enthusiastic and hopeful about what you think might happen, you will probably communicate a sense of excitement, which will make the invitation attractive and make your family members want to try along with you. By setting your request in a simple straightforward question—Will you participate with me in an experiment that I think might be useful to us?—you maximize the opportunity for a positive response.

The problem most people encounter is that they try to badger or demand or nag their family members to go along with them. This turns the transaction into a power struggle, which usually works in the opposite direction. It is possible that at this point in time, things are so ruptured nothing can be done. The chances are pretty good that if your family members live under the same roof, they will be willing to at least try.

I have seen much pain in families. Each one has moved me deeply. Through this book I hope to ease that pain in families whom I may never have a chance to meet personally. In doing so, I hope also to prevent the pain from continuing into the families their children will form. Some human pain is unavoidable, of course. But as a people, we don't always put our efforts in the right place, to change what we can and to work out creative ways to live with what we can't change.

There is some possibility that just reading this book may evoke a little pain for you. After all, facing ourselves has its painful moments. But if you think there may be a better way of living together as a family than the way you are living now, I think you'll find this book rewarding.

2 What's *Your* Family Like?

Does it feel good to you to live in your family right now?

That question would never have occurred to most of the families I have worked with. Before they came to me, living together was something they just took for granted. If there was no visible family crisis, everyone assumed that everyone else was satisfied with the situation. I suspect many of the individual family members didn't dare face such a question—they felt stuck in the family, for better or for worse, and knew no ways to change things.

Do you feel you are living with friends, people you like and trust, and who like and trust you?

This question has usually brought me the same puzzled replies. "Gee, I've never thought about that; they're just my family"—as though family members were somehow different from people!

Is it fun and exciting to be a member of your family?

Yes, there really are families in which the members find home one of the most interesting and rewarding places they can be. But many people live year after year in families that are a threat to them, a burden, or a bore.

If you can answer "yes" to those three questions, I am certain you live in what I call a *nurturing* family. If you answer "no" or "not often," you probably live in a family that is more or less troubled.

After knowing hundreds of families, I find that each one can be placed somewhere along a scale from *very nurturing* to *very troubled*. The nurturing families are individual ones, yet I see many similarities in the way these families operate. Troubled families, too, no matter what the nature of their visible problems, seem to have much in common. I would like now to draw you a word picture of each type of family, as I have observed them. Of course, neither picture will fit any specific family exactly, but in one or the other you may recognize some part of your own family in action.

The atmosphere in a troubled family is easy to feel. Whenever I am with such a family, I quickly sense that I am uncomfortable. Sometimes it feels cold, as if everyone were frozen; the atmosphere is extremely polite, and everyone is obviously bored. Sometimes it feels as if everything were constantly spinning, like a top; you get dizzy and can't find your balance. Or, it may have an air of foreboding, like the lull before a storm, when thunder may crash and lightning strike at any moment. Sometimes the air is full of secrecy, as in a spy headquarters.

When I am in any of these kinds of troubled atmospheres, my body reacts violently. My stomach feels queasy; my back and shoulders soon ache, and so does my head. I used to wonder if the bodies of the people who lived in that family responded as mine did. Later, when I knew them better and they became free enough to tell me what life was like in their family, I learned that they did indeed feel the same way. After having this kind of experience over and over again, I began to understand why so many of the members of troubled families were beset with physical ills. Their bodies were simply reacting humanly to a very inhuman atmosphere.*

In troubled families the bodies and faces tell of their plight. Bodies are either stiff and tight, or slouchy. Faces look sullen, or sad, or blank like masks. Eyes look down and past people. Ears obviously don't hear. Voices are either harsh and strident, or barely audible.

There is little evidence of friendship among individual family members, little joy in one another. The family seems to stay together through duty, with people just trying to tolerate one another. Now and then I would see someone in a troubled family make an effort at lightness, but his words would fall with a thud. More often

*Perhaps you will find the reactions I describe here surprising. Everybody—every body—has some kind of physical reaction to the individuals around him, but many people are not aware of it. Most of us have been taught as we grew up to 'turn off' these feelings. With years of practice one may turn them off so successfully that he is totally unaware that he is reacting until, hours later, he has a headache or an aching shoulder or an upset stomach. Even then he may not understand why. As a therapist I have learned to be tuned in to these feelings in myself and to recognize the signs of them in my patients. They tell me a good deal about what is actually going on between us. I hope this book will help you learn to recognize these useful clues in yourself.

humor is caustic, sarcastic, even cruel. The adults are so busy telling their child what to do and what not to do that they never find out who he is, never get to enjoy him as a person. As a result, he never gets to enjoy his parents as people, either. It often comes as a great surprise to members of troubled families that they actually *can* enjoy one another.

When I would see whole families in my office who were trying to live together in such an atmosphere, I used to wonder how they managed to survive. I discovered that in some people simply avoided one another; they became so involved in work and other outside activities that they rarely had much real contact with the family.

It is a sad experience for me to be with these families. I see the hopelessness, the helplessness, the loneliness. I see the bravery of people trying to cover up—a bravery that can eventually kill them. There are those who are still clinging to a little hope, who can still bellow or nag or whine at each other. Others no longer care. These people go on year after year, enduring misery themselves or, in their desperation, inflicting it on others.

Traditionally, we have looked upon the family as the place where we could find love and understanding and support, even when all else failed; the place where we could be refreshed and "recharged" to cope more effectively with the world outside. But for millions of troubled families, this is a myth.

In our big urban, industrial society, the institutions we must live with have been designed to be practical, efficient, economical, profitable—but rarely to protect and serve the human part of human beings. Nearly everyone experiences either poverty or discrimination or unrelenting world pressures or other consequences of our inhuman social institutions. For people from troubled families, who find inhuman conditions at home, too, these difficulties are even harder to bear.

No one would intentionally pick this troubled way of living. Families accept it only because they know of no other way.

Stop reading for a few minutes and think about some families you know that would fit the description "troubled." Did the family you grew up in have some of these characteristics? Does the family you are living in now? Can you discover any signs of trouble that you haven't been aware of before?

How different it is to be with a nurturing family! Immediately, I can sense the aliveness, the genuineness, honesty, and love. I feel the heart and soul present as well as the head.

I feel that if I lived in such a family, I would be listened to and would be interested in listening to others; I would be considered and would wish to consider others; I could openly show my affection as well as my pain and disapproval; I wouldn't be afraid to take risks because everyone in my family would realize that some mistakes are bound to come with my risk-taking—that my mistakes are a sign that I am growing. I would feel like a person in my own right—noticed, valued, loved, and clearly asked to notice, value, and love others.

One can actually see and hear the vitality in such a family. The bodies are graceful, the facial expressions relaxed. People look *at* one another, not *through* one another or at the floor; and they speak in rich, clear voices. There is a flow and harmony in their relations with one another. The children, even as infants, seem open and friendly, and the rest of the family treats them very much as persons.

The house where these people live tends to have a lot of light and color. It is clearly a place where people *live,* planned for their comfort and enjoyment, not as a show-place for the neighbors.

When there is quiet, it is a peaceful quiet, not the stillness of fear and caution. When there is sound, it is the sound of meaningful activity, not the thunder of trying to drown out everyone else. Each person seems to know that he will have his chance to be heard. If his turn doesn't come now, it is only because there isn't time—not because he isn't loved.

People seem comfortable about touching one another and showing their affection, regardless of age. The evidence of loving and caring isn't limited to carrying out the garbage, cooking the meals, or bringing home the pay-check. People show it also by talking openly and listening with concern, by being straight and real with one another, by simply being together.

Members of a nurturing family feel free to tell each other how they feel. *Anything* can be talked about—the disappointments, fears, hurts, angers, criticisms as well as the joys and achievements. If Father happens to be bad-humored for some reason, his son can say frankly, "Gee, Dad, you're grouchy tonight." He isn't afraid that Father will bark back, "How dare you talk to your father that way!" Instead, Father can be frank, too: "I sure am grouchy. I had a hell of a day today!" To which his son may reply, "Thanks for telling me, Dad. I thought you might have felt grouchy with me."

Nurturing families show evidence of planning, but if something interferes with the plan, they can readily make adjustments This way they are able to handle more of life's problems without panicking. Suppose, for example, that a child drops and breaks his glass. In a troubled family, this accident could lead to a half-hour lecture, a spanking, and perhaps sending the child away to his room in tears. In a nurturing family, more likely someone would remark,

"Well, Johnny, you broke your glass. Did you cut yourself? I'll get you a Band-Aid, and then you take a broom and sweep up the pieces." If the parent had noticed that

Johnny had been holding the glass precariously, he might add, "I think the glass dropped because you didn't have both hands around it." Thus the incident would be used as

a learning opportunity, which raises the child's self-worth, rather than as a cause for punishment, which puts the self-worth in question. In the nurturing family it is easy to pick up the message that human life and human feelings are more important than anything else.

These parents see themselves as leaders, not bosses, and they see their job as primarily one of teaching their child how to be truly human in all situations. They readily acknowledge to the child their poor judgment as well as their good judgment; their hurt, anger, or disappointment as well as their joy. Their behavior toward him matches what they tell him. (How different from the troubled parent who tells his children not to hurt each other, but slaps them himself whenever they displease him.)

Vital, nurturing parents know they have to *learn* leadership; they didn't get it automatically the day their first child was born. Like all good leaders, they are careful of their timing, watching for an opportunity to talk to their child when he can really hear them. When a child has misbehaved, the father or mother moves physically close to him, to offer him support. This will help the offending child to overcome his fear and guilty feelings, and make the best use of the teaching the parent is about to offer.

Recently, I saw a mother in a nurturing family handle a troublesome situation very skillfully and humanly. When she noticed that her two sons, ages five and six, were fighting, she calmly separated the boys, took each by the hand, and sat down with one son on either side of her. Still holding their hands, she asked each of them to tell her what was going on. She listened to one and then the other intently, and by asking questions she slowly pieced together what had happened: the five-year-old had taken a dime from the six-year-old's dresser. As the two boys talked about their hurts and feelings of injustice, she was able to help them make new contact with one another, return the dime to its rightful owner, and pave the way for better ways of dealing with each other. Furthermore, the boys had a good lesson in constructive problem-solving.

Parents in nurturing families know that their children are not intentionally bad. If someone behaves destructively, they realize that there has been some misunderstanding or someone's self-esteem is dangerously low They know that a child can learn only when he is valuing himself and feeling valued, so they don't respond to his actions in a way that will make him feel devalued. They know that even when it is possible to change behavior by shaming or punishing, the scar that results is not easily or quickly healed.

When a child must be corrected, as all children must at one time or another, nurturing parents rely on listening, touching, understanding, careful timing, being aware of the child's feelings and his natural wish to learn and to please. These things all help them to be effective teachers.

Rearing a family is probably the most difficult job in the world. It resembles a merger of two business firms, putting their respective resources together to make a single product. All the potential headaches of that operation are present when an adult male and an adult female join to steer a child from infancy to adulthood. The parents in a nurturing family realize that problems will come along, simply because life offers them, but they will be alert to creative solutions for each new problem as it appears. Troubled families, on the other hand, put all their energies into the hopeless attempt to keep problems from happening; when they do happen—and, of course, they always do—these people have no resources left for solving them.

Perhaps one of the distinguishing features of nurturing parents is that they realize that change is inevitable: children change quickly from one stage to another, nurturing adults never stop growing and changing; and the world around us never stands still. They accept change as an unavoidable part of being alive and try to use it creatively to make their families still more nurturing.

Can you think of a family that you would call nurturing at least part of the time? Can you remember a time recently when your own family could be described as nurturing? Try to remember how it felt to be in your family then. Do these times happen often?

Some people may scoff at my picture of the nurturing family and say it isn't possible for any family to live that way. To them I would say, I have had the good fortune to know a number of these kinds of families intimately, and *it is possible.* Alas, only four families in perhaps a hundred know how to do it.

Others may protest that with all the pressures of daily living there just isn't time for most people to overhaul their family lives. To them I would say, we had better find the time; *it is a matter of survival.* I consider this our first priority. Troubled families make troubled people and thus contribute to crime, mental illness, alcoholism, drug abuse, poverty, alienated youth, political extremism, and many other social problems. If we don't give our best efforts to developing the family and making people who are more truly human, I see our present social problems growing worse and worse, perhaps ending in extinction for us all.

But if the price of failure is high, so is the reward if we succeed. Everyone who holds a position of power or influence in the world was once an infant. How he uses his power or influence depends a good deal on what he learned in the family as he was growing up. If only we can help troubled families become nurturing—and nurturing ones even more nurturing—the impact of their increased humanity will filter out into government, education, business, religion, all the fields that determine the quality of our lives.

I am convinced that any troubled family can become a nurturing one. Most of the things that cause families to be troubled are learned after birth. Since they are learned, they can be unlearned; and new things can be learned in their place. The question is, how?

First, you need to recognize that your family is a troubled family.

Second, you need to have some hope that things can be different.

Third, you need to take some action to start the changing process.

As you begin to see the troubles in your family more clearly, it will help you to realize that, whatever may have happened in the past, it represented the best you knew how to do at the time. There is no reason for anyone to feel guilty himself or to blame others in the family. The chances are that the causes of your family pain have been invisible to all of you—not because you don't want to see them but because either you don't know where to look for them or you have been taught to view life through mental "glasses" that keep you from seeing certain things.

In this book you will begin to take off those glasses and look directly at the things that cause joy or pain in family life. The first is *self-worth*.

3   Self-Worth: The Pot That Nobody Watches

When I was a little girl, I lived on a farm in Wisconsin. On our back porch was a huge black iron pot, which had lovely rounded sides and stood on three legs. My mother made her own soap, so for part of the year the pot was filled with soap. When threshing crews came through in the summer, we filled the pot with stew. At other times my father used it to store manure for my mother's flower beds. We all came to call it the "3-S pot." Whenever anyone wanted to use the pot, he was faced with two questions: What is the pot now full of, and how full is it?

Long afterward, when people would tell me of their feelings of self-worth—whether they felt full or empty, dirty, or even "cracked"—I would think of that old pot. One day several years ago, a family was sitting in my office, and its members were trying to explain to one another how they felt about themselves. I remembered the black pot and told them the story. Soon the members of the family were talking about their own individual "pots," whether they contained feelings of worth or of guilt, shame, or uselessness.

Before long this simple shorthand word was helping many of my families express feelings that had been difficult to talk about before. A father might say, "My pot is high today," and the rest of the family would know that he felt on top of things, full of energy and good spirits, secure in the knowledge that he really mattered. Or a son might say, "I feel low-pot." This told everyone that he felt that he did not matter, that he felt tired or bored or bruised, not particularly lovable. It might even mean that he had always felt he was no good; that he had to take what was handed to him and could not complain.

Pot is a plain word, in this use almost a nonsense word. Incidentally, I had this word long before marijuana became popular, so I lay first claims to it. So many of the words professional people use to talk about human beings sound sterile and lack life-and-breath images. Families seem to find it easier to express themselves in "pot" terms and to understand when other people express themselves that way. They seem suddenly more comfortable, released from our culture's foolish taboo against talking about one's feelings. A wife, who would hesitate to tell her husband that she feels inadequate, depressed, worthless, can say frankly, "Don't bother me now—my pot is dragging!"

So, in this book when I say "pot," I mean *self-worth* or *self-esteem*. And pot is what we are going to talk about in this chapter.

In my many years of teaching young children, treating families of all economic and social levels, training people from all walks of life—from all the day-to-day experiences of my professional and personal living, I am convinced that the crucial factor in what happens both *inside* people and *between* people is the picture of individual worth that each person carries around with him—his *pot*.

128,852

Integrity, honesty, responsibility, compassion, love —all flow easily from the person whose pot is high. He feels that he matters, that the world is a better place because he is here. He has faith in his own competence. He is able to ask others for help, but he believes he can make his own decisions and is his own best resource. Appreciating his own worth, he is ready to see and respect the worth of others. He radiates trust and hope. He doesn't have rules against anything he feels. He accepts all of himself as human.

Vital people feel high-pot most of the time. True, everyone experiences times when he would just as soon chuck it all; when fatigue overwhelms him and the world has dealt him too many disappointments too quickly; when the problems of life suddenly seem more than he can manage. But the vital person treats these temporary low-pot feelings as just what they are—a crisis of the moment from which he can emerge whole and something he can feel uncomfortable about but does not have to hide.

Other people, however, spend most of their lives in a low-pot condition. Because they feel they have little worth, they expect to be cheated, stepped on, deprecated by others. Expecting the worst, they invite it and usually get it. To defend themselves, they hide behind a wall of distrust and sink into the terrible human state of loneliness and isolation. Thus separated from other people, they become apathetic, indifferent toward themselves and those around them. It is hard for them to see, hear, or think clearly, and therefore they are more prone to step on and deprecate others.

Fear is a natural consequence of this distrust and isolation. Fear constricts and blinds you; it keeps you from risking new ways of solving your problems and so gives rise to still more self-defeating behavior. (Fear, incidentally, is always fear of some *future* thing. I have observed that as soon as a person confronts or challenges whatever he is afraid of, the fear vanishes.)

When the perennially low-pot person experiences defeats—the kinds that would make even a vital person feel low-pot for a while—he feels desperate. How can such a worthless person as he cope with such troubles? he asks himself. It is not surprising that occasionally a low-pot person under overwhelming pressure will resort to drugs or suicide or murder. I truly believe that most of the pain, problems, ugliness in life—even wars—are the result of someone's low pot, which he really can't talk straight about.

Can you remember some time recently when your spirits were up? Perhaps the boss had just told you that you had been promoted; or you wore a becoming new dress and received several compliments; or you handled a difficult problem with one of the children and everything turned out happily. Try to go back now and feel again the feelings you had that day. That is what it is like to feel high pot.

Can you remember another occasion, when you made an embarrassing slip, or a costly error; or you were scolded angrily by your boss or your spouse; or you felt helpless in handling a problem with the children? Again, go back and relive the feelings you had, even though it is painful. That is what it is like to feel low pot.

Feeling low is not really the same as low pot. Low pot essentially means that you are experiencing undesirable feelings at the moment and are trying to behave as though those feelings did not exist. It takes a lot of trust to express your low self-esteem feelings. Low pot is a form of lying to yourself and others.

Now relax for a moment, then feel the state of your pot today. Is it high or low? Has something special happened to give you this feeling, or do you feel this way most of the time?

I hope that several members of your family will try this experiment together. Tell one another your feelings. Compare the things that make you feel low pot or high pot. You may find new dimensions to the people you've been living with all these years, and feel closer to one another as a result.

I am convinced that there are no genes to carry the feeling of worth. *It is learned.* And the family is where it is learned. You learned to feel high pot or low pot in the family your parents created And your children are learning it in your family right now

An infant coming into the world has no past, no experience in handling himself, no scale on which to judge his own worth. He must rely on the experiences he has with the people around him and the messages they give him about his worth as a person. For the first five or six years, the child's pot is formed by the family almost exclusively. After he starts school, other influences come into play, but the family remains important all through his adolescence. Outside forces tend to reinforce the feelings of worth or worthlessness that he has learned at home: the high-pot child can weather many failures in school or among peers; the low-pot child can experience many successes yet feel a gnawing doubt about his own value.

Every word, facial expression, gesture, or action on the part of the parent gives the child some message about his worth. It is sad that so many parents don't realize the effect these messages have on the child, and often don't even realize what messages they are sending. A mother may accept the bouquet clutched in her three-year-old's hand and say, "Where did you pick these?"—her voice and smile implying "How sweet of you to bring me these! Where do such lovely flowers grow?" This message would strengthen the child's feelings of worth. Or she might say, "How pretty!" but add, "did you pick these in Mrs. Randall's garden?"—implying that the child was bad to steal them. This message would make him feel wicked and worthless. Or she might say, "How pretty! Where did you pick them?" but wear a worried, accusing expression that added, "Did you steal them from Mrs. Randall's garden?" In this case, she is building low pot but probably does not realize it.

What kind of self-worth is your family building? You can begin to find out with this little experiment.

Tonight, when the family has settled around the table for dinner, try to feel what is happening to your pot each time another member speaks to you. There will be some remarks that have no "pot-content," of course. But you may be surprised to find that even "Pass the potatoes, please" can make you feel valued or deprecated, depending on the tone of voice, the facial expression, the timing (did it interrupt you or serve as a way of ignoring something you said?).

When dinner is about half finished, change the game. Listen to what you are saying to others. Is your remark likely to make the other person feel better about himself? Does his reply or his facial expression fit that prediction? If not, your face or tone or gestures may be communicating some message of which you are not aware. Try to be spontaneous and say what you would have said if you weren't trying this experiment. That won't be easy. Just being aware of what you say will make you tend to say pot-building things. But then that is another value of the experiment.

Tomorrow night explain this little game to the other members of the family. If they are old enough, let them read this chapter before dinner. Then all of you try the experiment at the same time. After dinner, talk together about what you discovered and how you felt.

Feelings of worth can only flourish in an atmosphere where individual differences are appreciated, mistakes are tolerated, communication is open, and rules are flexible—the kind of atmosphere that is found in a nurturing family. It is no accident that the children of these families usually feel good about themselves, or that the children of troubled families so often feel worthless, growing up as they must amid "crooked" communication, inflexible rules, criticism of their differentness, and punishment for their mistakes.

These same differences in self-worth can be seen in the adults in nurturing and troubled families. But here I think it is not so much that the family affects the adult's pot (although that certainly happens) as that high-pot parents are more likely to create nurturing families, and low-pot parents troubled families.

After years of working with families, I find that I no longer feel like blaming parents, no matter how foolish or destructive their actions. Instead, I try to find ways to raise their pot. This is a good first step to improving the whole family situation.

Happily, it is possible to raise anyone's pot, no matter what his age. Since the feeling of worth has been learned, it can be unlearned, and something new can be learned in its place. The possibility for this learning lasts from birth to death, so it is never too late. At any point in a person's life he can begin to feel better about himself.

I mean this to be the most important message in this book: *there is always hope that your life can change because you can always learn new things.* Human beings can grow and change all their lives. It is a little harder as we grow older, and it takes a little longer. But knowing that change is possible, and wanting to do it, are two first big steps. We may be slow learners, but we are all educable.

I want to close this chapter with a bit of prose which contains my feelings and ideas about self-worth.

MY DECLARATION OF SELF-ESTEEM

I am me.

In all the world, there is no one else exactly like me. There are persons who have some parts like me, but no one adds up exactly like me. Therefore, everything that comes out of me is authentically mine because I alone chose it.

I own everything about me—my body, including everything it does; my mind, including all its thoughts and ideas; my eyes, including the images of all they behold; my feelings, whatever they may be—anger, joy, frustration, love, disappointment, excitement; my mouth, and all the words that come out of it, polite, sweet or rough, correct or incorrect; my voice, loud or soft; and all my actions, whether they be to others or to myself.

I own my fantasies, my dreams, my hopes, my fears.

I own all my triumphs and successes, all my failures and mistakes.

Because I own all of me, I can become intimately acquainted with me. By so doing I can love me and be friendly with me in all my parts. I can then make it possible for all of me to work in my best interests.

I know there are aspects about myself that puzzle me, and other aspects that I do not know. But as long as I am friendly and loving to myself, I can courageously and hopefully look for the solutions to the puzzles and for ways to find out more about me.

However I look and sound, whatever I say and do, and whatever I think and feel at a given moment in time is me. This is authentic and represents where I am at that moment in time.

When I review later how I looked and sounded, what I said and did, and how I thought and felt, some parts may turn out to be unfitting. I can discard that which is unfitting, and keep that which proved fitting, and invent something new for that which I discarded.

I can see, hear, feel, think, say, and do. I have the tools to survive, to be close to others, to be productive, and to make sense and order out of the world of people and things outside of me.

I own me, and therefore I can engineer me.

I am me and I am okay.*

*Reprinted by permission of the publisher from V. Satir, "A Goal of Living," ETCETERA, December 1970.

4 Communication: Talking and Listening

I see communication as a huge umbrella that covers and affects all that goes on between human beings. Once a human being has arrived on this earth, *communication is the largest single factor determining what kinds of relationships he makes with others and what happens to him in the world about him.* How he manages his survival, how he develops intimacy, how productive he is, how he makes sense, how he connects with his own divinity—all are largely dependent on his communication skills.

Communication is the gauge by which two people measure one another's "pot level," and it is also the tool by which that level can be changed for them both. Communication covers the whole range of ways people pass information back and forth; it includes the information they give and receive, and the ways that that information is used. Communication covers how people make meaning of this information.

All communication is learned. By the time we reach the age of five, we probably have had a billion experiences in sharing communication. By that age we have developed ideas about how we see ourselves, what we can expect from others, and what seems to be possible or impossible for us in the world. Unless we have some exceedingly unusual experiences, those ideas will become fixed guides for the rest of our lives.

Once a person realizes that all of his communication is learned, he can set about changing it if he wants to. It will be helpful to remember that every baby who comes into this world comes only with raw materials. He has no self-concept, no experience of interacting with others, and no experience in dealing with the world around him. He learns all these things through communication with the people who are in charge of him from his birth on.

First, I want to review the elements of communication. At any point in time, with few exceptions such as blindness and deafness, everyone brings the same elements to his communication process.

He brings his *body*—which moves, has form and shape.

He brings his *values*—those concepts that represent his way of trying to survive and live the "good life" (his "oughts" and "shoulds" for himself and others).

He brings his *expectations* of the moment, gleaned from past experience.

He brings his *sense organs*—eyes, ears, nose, mouth, and skin, which enable him to see, hear, smell, taste, touch, and be touched.

He brings his *ability to talk*—his words and voice.

He brings his *brain*—which is the storehouse of his knowledge, including what he has learned from his past experience, what he has read, and what he has been taught.

Communication is like a film camera equipped with sound. It works only in the present, right here, right now, between you and me.

This is how it works. You are face to face with me; your senses take in what I look like, how I sound, what I smell like, and, if you happen to touch me, how I feel to you.

Your brain then reports what this means to you, calling upon your past experience, particularly with your parents and other authority figures, your book learning, and your ability to use this information to explain the message from your senses. Depending upon what your brain reports, you feel comfortable or uncomfortable—your body is loose or tight.

Meanwhile, I am going through something similar. I too, see, hear, feel something, think something, have a past, have values and expectations, and my body is doing something. You don't really know what I am sensing, what I am feeling, what my past is, what my values are and exactly what my body is doing. You have only guesses and fantasies, and I have the same about you. Unless the guesses and fantasies are checked out, they become "the facts" and as such can often lead to traps and ruptures.

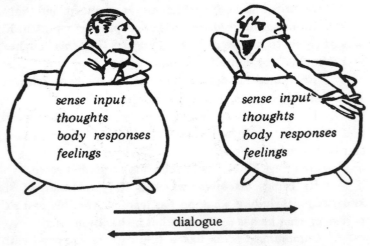

sense input
thoughts
body responses
feelings

sense input
thoughts
body responses
feelings

dialogue

This is a picture of communication between two people.

To illustrate the sensory message, the brain's interpretation of it, and the consequent feelings and feelings *about* the feelings, let's consider the following.

I am in your presence; you are a man. I think, "Your eyes are very wide apart, you must be a deep thinker." Or, "You have long hair, you must be a hippie." To make sense out of what I see, drawing on my experience and knowledge, what I tell myself influences me to have certain feelings both about myself and about you before a word is spoken.

For example, if I tell myself you're a hippie, and I'm afraid of hippies, then I might feel fear in myself and anger at you. I might get up and leave this frightening situation, or I might slug you. Perhaps I would tell myself you look like a scholar. Since I admire smart people, and I feel you are like me, I might want to start a conversation. One the other hand, if I felt myself to be stupid, your being a scholar would make me feel ashamed, so I would bend my head and feel humiliated.

Meanwhile you are also taking me in and are trying to make sense out of me. Perhaps you smell my perfume, decide I am a nightclub singer, which is offensive to you, so you turn your back. On the other hand, maybe my perfume would make you decide I am a neat gal, and you would search for ways to contact me. Again, all this takes place in a fraction of a second before anything is said.

I have developed a set of games or exercises that will help deepen your awareness and appreciation of communication with the emphasis in this chapter on looking, listening, paying attention, getting understanding, and making meaning.

It is best to try these games with a partner. Choose any member of your family that you wish. If no one feels free to join you, then try it alone in your imagination, but you will all learn and grow if you all take part in these exercises.

Sit directly in front of your partner, close enough to be able to touch him easily. You may not be used to doing what I'm going to ask you to do; it may even seem silly or uncomfortable. If you feel that way, try to go along anyway and see what happens.

Now imagine you are two people, each with a camera, photographing the other. This is how it is when two people are face-to-face. There may be other people present, but at any moment in time, only two people can be eye-to-eye.

A picture must be processed to see what was actually photographed. Human beings process their pictures in the brains, which interpret them, and then *maybe* people know what the picture is.

First, sit back comfortably in your chair and just look at the person in front of you. Forget what Mama or Papa said about its being impolite to stare. Give yourself the luxury of fully looking, and don't talk. Notice each movable part of his face. See what the eyes, eyelids, eyebrows, nostrils,

*facial and neck muscles are doing, and how the skin is coloring.
Is it turning pink, red, white, blue? You'll observe the body,
its size, form and the clothing on it. And you'll be able to
see how the body is moving—what the legs and arms are
doing, how the back is held.*

*Do this for about one minute and close your eyes.
See how clearly you can bring this person's face and body to
your mind's eye. If you've missed something, open your
eyes and pick up on the details you may have missed.*

This is the picture-taking-process. Our brains could
develop the picture as follows: "His hair is too long; he
should sit up straight. He is just like his mother." Or, "I like
his eyes. I like his hands. I don't like the color of his shirt.
I don't like his frown." Or you may ask yourself, "Does he
frown all the time? Why doesn't he look at me more? Why is

he wasting himself?" You may compare yourself to him. "I could never be as smart as he is." You may remember old injuries. "He had an affair once; how can I trust him?"

This is part of your internal dialogue. Are you aware that dialogue of some kind is going on in your head all the time? When your senses are focused on something, this inner dialogue is emphasized.

As you become aware of your thoughts, you may notice some of them make you feel bad, and your body responds. It may stiffen, your stomach could get butterflies, your hands become sweaty, your knees weak, and your heart beat faster. You could get dizzy or blush. If, on the other hand, you're having thoughts that make you feel good, your body may relax.

All right. We're ready to go on with the exercise. You have really looked at your partner. Now close your eyes. Does he remind you of anyone? Almost everyone reminds one of someone else. It could be a parent, a former boy or girl friend, a movie star—anybody. If you find a resemblance, let yourself be aware of how you feel about that person. Chances are that if the reminders are strong, you could sometimes get that person mixed up with the one in front of you. You could have been reacting to him as someone else. Should this happen the other person will be in the dark and feel unreal about what is happening.

After about a minute open your eyes and share what you've learned with your partner. If you found another person while your eyes were closed, tell your partner who it was and what part of him reminded you of your partner. Add how you feel about this. Of course, your partner will do the same thing.

When this kind of thing goes on, communication is taking place with shadows from the past, not real people. I have actually found people who lived together for thirty years treating one another as someone else and constantly suffering disappointment as a result. "I am not your father!" cries the husband in a rage.

As mentioned, all of these responses take place almost instantly as you look. What words come out depend upon how free you and your partner feel with one another, how sure you are about yourself and how aware you are in expressing yourself.

So you have looked at your partner, and you have become aware of what is going on inside of you.

Close your eyes for a minute. Let yourself become aware of what you were feeling and thinking as you looked— your body feelings and also how you felt about some of your thoughts and feelings. Imagine telling your partner all that you can about your inner space activity. Does the very thought of it make you quake and feel scared? Are you excited? Do you dare? Put into words all you want to and/or can about your inner space activity, talking quietly about what went on within you with a sharing attitude.

How much of your inner space activity were you willing to share with your partner? The answer to this question can give you a pretty good idea of where you stand in terms of freedom with your partner. If you quaked at the thought of sharing, you probably didn't want to tell much. If you had negative feelings, you probably wanted to hide them. If there is very much of this negative kind of response, you've probably been troubled about your relationship. If you felt you had to be careful, could you let yourself know why? Could you be honest and direct?

If you keep too much of your inner space to yourself, barriers are quickly built up, which often leads to loneliness and a first step toward emotional divorce. Emotional divorces can exist between parents and children and between siblings as well as the married pair. If you can risk sharing your insides, some of the barriers may begin to tumble.

Now we are ready for the sound part of your camera

to become active. When your partner starts breathing heavily, coughing, making sounds or talking, your ears report it to you. Your hearing stimulates inner space experience just as seeing does.

The other person's voice usually puts other sounds in the background except to someone who has broadened his ability to hear. His voice is loud, soft, high, low, clear, muffled, slow, fast. Again, you have thoughts and feelings about what you hear. Almost everyone notices and reacts to voice quality—sometimes to the extent that the words may escape you and you have to ask your partner to repeat.

I'm convinced that few people would talk as they do if they knew how they sounded. Voices are like musical instruments—they can be in or out of tune. But the tunes of our voices are not born with us; so we have hope. If people could really hear themselves, they could change their voices. I am convinced that people don't hear how they really sound, but how they *intend* to sound.

Once a woman and her son were in my office. She was saying in loud tones to him, "You are always yelling!" The son answered quietly, "You are yelling now." The woman denied it. I happened to have my tape recorder on, and I asked her to listen to herself. Afterward she said rather soberly, "My goodness that woman sounded loud!" She was unaware of how her voice sounded; she was aware only of her thoughts, which were not getting over because her voice drowned them out. You all probably have been around people whose voices were high-pitched and harsh, or low and barely audible, who talked as if they had a mouthful of mush, and you have experienced the resultant injury to your ears. A person's voice can help you or hinder you in understanding the meaning of his words.

Share with your partner how his voice sounds to you, and ask him to do the same.

When more of us know how to hear our voices, I think they will change considerably. If you have a chance to hear yourself on a tape recorder, by all means do it. Prepare yourself for a surprise. If you listen to it in the presence of others, you will probably be the only one who feels your recorded voice sounds different. Everyone else will say it's right on. There is nothing wrong with the tape recorder.

We're ready for another exercise.

Again sit within touching distance of your partner, and look at each other for one minute. Then take each other's hands and close your eyes. Slowly explore the hands of your partner. Think about their form, their texture. Let yourself be aware of any attitudes you have about what you're dis-covering in these hands. Experience how it feels to touch these hands and be touched by them. See how it feels to feel the pulses in your respective fingertips.

After about two minutes open your eyes and continue touching at the same time you are looking. Let yourself experience what happens. Is there a change in your touching experience when you look? After about thirty seconds close your eyes, continuing to touch and experience any possible changes. After a minute disengage your hands with a "parting but not a rejection" and sit back and let yourself feel the impact of the whole experience. Open your eyes and share your inner space with your partner.

Try this variation: one closes his eyes, and the other uses his hands to trace all the parts of the other's face, keeping awareness on touch. Reverse this and share your experience.

At this point in the experiment many people say they become uncomfortable. Some say their sexual responses get stirred up, and it is like having intercourse in public. My comment at this point is, "It was your *hands* and *faces* you were touching!" Some say they feel nothing; the whole thing seems stupid and silly. This saddens me as it could mean these people have constructed walls around themselves so they never can get the joy of physical comfort. Does anyone ever really outgrow his wish and need for physical comforting?

I have noticed that when couples with these feelings gradually let down and begin to enjoy touching, their relationship improves in all areas. The taboo against touching and being touched goes a long way to explain sterile, unsatisfying, monstrous experiences many people have in their sexual lives.

This taboo also does much to explain to me why the younger person gets into so much premature sex. They feel the need for physical comforting and think the only proper avenue open to them is intercourse.

As you went through all these experiments, you probably also realized that they are subject to individual interpretation. When our hands touch, you and I each feel the touch differently. I think it is so important for people to tell each other how the touch of the other feels. If I intend a loving touch and you experience it as harsh, I think it is pretty important for me to know that. This not knowing how we look, sound, or how our touch feels to someone else is very common, and it is also responsible for much disappointment and pain in relationships.

Now try smelling each other This may sound a little vulgar. However, any woman who has ever used perfume knows that the sense of smell is important in the way she is perceived. Many a potentially intimate relationship has been aborted or remained at a distance because of bad odors or scents. See what happens as you break your taboos against smelling, and let yourself tell and be told about your smells.

By this time it is possible that as you made contact with your eyes, ears, skin, and sharing one another's inner space activities you already have a heightened appreciation of each other. It is equally possible that as you first looked, memories of old hurts were so strong that that was all you could see. I call this "riding the garbage train." As long as you look now, but see yesterday, the barriers will only get higher. If you encounter the "garbage train," say so and dump it.

What is so important to remember is to look at one another in the present, in the here and now. Eyes clouded with regret for the past or fear for the future limit your vision and offer little chance for growth or change.

Believe it or not, I have met hundreds and hundreds of family pairs who have not touched each other except in rage or sex, and who have never looked at one another except in fantasy or out of the corners of their eyes.

The next set of exercises are concerned with physical positions and how they affect communication.

Turn your chairs around back to back, about eighteen inches apart, and sit down. Talk to each other. Very quickly you will notice some changes. You become physically uncomfortable, your sense of enjoyment of the other decreases, and it's hard to hear.

Add another dimension to the exercise and move your chairs about fifteen feet apart, remaining back to back. Notice the drastic changes in your communication. It is even possible to "lose" your partner entirely.

One of my first discoveries after beginning the study of families in operation was how much of their communication was carried on in precisely this way. The husband is in the den behind his newspaper; the wife is doing the ironing. Each has his attention elsewhere, yet they are talking about something important. "I hope you made the mortgage payment today." The other one grunts. Two weeks later there is the eviction notice. You can probably think of many, many examples of your own.

Don't be fooled by thinking that in order to be polite there must be great physical distances between people. I think if there is more than three feet between people, a great strain is put on their relationship.

Now let's try something else.

Decide which of you will be A and which B. In the first round A stands and B sits on the floor directly in front of him. Talk about how this feels. Stop after two minutes. Share how it feels to talk in this positon. Then change places and share again.

At one time we were all in the on-the-floor position in relation to the adults around us. It is the position any young children in your family are in right now.

Still in these positions let yourselves become aware of how your bodies feel. The sitter has to look up. Within thirty seconds his neck and shoulders will begin to ache, his eyes and eye muscles will become strained and his head will probably begin to ache. You, the stander, will have to arch your back to look down, and your back and neck muscles will begin to ache. It will probably become more difficult to see as the strain grows.

(Give yourself just thirty seconds in these positions so you'll know what I'm talking about. They become really horrible by sixty seconds.)

Everyone was born little, and each of us spends from ten to fifteen years (sometimes longer) being shorter than our parents. Considering the fact that most of our communication takes place in the positions described above, there is little wonder so many people *feel* so little all their lives. Understanding this, we can also understand why so many grow up with distorted views about themselves and their parents as people.

Let's look at this exercise from a slightly different perspective.

Again, in the position of the last exercise, both of you look straight ahead and notice the scenery. From the floor you see knees, legs, and if you look down, you see feet and very big ones. Look up and you see all the protrusions—genitals, bellies, breasts, chins, and noses.

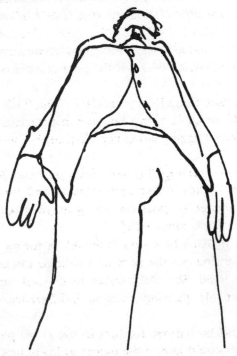

So often I have heard reports from people about their parents' mean looks, huge breasts, bellies, huge genitals and chins, and so on. Then when I met the parents I often saw quite the opposite. The child had formed his menacing picture from his out-of-perspective position.

The parent sees the child out of perspective as well. He could always envision you as little. These images, formed early in childhood, become bases upon which other experiences follow and which, for many, many people, never change.

Try this variation. You are in the same up and down positions. Make hand contact. The one on the floor obviously has to hold his hand and arm up; the one standing has his arm down. Thirty seconds is enough time for the upraised arm to get numb.

Inasmuch as the adult enjoys a more comfortable position with his arm down, he might find it difficult to realize the discomfort he is inflicting on the child. The child might struggle to get away, and the adult could become irritated at this "negative behavior" when all the poor kid wants is to get comfortable.

How many times have you seen a child, both arms up, being virtually dragged along between his parents? Or a hurrying mother dragging along her offspring by one arm on the bias?

Get into your standing and sitting positions for thirty seconds again. Then break eye contact, and notice how quickly this change in position will give your neck, eyes, shoulders, and back some relief.

Again, imagine how easy it would be for an adult to interpret this action on the part of a child as disrespectful. On the other hand, the child trying to contact his parent could interpret his glancing away as indifference or even rejection.

It would be natural for him to tug at his parent for attention. This could annoy the parent to the extent that he could slap the pesky child or box his ears. All of this would be humiliating, "pot lowering," and the child could get hurt. This whole interaction is fertile breeding ground for engendering feelings of fear and hate in the child and rejection on the part of the adult.

Suppose the parent responds to the tugging by what he supposes is a reassuring pat on the head but doesn't gauge his force very well?

You the stander give the sitter a rather obvious pat on the head. Is it experienced as comforting or as a "cranial explosion"?

The significance of eye contact can be seen in this last set of exercises. In order for people to really contact one another successfully, they need to be on eye level, each supported by his own two feet and facing one another. I hope we've established how essential eye level contact is between adults and children when images and expectations of one another are being formed. We must never forget that first experiences have great impact and unless something happens to change it, that experience will be the reference point for all of the future.

If you have young children, work it out so you contact them at eye level. Most of the time this means that adults will have to squat and build eye level furniture.

Now I would like to undertake some exercises that will help deepen understanding and make meaning between two people.

Good human relations depend a great deal on people's getting one another's meaning, whatever words they happen to use. Also, since our brains work so much faster than our mouths, we often use a kind of "shorthand," which might have an entirely different meaning for the other person than what we intended.

We learned from the seeing exercise that although we

thought we were seeing, we were actually making up much of what we "saw." This same kind of thing is possible with words. Let's try this exercise.

Make what you believe to be a true statement to your partner. He is then to repeat it to you verbatim, mimicking your voice, tone, inflection, facial expression, body position, movement. Check him for accuracy, and if it fits, say so. If it doesn't, produce your evidence. Be explicit; don't make a guessing game out of this. Then reverse roles.

This exercise helps to focus on really listening to and really seeing another person. Listening and looking require one's full attention. We pay a heavy price for not seeing and not hearing accurately as we end up by making assumptions and treating them as facts.

A person can look either with attention or without attention. Whoever is being locked at may not know the difference and assume he's being seen when he is not. And what a person thinks he sees is what he reports. If that individual happens to be in a position of power—a parent, a teacher, or an administrator—he can cause personal pain to another.

Let's consider words a moment. When someone is talking to you, do his words make sense? Do you believe them? Are they strange, or do they sound like nonsense? Do you have feelings about the other person and yourself? Do you feel stupid because you don't understand? Puzzled because you can't make sense? If so, can you say so and ask questions? If you can't, do you just guess? Do you not ask questions for fear you'll be thought stupid, and thus you remain stupid? What about the feeling of *having* to be quiet?

If you concentrate on these kinds of questions, you stop listening. I say it this way, "To the degree that you are involved with internal pot dialogue, you stop listening."

As you literally try to hear the other person, you are, at the very least, in a kind of three-ring circus. You are paying attention to the sound of the other person's voice, experiencing past and future fears concerning you both, becoming aware of your own freedom to say what you are feeling, and finally concentrating on efforts to get the meaning from your partner's words.

This is the complicated inner space activity each person has, out of which communication develops and on which interaction between any two people depends.

Let's go back to the exercises.

Could you begin to feel how it was to use yourself fully to get the other's meaning? Do you know the difference between full listening and half listening? When you were imitating did you find that your attention wandered and you made more errors in seeing?

My hope is that you can learn to engage yourself fully when listening and not make believe. If you don't want to or can't listen, don't pretend. You'll make fewer mistakes that way. This is particularly true between adults and children.

Now let's go to the next part of the meaning exercises.

Sit face-to-face with your partner as before. Now one of you make a statement you believe to be true. The other responds with, "Do you mean . . . " to indicate whether or not he has understood. Your aim is to get three yeses. For example:

"I think it's hot in here."

"Do you mean that you're uncomfortable?"

"Yes."

"Do you mean that I should be hot, too?"

"No."

"Do you mean that you want me to bring you a glass of water?"

"No."

"Do you mean that you want me to know that you're uncomfortable?"

"Yes."

"Do you mean that you want me to do something about it?"

"Yes."

At this juncture at least one has understood the other's meaning. If the partner were not able to get any yeses, then the other would simply have to tell what he meant.

Try this several times with the same statement, changing partners each time. Then try a question. Remember you are trying to get the meaning of the question, not to answer it. Do several rounds.

You are probably discovering how easy it is to misunderstand someone by making assumptions about what he meant. This can have serious results, as we've indicated, but they can also be funny.

I remember a young mother who was eager to clue into her young son's sexual questions. Her opportunity came one day when he asked her, "Mommy, how did I get here?" Believe me, she made the most of her opportunity. When she finished, her son, looking extremely puzzled, said, "I meant, did we come by train or by airplane?" (The family had moved some months previously.)

As you were doing the meaning exercises, were you able to become more fully aware of the trust and enjoyment that can come from engaging in a deliberate effort to understand?

Has this ever happened at your house? You and your spouse meet at the end of the day. One of you says, "So, how was your day?" The other answers, "Oh, nothing special."

What meanings are evident in this exchange? One woman who went through this fairly frequently said that this was her husband's way of turning her off. Her husband told me this was the way his wife showed him she didn't care.

"So, how was your day?" can mean, "I had a tough day, and I'm glad you're here. I hope it will go better now."

It can mean, "You're usually such a grouch. Are you still grouchy?"

It can mean, "I am interested in what happens to you. I would like to hear about anything exciting that happened to you."

"Oh, nothing special" can mean "Are you really interested? I'd like that."

It can mean "What are you trying to trap me in now? I'll watch my step."

How about some examples from your family?

There are a couple of very common communication traps based on the assumption so many people make that everyone else already knows everything about them.

There is the *hint method*, using one-word answers. Remember this old story that is illustrative of the point?

An inquiring reporter visited a rather plush old men's home. As the director proudly escorted him around, the reporter heard someone call out "31" from a nearby room. This was followed by great laughter. This procedure went on with several other numbers, all of which got the same response. Finally someone called out, "Number 11!" There was a dead silence. The reporter asked what was going on, and the director replied that these men had been there so long they knew all each other's jokes. To save energy they had given each joke a number. "I understand that," said the reporter. "But what about Number 11?" The director responded, "That poor guy never could tell a joke well."

The other communication trap is that so often people assume that no matter what they actually say, everyone else should understand them (the *mind-reading method*).

I am reminded of a young man whose mother was accusing him of violating an agreement to tell her when he was going out. He insisted he had told her. As evidence he said, "You saw me ironing a shirt that day, and you know I never iron a shirt for myself unless I am going out."

I think we've established at least so far that in human communication there is always mutual picture-taking, but that the people involved may not share their pictures, the meanings they give the pictures, nor the feelings the pictures arouse. The meanings are then guessed at, and the tragedy is that the guesses are then taken as facts.

At this point there can't be much doubt that our guesses about one another are anything but 100 percent accurate. I believe this guessing procedure is responsible for a great deal of unnecessary human estrangement.

Part of the problem is that we are such sloppy talkers! We use words such as *it*, *that*, and *this* without clarifying them. This is particularly difficult for the child because he has fewer clues from experience to help him. Anyone in this situation is in an impossible bind if his rules require that he act as though he understood.

Thousands of times I've heard one person say to another, "Stop that!" What is *that*? The second person may have no idea. Just because I see you doing something I want you to stop doesn't mean you know what I'm talking about. Many, many harmful pot reactions can be avoided simply by remembering to say to someone else what you are literally seeing and hearing.

This brings us to what I consider one of the most impossible hurdles in human relationships. That is the assumption that *you* always know what *I* mean. The premise appears to be that if we love each other, we also can and should read each other's minds.

The most frequent complaint I have heard people make about their family members is, "I don't know how he feels," which results in a feeling of being left out. This puts a tremendous strain on any relationship, particularly a family one. People tell me they feel in a kind of no-man's-land as they try to make some kind of a bridge to a family member who doesn't show or say what he feels.

It's important to point out, however, that many people who are accused of this are often feeling very strongly, but are unaware they aren't showing it. They believe themselves to be as transparent to others as they are to themselves.

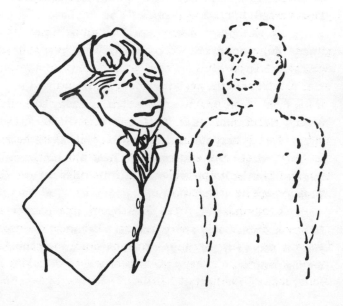

I have a little experiment I use to help people in the problem of awareness. I ask two people to discuss something, and video tape it. Then I play back the tape and ask each to respond to what they see in comparison to what they remember feeling as it happened. Many people are astonished as they see things of which they were not even in the remotest way aware when the tape was being made.

I remember a terrible ruckus in a family because the father sent his son to the lumber yard for a longer board. The child was obedient, wanted to please his dad, and thought he knew what was expected. He dutifully went and came back with a board that was three feet too short. His father, disappointed, became angry and accused his son of being stupid and inattentive. The father knew how long a board he wanted, but it apparently had not occurred to him that his son wouldn't know also. He literally had never thought of this and did not see it until we discussed it in the session.

Here is another example. A sixteen-year-old son says at 5:30 P.M. on a Friday night, "What are you doing tonight, Dad?" Ted, his father, replies, "You can have it!" Tom, the son, answers, "I don't want it now." With irritation Ted snaps, "Why did you ask?" To which Tom responds angrily, "What's the use?"

What are they talking about? Tom wanted to find out if his father were planning to watch him play basketball that night. Tom didn't ask his father directly because he was afraid he might say no, so he used the hinting method.

Ted got the message that Tom was hinting, all right, but he thought it was a request for the family car that night. Tom thought his dad was putting him off. Ted then thought Tom was ungrateful. These interactions ended with both father and son being angry and each feeling the other didn't care. I believe these kinds of exchanges are all too frequent among people.

Sometimes people have become so used to saying certain things in certain situations that their responses become automatic. If a person feels bad and he's asked how he feels, he will answer, "Fine," because he's told himself so many times in the past that he *should* feel fine. Besides, he probably concludes, no one is really interested anyway, so why not pick the expected answer? He has programmed himself to have only one string on his violin, and with only one string he has to use it with everything, whether it applies or not.

People can process their mental pictures by *describing* what they see or hear—by using *descriptive* not judging language. Many people intend to describe, but their pictures are distorted because they use judgmental words. If I can tell you what meaning I make of a given picture, avoid being judgmental, and tell you what I feel about it, and you do the same with me, at least we are straight with each other. We might not like the meaning we discover, but at least we understand. For example my camera picture is that you have a dirt smudge on your face. If I say, "For the love of heaven, what a slob!" I am being judgmental. If I use descriptive words, I would say, "I see a dirt smudge on your face."

Two traps are implicit here: *I read you in my terms* and *I hang a label on you.* To me the label *is* you. For example, you are a man, and I see tears in your eyes. Since I think men should never cry because that shows weakness, I conclude that you are weak, and I treat you accordingly. (Personally I happen to feel just the opposite, but the above is a popular view.)

I think you are ready now to try the ultimate risk with your partner.

This time assign yourself the task of confronting him with three statements you believe to be true about him and three you believe to be true about yourself. You'll probably be aware that these are your truths as of now; they are not the real truths for all time. To keep focused on telling your now truths, try beginning with the following words, "At this point in time I believe such and such to be true about you." If you have a negative truth, see if you can put words to that. In my opinion no relationship can be a nurturing one unless all states and aspects can be openly and freely commented upon.

I used to tell my students that they had it made when they could say straight to someone that he had a bad smell about him, in such a way that he received the information as a gift. It is painful at the outset, but definitely useful in the long run. Many people have reported to me that contrary to their expectations, relationships stood on firmer and more nurturing and trusting ground when they found they could be straight with negative as well as positive content.

On the other hand many people never put words to expressing appreciation. They just assume the others know of it. This, coupled with the fact that most people aren't a bit shy about voicing objections, results in estrangment and resentment. Who doesn't like (and need!) a pat on the head from time to time?

I recommend that families have the same kind of confrontation as the exercise just described at least once a week if not daily. After all, the first and basic learning about communication comes in the family. Sharing your inner space activity with one another accomplishes two important things: becoming really acquainted with the other person and thus changing strangeness to something familiar, and also making it possible to use your communication to develop nurturing relationships—something we all continue to need.

You should now be more aware that every time two people are together, each has an experience that affects him in some way. The experience can serve to reinforce what was expected—either positively or negatively. It may create doubts about the other's worth and thus create distrust, or it may deepen and strengthen the worth of each, and the trust and closeness between them. Every interaction between two people has a powerful impact on the respective worth of each and what happens between them.

If encounters between a couple become doubt-producing, the individuals involved begin to feel low pot about themselves. They begin to look elsewhere—to work, to children, to other heterosexual partners. If a husband and wife begin to have sterile and lifeless encounters, they eventually become bored with one another. Boredom leads to indifference, which is probably one of the worst human feelings there is and, incidentally one of the real causes of divorce. I am convinced that anything exciting, even if it's dangerous, is preferable to boredom. Fighting is better than being bored. You might get killed from it, but at least you feel alive while it's going on.

If, on the other hand, communication between a couple produces something new and interesting, then aliveness and/or new life comes into being; there develops a deepening, fulfilling relationship, and each feels better about himself and the other.

I hope that now after the many exercises you have experienced, my earlier words about the communication process will have more meaning: *communication is the greatest single factor affecting a person's health and his relationship to others.*

5   Patterns of Communication

After thirty years of listening to literally thousands of interactions among people, I gradually became aware of certain seemingly universal patterns in the way people communicated.

Whenever there was any stress, over and over again I observed four ways people had of handling it. These four patterns occurred only when one was reacting to stress *and at the same time* felt his self-esteem was involved—"his pot got hooked." In addition, the "hooked" one felt he could not say so. Presence of stress alone need not hook your pot, incidentally. Stress might be painful or annoying, but that isn't the same as doubting your own worth.

The four patterns of communication (which will be dealt with in detail later in this chapter) are: *placating*, *blaming*, *computing*, and *distracting*.

As I went into this more deeply I began to see that the self-esteem (pot) became hooked more easily when a person had not really developed a solid, appreciative sense of his own worth. Not having his own, he would use another's actions and reactions to define himself. If someone called him green, he would agree with no checking and take the other's comment as one fitting him. He was green because the other person said so. It's easy for anyone with doubts about his own worth to fall into this trap.

Do you know your internal feeling when your pot gets hooked? When mine does, my stomach gets knots, my muscles get tight, I find myself holding my breath, and I sometimes feel dizzy. While all this is going on I find that my thoughts concern the pot dialogue I am having with myself. The words are variations of "Who cares about me? I am unlovable. I can never do anything right. I am a nothing." Descriptive words for this condition are embarrassed, anxious, incompetent.

What I say at this point might be quite different from anything I am feeling or thinking. If I feel the only way out of my dilemma is to make things right with you so you will think I am lovable, etc., I will say whatever I think would fit. It would not matter if it were true or not. What matters is my survival, and I have put that in your hands.

Suppose, instead, I keep my survival in my hands. Then when my pot is hooked, I can say straight out what I think and feel. I might feel some initial pain at exposing my "weaknesses" and taking the risk that I believe goes with that, but I avoid the greater pain of hurting myself physically, emotionally, intellectually, socially, and spiritually, as well as avoiding giving you double-level messages.

It's important at this point to understand that every time you talk, all of you talks. Whenever you say words, your face, voice, body, breathing, and muscles are talking, too. A simple diagram is as follows:

Verbal communication   =   words

Body/sound communication = facial expression
body position
muscle tonus
breathing tempo
voice tone

What we are essentially talking about in these four patterns of communication are *double-level* messages. In all four instances your voice is saying one thing, and the rest of you is saying something else. Should you be interacting with someone who responds in double-level messages, too, the results of your interactions are often hurtful and unsatisfactory.

The troubled families I have known all have handled their communication through double-level messages. Double-level messages come through when a person holds the following views:

1. He has low self-esteem (low pot) and feels he is bad because he feels that way.
2. He feels fearful about hurting the other's feelings.
3. He worries about retaliation from the other.
4. He fears rupture of the relationship.
5. He does not want to impose.
6. He does not attach any significance to the person or the interaction itself.

In nearly all of these instances the person is unaware that he is giving double-level messages.

So the listener will be confronted by two messages, and the outcome of the communication will be greatly influenced by his response. In general, these are the possibilities: pick up the words and ignore the rest; pick up the non-word part and ignore the words; ignore the whole message by changing the subject, leaving, going to sleep, or commenting on the double-level nature of the message.

For example, if I have a smile on my face and the words, "I feel terrible," come out of my mouth, how will you respond? Picking up on the possibilities outlined in the last paragraph, you might respond to the words and say, "That's too bad," to which I can respond, "I was just kidding." Your second choice is to respond to the smile and say, "You look great," in which case I can say, "How can you say that!" Your third choice is to ignore the whole thing and go back to your paper, in which case I would respond, "What's the matter? Don't you give a damn?" Your fourth choice is to comment on my double message: "I don't know what you're telling me. You're smiling, yet you tell me you're feeling bad. What gives?" In this case I have a chance to repond, "I didn't want to impose on you," and so on.

Let yourself imagine what kinds of results there could be if each of the above were the basis of communication between two people.

I feel terrible

It is my belief that any family communication not leading to realness or straight, single levels of meaning cannot possibly lead to the trust and love that, of course, nourish members of the family.

Remember that what goes on in a moment in time between two people has many more levels than are visible on the surface. The surface represents only a small portion of what is going on, much in the same way that only a very small part of an iceberg is visible.

Thus in the following:

"Where were you last night?"

"You are always nagging me!"

Something is happening to each person in relation to himself.

Something is happening to the perception by each of the other.

The ensuing direction of the relationship can go toward distrust, personal low pot, frustration, or, on the other hand, it can be the beginning of new depth and trust.

Let's take a closer look at these universal patterns

of response people use to get around the threat of rejection. In all cases the individual is feeling and reacting to the threat, but because he doesn't want to reveal "weakness" he attempts to conceal it in the following ways:

1. *Placate* so the other person doesn't get mad;
2. *Blame* so the other person will regard you as strong (if he goes away it will be his fault, not yours);
3. *Compute* with the resultant message that you are attempting to deal with the threat as though it were harmless, and you are trying to establish your self-worth by using big words;
4. *Distract* so you ignore the threat, behaving as though it were not there (maybe if you do this long enough, it really will go away).

Our bodies have come to accommodate our feeling of self-worth whether we realize it or not. If our self-worth is in question, our bodies show it.

With this in mind I have devised certain physical stances to help people get in touch with parts of themselves that are obvious to other people but not to themselves. All I did was exaggerate and expand the facial and voice messages into the whole body and make it so exaggerated that nobody could miss it.

To help clarify the responses (we are actually going to play out these roles in communication games in the next chapter), I have included a simple word-diagram with each descriptive section.

PLACATER

(1) Words   agree   ("Whatever you want is okay. I am just here to make you happy.")

| Body | placates | ("I am helpless.") |

| Insides | | ("I feel like a nothing; without him I am dead. I am worthless.") |

The *placater* always talks in an ingratiating way, trying to please, apologizing, never disagreeing, no matter what. He's a "yes man." He talks as though he could do nothing for himself; he must always get someone to approve of him. You will find later that if you play this role for even five minutes, you will begin to feel nauseous and want to vomit.

A big help in doing a good placating job is to think of yourself as really worth nothing. You are lucky just to be allowed to eat. You owe everybody gratitude, and you really are responsible for everything that goes wrong. You know you could have stopped the rain if you used your brains, but you don't have any. Naturally you will agree with any criticism made about you. You are, of course, grateful for the fact that anyone even talks to you, no matter what they say or how they say it. You would not think of asking anything for yourself. After all, who are you to ask? Besides, if you can just be good enough it will come by itself.

Be the most syrupy, martyrish, bootlicking person you can be. Think of yourself as being physically down on one knee, wobbling a bit, putting out one hand in a begging fashion, and be sure to have your head up so your neck will hurt and your eyes will become strained so in no time at all you will begin to get a headache.

When you talk in this position your voice will be whiny and squeaky because you keep your body in such a lowered position that you don't have enough air to keep a rich, full voice. You will be saying "yes" to everything, no matter what you feel or think. The placating stance is the body position that matches the placating response.

BLAMER

(2)	Words	disagree	("You never do anything right. What is the matter with you?")
	Body	blames	("I am the boss around here.")
	Insides		("I am lonely and unsuccessful.")

The *blamer* is a fault-finder, a dictator, a boss. He acts superior, and he seems to be saying, "If it weren't for you, everything would be all right." The internal feeling is one of tightness in the muscles and in the organs. Meanwhile the blood pressure is increasing. The voice is hard, tight, and often shrill and loud.

Good blaming requires you to be as loud and tyrannical as you can. Cut everything and everyone down.

As a blamer it would be helpful to think of yourself pointing your finger accusingly and to start your sentences with "You never do this or you always do that or why do you always or why do you never . . ." and so on. Don't bother about an answer. That is unimportant. The blamer is much more interested in throwing his weight around than really finding out about anything.

Whether you know it or not, when you are blaming you are breathing in little tight spurts, or holding your breath altogether, because your throat muscles are so tight. Have you ever seen a really first-rate blamer whose eyes were bulging, neck muscles and nostrils standing out, who was getting red and whose voice sounded like someone shoveling coal? Think of yourself standing with one hand on your hip and the other arm extended with your index finger pointed straight out. Your face is screwed up, your lips curled, your nostrils flared as you tell, call names, and criticize everything under the sun. Your blaming stance looks like this:

You don't really feel you are worth anything, either. So if you can get someone to obey you, then you feel you count for something.

COMPUTER

(3) Words   ultra-   ("If one were to observe carefully,
            reasonable   one might notice the workworn
                           hands of someone present here.")

Body   computes   ("I'm calm, cool, and collected.")

Insides   ("I feel vulnerable.")

The *computer* is very correct, very reasonable with no semblance of any feeling showing. He is calm, cool, and collected. He could be compared to an actual computer or a dictionary. The body feels dry, often cool, and disassociated. The voice is a dry monotone, and the words are likely to be abstract.

When you are a computer, use the longest words possible, even if you aren't sure of their meanings. You will at least sound intelligent. After one paragraph no one will be listening anyway. To get yourself really in the mood for this role, imagine that your spine is a long, heavy steel rod reaching from your buttocks to the nape of your neck, and you have a ten-inch-wide iron collar around your neck. Keep everything about yourself as motionless as possible, including your mouth. You will have to try hard to keep your hands from moving, but do it.

When you are computing, your voice will naturally go dead because you have no feeling from the cranium down. Your mind is bent on being careful not to move, and you are kept busy choosing the right words. After all, you should never make a mistake. The sad part of this role is that it seems to represent an ideal goal for many people. "Say the right words; show no feeling; don't react."

Your computer position stance will look like this:

DISTRACTER

(4) Words   irrelevant (the words make no sense)

    Body   angular and off somewhere else

    Insides   ("Nobody cares. There is no place for me.")

Whatever the *distracter* does or says is irrelevant to what anyone else is saying or doing. He never makes a response to the point. His internal feeling is one of dizziness. The voice can be singsong, often out of tune with the words, and can go up and down without reason because it is focused nowhere.

When you play the distracting role, it will help you to think of yourself as a kind of lopsided top, constantly spinning, but never knowing where you are going, and not realizing it when you get there. You are too busy moving your mouth, your body, your arms, your legs. Make sure you are never on the point with your words. Ignore everyone's questions; maybe come back with one of your own on a different subject. Take a piece of imaginary lint off someone's garment, untie shoelaces, and so on.

Think of your body as going off in different directions at once. Put your knees together in an exaggerated knock-kneed fashion. This will bring your buttocks out, and make it easy for you to hunch your shoulders and have your arms and hands going in opposite directions.

At first this role seems like a relief, but after a few minutes of play, the terrible loneliness and purposelessness arise. If you can keep yourself moving fast enough, you won't notice it so much.

You will look like this:

As practice for yourself, take the four physical stances I have described, hold them for just sixty seconds and see what happens to you. Since many people are unaccustomed to feeling their body reactions, you may find at first that you are so busy thinking you aren't feeling. Keep at it, and you will begin to have the internal feelings you've experienced so many times before. Then the moment you are on your own two feet and are freely relaxed and able to move, you find your internal feeling changes.

It is my hunch that these ways of communicating are learned early in childhood. As the child tries to make his way through the complicated and often threatening world in which he finds himself, he uses one or another of these means of communicating. After enough use he can no longer distinguish his response from his feeling of worth or his personality.

Use of any of these four responses forges another ring in an individual's feeling of low self-worth or low pot. Attitudes prevalent in our society also reinforce these ways of communicating—many of which are learned at our mother's knee.

"Don't impose; it's selfish to ask for things for yourself," helps to reinforce placating.

"Don't let anyone put you down; don't be a coward," helps to reinforce blaming.

"Don't be so serious. Live it up! Who cares?" helps to reinforce distracting.

At this point you may well be wondering if there is any hope for us at all if these four crippling modes of communication are all we have. Of course they are not.

There is a fifth response that I have called *leveling* or flowing. In this response all parts of the message are going in the same direction—the voice says words that match the facial expression, the body position, and the voice tone.

Relationships are easy, free and honest, and there are few threats to self-esteem. With this response there is no need to blame, retreat into a computer, or to be in perpetual motion.

Of the five responses only the leveling one has any chance to heal ruptures, break impasses, or build bridges between people. And lest leveling seem too unrealistic to you, let me assure you that you can still placate if you choose, blame if you like, be on a head trip, or be distracting. The difference is you know what you are doing and are prepared to take the consequences for it.

So when you are leveling you apologize in reality when you realize you've done something you didn't intend. You are apologizing for an act not for your existence. There are times when you need to criticize and evaluate. When you do this in a leveling way, you are evaluating an act, not blaming the person, and there is usually a new direction you have to offer. There are times when you're talking about intellectual kinds of things such as giving lectures, making explanations, giving directions, and so on, where precise word meanings are essential. When you are leveling in this area, you are still showing your feelings, moving freely while you're explaining. You aren't coming off like a machine. So many people who make their livings with their brains—scientists, mathematicians, accountants, teachers, and therapists—come off like machines and epitomize the computing response. In addition, there are times when you want to or need to change the subject. In the leveling response you can say what you want to instead of hopping all over the place.

The leveling response is real for whatever is. If a leveler says, "I like you," his voice is warm and he looks at you. If his words are, "I am mad as hell at you," his voice is harsh, and his face is tight. The message is single and straight.

Another aspect of the leveling response is that it represents a truth of the person at a moment in time. This is in contrast, for example, to a blaming response where the person is feeling helpless, but is acting angry—or is hurting, but is acting brave.

A third aspect of the leveling response is that it is whole, not partial. The body, sense, thoughts, and feelings all are shown, in contrast to computing, for example, where nothing moves but the mouth and that only slightly.

There is an integration, a flowing, an aliveness, an openness and what I call a *juiciness* about a person who is leveling. You trust him, you know where you stand with him, and you feel good in his presence. The position is one of wholeness and free movement. This response is the only one that makes it possible to live in an alive way, rather than a dead way.

Now, to help you distinguish more clearly between a given subject and the different ways of expressing oneself about that subject, let me present five ways of apologizing in the five ways of communicating. This can also serve as a kind of demonstration before actually playing the games in the next chapter. Let's imagine that I have just bumped your arm.

Placating (looking down, wringing hands): "Please forgive me. I am just a clumsy oaf."

Blaming: "Ye gods, I just hit your arm! Keep it in next time so I won't hit it!"

Computing: "I wish to render an apology. I inadvertently struck your arm in passing. If there are any damages, please contact my attorney."

Distracting (looking at someone else): "Gee, some guy's mad. Must've got bumped."

Leveling (looking directly at the person): "I bumped you. I'm sorry. Are you hurt?"

Let's take another imaginary situation. I am your father, and there is something wrong in what you, my son, are doing.

Placating (coming up with a hushed voice, downcast face): "I'm — uh — uh — gosh, gee, Jim, I — am sorry — you feeling okay? You know — promise me you won't get mad — no, you're doing okay, it's just — maybe you could do a little better? Just a little, maybe? Hm?"

Blaming: "For Christ's sake, don't you know anything, you dumb cluck?"

Computing: "We are making a survey of our family efficiency. We find that in this department, namely with you, that efficiency is beginning to go down. Would you have any comments to make?"

Distracting (talking to his other son, standing next to Jim): "Say, Arnold, is your room about the same as Jim's? No, nothing wrong—I was just taking a walk through the house. Tell Jim to see his mother before he goes to bed."

Leveling: "Jim, your room is in bad shape. You haven't made your bed since yesterday. We need to stop, take a look, and see what's wrong."

It's anything but easy to break old habit patterns and become a leveler. One way in which you might be helped to achieve this goal is through learning what some of the fears are that keep you from leveling. To thwart the rejection we so fear, we tend to threaten ourselves in the following ways:

1. I might make a mistake.
2. Someone might not like it.
3. Someone will criticize me.
4. I might impose.
5. He will think I am no good.
6. I might be thought of as imperfect.
7. He might leave.

When you can tell yourself the following answers to the foregoing statements, you will have achieved real growth:

1. You are sure to make mistakes if you take any action, especially new action.
2. You can be quite sure that there will be someone who won't like what you do. Not everyone likes the same things.
3. Yes, someone will criticize you. You really aren't perfect. Some criticism is useful.
4. Sure! Every time you are in the presence of another person, speak to him, and interrupt him, you impose!
5. So maybe he will think you're no good. Can you live through it? Maybe sometimes you aren't so hot. Sometimes the other person is "putting his trip on you." Can you tell the difference?
6. If you think of yourself as needing to be perfect, the chances are you will always be able to find imperfection.
7. So he leaves. Maybe he should leave, and anyway, you'll live through it.

These attitudes will give you a good opportunity to stand on your own two good feet. It won't be easy and it won't be painless, but it might make the difference as to whether or not you grow.

With no intention of being flippant, I do think that most of the things we use to threaten ourselves and that affect our self-worth turn out to be tempests in teapots. One way I helped myself through these threats was to ask myself if I would still be alive if all these imagined threats came true. If I could answer yes, then I was okay. I can answer yes to all of them now

I will never forget the day I found out that lots of other people worried about these same silly threats as I did. I had thought for years I was the only one, and I kept myself busy trying to outwit them, and at the same time doing my best to conceal the threats. My feeling was—what if somebody found out? Well, what if somebody did? We all use these same kinds of things to threaten ourselves.

By now you must realize that this isn't some kind of a magical recipe, but the leveling response is actually a way of responding to real people in real life situations that permit you to agree because you really do, not because you think you should; disagree because you really do, not because you think you won't make points unless you do; use your brain freely, but not at the expense of the rest of you; to change courses, not to get you off the hook, but because you want to and there is a need to do so.

What the leveling response does is make it possible for you to live as a whole person—real, in touch with your head, your heart, your feelings, and your body. Being a leveler enables you to have integrity, commitment, honesty, intimacy, competence, creativity, and the ability to work with real problems in a real way. The other forms of communication result in doubtful integrity, commitment by bargain, dishonesty, loneliness, shoddy competence, strangulation by tradition, and dealing in a destructive way with fantasy problems.

It takes guts, courage, some new beliefs, and some new skills to become a leveling responder. *You can't fake it.*

Unfortunately there is little in society that reinforces this leveling response. Yet people are actually hungry for this kind of straightness and honesty. When they become aware of it and are courageous enough to try it, distances between people are shortened.

I did not come to this formulation via religion or through the study of philosophy. I came to it through a tough, trial-and-error way, trying to help people who had serious life problems. I found that what healed people was getting them to find their hearts, their feeling, their bodies, their brains, which once more brought them to their souls and thus to their humanity. They could then express themselves as whole people, which, in turn, helped them to greater feelings of self-worth (high pot), to nurturing relationships and satisfying outcomes.

None of these results is possible through the use of the four crippling ways of communication. I have found these, incidentally, as inevitable outcomes of the way authority is taught in famliies and reinforced by much of our society. What is so sad is that these four ways have become the most frequently used among people and are viewed by many as the most possible ways of achieving communication.

From what I have seen I've made some tentative conclusions about what to expect when I meet new groups of people. Fifty percent will say yes no matter what they feel or think (placate); 30 percent will say no, no matter what they feel or think (blame); 15 percent will say neither yes nor no and will give no hint of their feelings (compute); and 1/2 percent will behave as if yes, no, or feeling did not exist (distracting). That leaves only 4 1/2 percent whom I can expect to be real and to level. My colleagues tell me I am optimistic, saying the leveling response is probably found in only 1 percent of our population. Remember this is not validated research. It is only a clinical hunch. In the vernacular it would seem we are all a bunch of crooks—hiding ourselves and playing dangerous games with one another.

At this point I want to make an even more drastic statement. If you want to make your body sick, become disconnected from other people, throw away your beautiful brain power, make yourself deaf, dumb, and blind, using the four crippling ways of communication will in great measure help you to do it.

I feel very strongly as I write this. For me, the feelings of isolation, helplessness, feeling unloved, low pot, or incompetence comprise the real human evils of this world. Certain kinds of communication will continue this and certain kinds of communication can change it. What I am trying to do in this chapter is make it possible for each person to understand the leveling response so he can recognize and use it.

I would like to see each human being value and appreciate himself, feel whole, creative, competent, healthy, rugged, beautiful, and loving.

Despite the fact that I have exaggerated these different ways of communication for emphasis, and they may even seem amusing, I am deadly serious about the killing nature of the first four styles of communication.

In the next chapter, when you play the games I have invented, you will be able to experience exactly what these ways of communication are like, and you will be able to understand very quickly the toll they take of your body, the distrust that is formulated in your relationships with others and the blah, disappointing, and many times disastrous outcomes that ensue.

6 Communication Games

Now we are ready to actually play the games. I'm going to spell them out in detail in the hope that you'll be challenged and curious enough to try them out in earnest.

You know that reading about something is far different from seeing and doing it. I'd like you to have all three experiences—reading about the games, doing them, and then interesting another group in doing them so you can watch. Each approach will add something different to your learning.

You can read about swimming, you can watch others swim, but you don't really know what it's all about until you take the plunge yourself.

I have introduced these games to thousands of people, from preschool children (who call it "playing house") to various adult groups—businessmen, clergymen, hospital staffs and personnel as well as hundreds and hundreds of family groups. I've never met anyone who couldn't play. I've met a few here and there who wouldn't, but I believe they were too scared to try and covered up by saying they couldn't.

It may seem strange, but the minute people start to play the games, they know the dialogue. For me this is a validation of the fact that my games reflect the actual experiences so many have had in their families and, as they grow up, in their society. Regardless of economic status, race, age, sex, nationality or religion, everybody knows the communication games language.

By the way, and as immodest as it may seem, I am grateful to myself for having originated them. They've been very useful in getting back my perspective when I have temporarily lost it, and they certainly are a means of growing further You might have a similar experience.

I urge you to take the plunge into these games. You have no idea how surprised you'll be at what you'll learn about yourself and the other members of your family and how you all function within your family. After playing them, most people say they were a means of opening new doors into greater understanding. I know that every time I play them I learn something new. Go ahead!

Apart from the learning and growth, the games can provide you with a lot of fun.

To begin, then, let's play with three people at a time—a triad, with the others watching. I start with a triad because that is the basic family unit (mother, father and child). This is where we all learned our communication patterns. You can start with any three in your family, but I suggest you start with the oldest children first. Incidentally, the children will probably have to be at least three years old before they can enter in well.

The first triad could be husband, wife, and the first child. To really make the plunge in your efforts to understand the communication in your family, I suggest that you play with all your possible triads and play them one triad at a time. If you are a family of five, your triads would be as follows:

> *Husband, wife, and first child*
> *Husband, wife, and second child*
> *Husband, wife, and third child*
> *Father, first child, and second child*
> *Father, second child, and third child*
> *Father, first child, and third child*
> *Mother, first child, and second child*
> *Mother, second child, and third child*
> *Mother, first child, and third child*
> *First, second, and third child*

This makes ten triads altogether, and it will probably take three to four hours. Don't push yourselves. If you find that some helpful material gets opened up, allow it to happen. Don't push! There will be another day.

If you happen to have access to an audio or video tape recorder, use it. Later look and/or listen to it, and be prepared for some surprises.

All right. Three of you have agreed to play the game. Seat yourselves in chairs near one another. Then each of you take names other than your own, including a different family name. Announce your new name out loud. It seems that more learning is possible when people use different names.

You may need to refer back to the part where I discussed the different ways of communicating: placating, blaming, computing, distracting, and leveling.

To do these games, each of you select a way of communicating. For instance, one of you could blame, one could placate, and the third might also blame. The next time around, the one who blamed might now placate. The one who placated might now blame. The third one who blamed might now also placate. The third time around, the first one might try computing (being super-reasonable), the second, irrelevant and the third might stay blaming.

Below are listed combinations that I see frequently:

Person 1	Person 2	Person 3
Blaming	*Placating*	*Blaming*
Placating	*Blaming*	*Placating*
Blaming	*Blaming*	*Placating*
Computing	*Blaming*	*Irrelevant*
Blaming	*Computing*	*Irrelevant*
Computing	*Computing*	*Blaming*
Irrelevant	*Computing*	*Placating*
Computing	*Irrelevant*	*Blaming*
Placating	*Placating*	*Irrelevant*

As you play these, you may come upon some combinations that seem to be familiar to you.

Now that you have decided who is going to do which kind of communication, tell each other out loud. Start out by taking the physical position that matches your communication. You remember the communication stances that we discussed before that correspond to placating, blaming, being super-reasonable, and irrelevant. Here are the stances shown in combination with each other.

Now take these positions and hold the stances for one minute. While you are doing this, allow yourself to be aware of how you feel about yourself and the others. Then

*sit down and play these same communication stances but use
conversation.*

Here is an example of a possible interaction.

Sam   *(father-husband) - (blaming):*
Why haven't you got our vacation planned?

Elsa   *(mother-wife) - (blaming):*
*What are you yelling about? You've got as much time
as I have.*

Carl   *(son) - (blaming):*
*Aw, shut up. You two are always yelling. I'm not
going on any vacation, anyway.*

Sam   *(blaming):*
*You keep your trap shut. I am the one who makes
the rules around here.*

Elsa   *(blaming):*
*Says who? Besides young man, keep your nose out
of this.*
Or:

Sam   *(placating):*
Where would you like to go, dear?

Elsa   *(super-reasonable):*
According to the last issue of Woman's Day, *they say
that making a change of pace is a good way to plan a
vacation.*

Sam   *(placating):*
Whatever you would like to do, dear.

Carl   *(placating):*
You always plan nice times, Mother.

Elsa   *(super-reasonable):*
That's good. I will begin to make lists in the morning.

*Set the oven timer for five minutes. If there is any
particular conflict brewing in your family, use this as your
topic. If you do not have such a situation, they try to plan*

*something together—a meal, a vacation, a garage clean-up,
or anything else your family might conceivably plan together.
When you play, don't be afraid to exaggerate your communication. When the timer rings, stop, even if you are in
the middle of a sentence. Immediately sit back, close your
eyes and let yourself become aware of your breathing, your
thoughts, your feelings, how your body feels, and how you
feel about your partners.*

*Try to feel how it would be to live in this way in
your family all the time.*

*It could be that your blood pressure may be rising;
you might be beginning to sweat or experiencing aches of
various kinds. Just let yourself relax, still with your eyes
closed. Move about a bit to loosen up tight muscles if you
need to. Then mentally take off your role-playing name and
say your real name quietly to yourself.*

*Gradually open your eyes, then, and tell your partners
about your inner experiences as you were playing your role.
What actually happened? What were your thoughts, feelings,
and what parts of the past and present came to the fore?
What was your body doing? Say how you felt toward the
other members in your group while you were enacting your
role and tell them about it.*

You may be becoming aware that the fate of any
planning or conflict-solving is related to your communication.
Try another kind of communication and the outcome would
be different.

The painful part that people experience in these games
is that some of the combinations are very similar to the
kinds of communication patterns they were actually using to
interact with one another. Playing the games can also bring
back memories of what your life was like, perhaps some of the
time, with your parents when you were a child. If this is the
case, treat it as a discovery rather than a club with which to

punish yourself. Instead of telling yourself how bad or stupid you are or they are, use the discovery as a point from which to go forward.

Try again with a different set of communication stances. Maybe you could also experiment with changing roles. The male who was father might now become son, for example.

At the end of each game, take as much time as you need to express your inner experience to your partners. Then put on your role hats, set the timer and go on to the next set and then the next until you finish.

When you are sharing your inner experience, you may find yourself feeling uncomfortable. This will begin to ease as you put words to your discomfort. You will also find that you use a different voice when you are talking about your inner self. At this point you will be coming close to using a leveling response.

When people first start playing these games they are often revolted by being asked to do openly what they secretly fear they have been doing all along. Men, for instance, can actually feel nauseous at the thought of placating. Women react strongly against blaming because they don't want to be bitches.

You will learn a great deal if you let yourself develop your rules fully. Remember, *you can choose* whether or not to let it rub off.

If you are a woman and worry about being a bitch and handle it by never, never letting yourself be bitchy, you will be ruling yourself with an iron hand. That hand can get awfully heavy, and you will have to set it down sometimes. Then, bingo! Out comes the bitch. This is in contrast to choosing your behavior at any point in time. Bitchiness properly nurtured turns into healthy aggression, which all women need.

This concept can be compared to keeping three hungry dogs in a cage with a thick iron fence, who are always clamoring to get out, and three who are well fed and come quickly when called. If you forget to close the door, the hungry ones will get out and may even devour you. In the other situation, if the door is open, they may run out and even run away, but they won't eat you.

So you have a tendency to be bitchy. Take it out, dress it up, and honor this tendency as part of yourself. Love it and give it a place with the rest of your feelings. You can do the same with all your tendencies. This way one tendency won't stamp all over the rest of you; it will come out and "act nice" at your bidding. And it may turn out that you summon it less and less and then, like a formal gown you have outgrown or is no longer in style, you perhaps reshape it into a play gown for your young daughter, give it away, or use it to dust with.

If you try to hide or bridle your tendencies, however, you won't be able to do this very well. They will be waiting for the chance to escape and act up behind your back.

If you are a man and worry about appearing like Mr. Milquetoast, and handle it by being Mr. Big or Mr. Terrible, you are in the same spot as the lady who fears her bitchiness. It is always ready to do you in. Your Milquetoast quality—nurtured and reshaped a little—becomes your tenderness that you, as a man, sorely need because it enables you to keep your body juicy and healthy and to really make a loving connection with your wife and children, as well as your colleagues. Developing your tenderness does not have to eradicate your toughness. You need that, too. You can have both; you don't have to settle for only one.

Once a person decides he can look at all his parts, he can develop a sense of perspective and a sense of humor which aid him in making better choices. He will be helped to neutralize his negative attitudes toward his negative tendencies, and he will have clues as to how he can use these tendencies more positively.

Since none of us is 100 percent in self-awareness, the techniques involved in these games help to keep perspective. Many families have told me when they feel things are going badly, they sit down and play the games to restore their perspective, which releases their resources to work for them rather than against them.

There is another useful experiment you can try with the games.

After all the triads have been played, play a game with the whole family. By now you will be quite familiar with the games, and all have developed some skill at playing them.

Again, take different names. Each of you then privately choose one of the four responses and don't tell the others which one you choose. Start your session by planning something together. Again use a tape recorder if you have one. Set your timer for thirty minutes. When you start to have internal feelings of discomfort, change your role.

If you've been placating, change to another—perhaps blaming. Use that until you again experience discomfort. When this happens tell your partners as fully as you can what you were feeling and thinking about them and yourself as you were playing. Long before the thirty minutes have passed you probably will feel uncomfortable and get relief only when you can talk fully about your experience. Again, this will bring you closer to the leveling response.

Something that frequently happens as a result of thoroughly learning these games is that each person realizes he had more talent than he thought. Everyone can develop skill in playing the various roles. You find that instead of being stuck with one possibility you have at least four and perhaps five. Realizing this enables you to be a chooser, and this brings up your pot level.

Say to yourself: I can be a placater, I can be a blamer, a computer, a distracter, and a leveler. *I can choose.* For me, Virginia, I prefer the leveling response. It has the best consequences, and it is, as you all must know by now, the hardest to learn.

To be able to apologize without placating, to disagree without blaming, to be reasonable without being inhuman and boring, to be able to change the subject without distracting gives me greater personal satisfaction, less internal pain, and more opportunities for growth and for more satisfactory relationships with others, to say nothing about increased competence. On the other hand, if I choose to do any of the others I can take responsibility for the consequences and accept what pain comes from that.

Could you feel the wear and tear on your body while you were playing these games? Common aches and pains such as headaches, backaches, high and low blood pressure, and digestive difficulties are much more understandable when we look at them as natural results from the way we do or do not communicate. Can you also imagine how little chance there would be for growing closer to anyone or understanding him if these patterns were all we had? Deterioration of the relationship would have to happen!

As you begin to feel the internal stress, the personal frustration, and the hopelessness that follow these kinds of communication responses, can you further imagine that if you were stuck in these relationships, how tempting it would be to think about getting sick, taking a lover, commiting suicide or even murder? Only a very strong rule on your part will stop you. And the chances are pretty good that if you put all your energy into keeping that rule, you'll die prematurely anyway. I'll have more to say about rules in a subsequent chapter.

You see, just about everyone I have found with serious problems in coping with life—school problems, alcoholism, adultery, whatever—was carrying on his communication in the ways with which you have been experimenting. If there are any people who successfully "make it" with these responses, I haven't seen them. I can hardly emphasize too many times that all of these ways of communication arise from low pot—low feelings of self-worth. More than anything else, what I want to do is to stimulate feelings of self-worth in you.

Now you could be able to see quite clearly how your pot is connected with your communication. Further, it will be easier to see how the actions of people grow out of their communications. It becomes like a merry-go-round. I have low pot to begin with; I have poor communication with someone; I feel worse, my behavior reflects it and around it goes.

Let's consider a common example. You woke up this morning grouchy and out of sorts. You have to go to work and face a boss whom you think has something against you. You have a rule that no one should know about your fears. Your wife notices your sour face, and she might comment, "So what's the matter with you?" "Nothing," you respond coldly, rushing out the door, all but knocking her down and without kissing her good-bye. You're not aware of how your behavior struck her.

But she knows now that you are a brute, and she plans retaliation. When you come home, you find a note that she has gone to see her mother. You eat a cold supper. When she does come home, she ignores your invitation to come to bed because she has ironing to do. And so it goes.

All four responses demonstrate that each person is making the other his choice-maker. He puts his fate on someone or something else, and doesn't live as though he were free to make his own choices about his own reactions. And then, of course, it is easy to complain about how badly he has been treated.

These experiments must have shown you that each person makes the other more of what he already is. The blamer makes the placater even more of a placater, and the placater makes the blamer even more blaming. This is the beginning of what I call a closed system, which I shall discuss more fully later.

After this kind of communication has gone on for several years, you get to thinking of yourself as blighted, that the world is tainted and impossible; you stop growing and start dying.

It is important that we realize the power of these kinds of responses with other people.

The placating response can evoke guilt.

The blaming response can evoke fear.

The computing response can evoke envy.

The distracting response can evoke longing for fun.

So,

If I evoke your guilt, you might spare me.

If I evoke your fear, you might obey me.

If I evoke your envy, you might ally with me.

If I evoke your longing for fun, your might tolerate me.

In no case, though, can you love me or trust me, which, in the final analysis, is what makes a growth producing relationship. All we can do is survive.

I think we need to discuss feelings a bit more at this point. I have met so many people who never openly share their insides—probably because they either don't know how or they are scared to. I hope you are finding out whether or not you can share your feelings.

Hiding your feelings, by the way, takes a kind of skill most people don't really have. So often their efforts turn out to be like the traditional ostrich with his head in the sand. He thinks he's safely hidden, but of course he is not. The person who deludes himself like the ostrich often feels misunderstood and betrayed by others.

Oh, there are ways to successfully hide yourself if you insist on doing it. You could keep your body in a big black box with only a small hole for your voice to come through. You will have to talk in a steady monotonous voice. You won't have much of a life, but you'll be hidden, all right.

As we learned in our elementary exercises, you can mask your feelings by always talking to someone whose back is to you. He can't see you; you won't hear each other well, but your feelings won't show. Or get thirty or forty feet away from a person. Your feelings can be hidden pretty successfully that way, particularly if you put something between you, such as other people or a big table. In many families, marital partners often try to achieve this by putting their children between them.

Be assured, however, that when someone tries to hide feelings—especially strong, intense ones—it usually shows somewhere on his body or face anyway. The net result is that the hider just turns out more like a liar or a hypocrite than anything else.

As mentioned, all four responses you've been experimenting with are forms of hiding or concealing parts of yourself. You could have been doing it for so long you are no longer aware of it. You may be consciously thinking that this is a way of getting along, or it could be that you just don't know any better.

In the placating response you hide your needs for yourself; in the blaming response you hide your needs for the other; the computer hides his emotional need for himself and for others. These same needs are ignored in the distracter, and in addition he hides any relationship to time, space, or purpose.

These, then, are the shields people use to hide their feelings so they won't be hurt. The problem is one of convincing them that it is *safe to* express their feelings. *This is 90 percent of a therapist's work*, and the biggest job an individual has—to know himself, and to know it is safe to express honest feelings.

My experience shows that people who either can't or don't show their feelings are very lonely, even though their behavior doesn't indicate it. Most people like this have been terribly hurt and neglected over long periods in their childhoods. Not showing their feelings is a way to keep from being hurt again. It takes time, a loving, patient partner, and some new awareness to change them. Even then it doesn't always work very well unless the person who is to undergo the change wants it and understands the need for it.

On the other hand, personal privacy is an important part of any relationship, too. There are times when you have no words or you simply don't want to share your feelings. In that case, can you openly say, "I don't want to tell you," or "I don't have the words to tell you?" Secrecy can hurt. To tell someone close to you that you don't want to tell him something could easily make him uncomfortable. However, if it is clearly understood between the two of you that you can give each other privacy—both internal and bathroom—then you can stand the discomfort. What is important is that you talk about the fact that you don't want to talk about your insides at that moment in time. This is being real and leveling. There is a big difference between saying, "I choose not to say what I am thinking and feeling now," and using shields to hide your feelings.

It can make you very uncomfortable if you're expected to "spill your guts" all the time. The key is your choosing when and how to talk, and finding a context in which this is possible. Having privacy is part of maintaining high pot.

What have you been accustomed to doing about your privacy? How well do you think it's working for you? How do you find out whether or not it's working?

As you look back over your experience in playing the games, if you played them seriously, you may have been surprised by the fact that your body, feelings, and thoughts got stirred up even though you knew you were only role-playing. Your response is a definite indication of how powerful these roles really are.

Something else of which you're probably well aware by now is how tired you got when playing the games. Suppose you knew of no other way to communicate except the game ways? You could feel tired and hopeless and unloved much of the time. Maybe all the tiredness you've been experiencing isn't all because you work so hard.

Remember how alone, helpless, and isolated you felt inside regardless of how you sounded and what you said? Did you notice how your sight, hearing, and thought processes were cut down?

I consider it tragic that I have found literally thousands of families who live out their lives in this way. They simply don't know anything else, and thus live miserable, isolated and meaningless existences.

I am sure that by now you have an idea of the kinds of communication patterns you follow with your family members when you are under stress. *If one comes close to yours, try positioning yourself in the various communication stances and see what happens.*

My guess is that you are finding it isn't so easy as you might have thought to be fully honest and complete in your responses when given the opportunity. If this is the case, you may be getting in touch with some of the barriers between you and the rest of your family.

In spite of whether or not you achieved the flowing, leveling, together response as fully as you would have liked, you are probably more fully aware now that you do have choices in how to respond, and that when you exercise these choices your pot level goes up.

Secondly, you probably realize that you have been responding in ways of which you hadn't been aware, and this realization can help you avoid the shock of being reacted to in ways you didn't expect.

Thirdly, you probably discovered you have been responding in ways you would never have used intentionally. Though painful at the outset, this realization can help you to a greater understanding of what has been happening to you. Understanding is the first step to change.

Lastly, after a bit, you will find that you can really have fun with these games. It may even turn out that you will develop a little do-it-yourself drama group and incidentally, in the process, find yourself doing something pretty exciting and dynamic about increasing your sense of humor.

7   The Rules You Live By

Webster states that a *rule* is an established guide or regulation for action, conduct, method, arrangement. I agree, but my intention in this chapter is to take the word from its flat definition form and show you that rules are actually a vital, dynamic, and extremely influential force in your family life.

Helping you as individuals and as families to discover the rules by which you live is my goal. I think you're going to be very surprised to discover that you may be living by rules of which you're not even aware.

Rules have to do with the concept of *should*. They form a kind of shorthand, which becomes important as soon as two or more people live together. The questions of who makes the rules, from what material are they made, what they do, and what happens when they are broken will be our concerns in this chapter.

When I first talk with families about rules, the first ones mentioned usually concern money, getting the chores done, planning for individual needs, dealing with infractions, and all the other contributing factors that make it possible for people to live together in the same house and grow or not grow.

To find out about the rules in your family, sit down with all family members present and ask yourself the following questions:

What are your current rules? Elect a secretary and have her write them down on a piece of paper to help you keep track of them. Don't enter into any arguments at this point about whether or not they're right, and this is not the time to find out whether or not they are being obeyed, either. Choose a time when you all will have two hours or so. Sit around a table or on the floor. You're not trying to "catch" anybody at this point. The exercise should be carried out in the spirit of making a discovery much in the manner of poking about in an old attic just to find out what's there.

Maybe you have a ten-year-old boy who thinks the rule is that he only has to wash the dishes when his eleven-year-old sister is *justifiably occupied somewhere else.* He figures he is a kind of backup dishwasher. His sister thinks the rule is that her brother washes the dishes *when his father tells him to.* Can you see the kind of misunderstanding that can result from this kind of thing? This may sound foolish, but don't kid yourself. It could be happening in your home. Irate parents tell me, "He knows what the rules are!" When I pursue the matter, I often find that this isn't the case. "You know what the rules are" is already starting on a potentially wrong assumption.

For many families simply sitting down and discovering their rules is something very new, and it often proves enlightening. This exercise can open some exciting new possibilities for more positive ways of living together.

Here, too, I've found that most people *assume* that everyone else knows what they know. Talking over your rule inventory with your family can clear the way to finding reasons for misunderstanding and behavior problems.

For example, how well understood are your rules? Were they fully spelled out, or did you think your family could read the rules in your mind? It is wise to determine the degree of understanding about rules before deciding somebody has disobeyed them. Perhaps you found that some of the rules were unfair or inappropriate.

After you have written down all the rules your family thinks exist and cleared up any misunderstanding about them, go on to the next phase.

Try to discover which of your rules are still up-to-date and which are out-of-date. As fast as the world changes it is easy to have out-of-date rules. Are you driving a modern car with Model T rules? Many families are doing just this. If you find that you are, can you bring your rules up-to-date and throw out the old ones?

One of the characteristics of a nurturing family is the ability to keep up-to-date with its rules.

Now ask yourself if your rules are really helping or are they obstructing? What do you want them to accomplish?

All right. We've seen that rules can be out-of-date, unfair, unclear, or inappropriate.

What have you worked out for making changes in your rules? Who is allowed to ask for changes? Our legal system provides for appeals. Does your family?

Go a little farther in this family confrontation. How are rules made in your family? Does just one of you make them? Is it the person who is the oldest, the nicest, the most handicapped, the most powerful? Do you get them from books? The neighbors? From the families where the parents grew up? Where do they come from?

So far the rules we've been discussing are fairly obvious and easy to find. There is another set of rules, however, which is submerged and much more difficult to get one's fingers on. These rules make up a powerful invisible force that moves through the lives of all members of families.

I'm talking about the "unwritten" rules having to do with *freedom to comment* of various members of the family. What can you say in your family about what you feel, think, see, hear, smell, touch, and taste? Can you comment only on what should be rather than what is?

There are four major areas involved with this question of freedom to comment.

What can you say about what you're seeing and hearing?

Can you express your fear, helplessness, anger, need for comfort, loneliness, tenderness, or aggression?

To whom can you say it?

You are a child who has just heard his father swear. There is a family rule against swearing. Can you tell him?

How do you go about it if you disagree or disapprove of someone or something?

If your seventeen-year-old son reeks of marijuana, can you say so?

How do you question when you don't understand (or do you)?

Do you feel free to ask for clarification if a family member doesn't make himself understood? Is your rule if *you* don't understand *me*, it is always because of *you*?

Living in a family provides all kinds of seeing and hearing experiences. Some of these bring joy to the heart, some pain, and perhaps some bring a feeling of shame. Whatever feelings are aroused, if family members cannot recognize them and comment on them, the feelings can go underground and gnaw away at the roots of the family well-being.

Let's think about this a moment. Are there some subjects that must never be raised in your family? These are the kinds of things I am referring to: your oldest son was born without an arm, your grandfather is in jail, your father has a tic, your mother and father fight, or either parent was previously married.

Perhaps the man in your family may be shorter than the average man. The rule honored by all members of the family is that no one talks about his shortness, and no one talks about the fact that they can't talk about his shortness, either.

How can you expect to behave as though these family facts simply don't exist? Family barriers erected against talking about what *is* or what *has been* provide a good source for breeding low pot.

Let's consider another angle to this perplexing situation. The family rule is that one can talk about only the good, the right, the appropriate, and the relevant. When this is the case, large parts of the reality that is presented can't be commented on. In my opinion there are no adults and few children living in the family or anywhere else who are consistently good, appropriate, and relevant. What can they do when the rules say that these kinds of things cannot be commented upon? As a result some children lie, some develop hatred for, and estrangement from, their parents. Worst of all they develop attitudes about their self-worth, which translates itself into helplessness, hostility, stupidity, and loneliness.

The simple fact is that whatever is seen or heard has its impact on the person seeing or hearing it. Anything that is seen and/or heard by a person asks that person to make an explanation to himself about it. As we've seen so many times before, if there is no opportunity to check out the explanation, then that explanation becomes the "fact." The "fact" may be accurate or inaccurate, but it will be the basis upon which the individual will base his actions and opinions.

This is the reason I believe so many children grow up to be adults who see themselves as versions of saints or devils instead of living, breathing human beings who *feel*.

All too often family rules permit expressing feeling only if it is justified, not becasue it *is*. This is when you hear expressions like "You shouldn't feel that way," or, "How could you feel like that—I never would." If you make a distinction between acting your feelings and telling your feelings, it might be easier to give up the rule, "Thou shalt have only justified feelings."

If your rules say that whatever feeling you have is human and therefore acceptable, the self can grow. This is not saying that all actions are acceptable. If the feeling is welcome, there are good chances for developing different courses of action and more appropriate action at that.

From birth to death, human beings continue to experience a wide range of feelings—fear, pain, helplessness, anger, joy, jealousy, and love—not because they are right, but because they *are*.

Giving yourself the ability to get in touch with *all* parts of your family life could dramatically change things for the better. I believe that anything that *is* can be talked about and understood in human terms.

Let's get into some real specifics. Take anger. Many people are not aware that anger is a necessary human emergency emotion for some. Because anger sometimes erupts into destructive actions, the belief is that the anger itself is destructive. It isn't the anger, but the action taken as a result of it that can be destructive.

Let's consider an extreme example. Suppose I spit at you. For you that could be an emergency. You might feel you have been attacked and feel bad about yourself and angry at me. You might think of yourself as unlovable (or else why would I have attacked you?). You feel hurt, experience low pot, feel lonely, and perhaps unloved. Although you are feeling *hurt*—of which you are only remotely aware—you act *angry*. How would you show what you are feeling? What would you say? What would you do?

You have choices. You can spit back. You can hit me. You can cry and beg me not to do it again. You can thank me. You can run away. You can express yourself honestly and tell me how angry you feel. Then you'll probably be in touch with your hurt, which you can tell me. Then you can ask me the questions you need to in order to have me explain how I happened to spit at you.

Your rules will be your guides in how to express this in the first place. If your rules permit questions, you can ask me and then understand. If your rules don't permit questions, you can guess, and maybe make a wrong guess. The spitting could represent many things. You could ask yourself, did she spit because she doesn't like me? Because she was angry with me? Because she is frustrated with herself? Because she has poor muscle control? Did she spit because she wanted me to notice her? These possibilities may seem far-fetched, but think about them awhile. They aren't really so far-fetched at all.

Let's talk about anger some more because it's important. It's not a vice, it is a respectable human emotion that can be used in an emergency. Human beings can't live out their lives without encountering some emergencies, and in the business of living, it is 100 percent predictable that at times we all will find ourselves in a state of anger.

If an individual wants to qualify as being a Good Person (and who doesn't?), he will try to hold in his occasional feeling of anger. He doesn't fool anybody, though. Have you ever seen anyone, obviously angry, but trying to talk as if he were not? His muscles tighten, his lips go tight, his breathing gets choppy, his skin color changes, his eyelids tighten; sometimes he'll even puff up.

As time goes on, the person whose rule is that anger is bad begins to tighten up further inside. His muscles, digestive system, heart tissue, artery and vein walls get tight, even though outside he looks calm, cool, and collected. Only an occasional steely look in the eye or a twitchy left foot will indicate what he's really feeling. Soon he is suffering from all the physical manifestations of sickness that come from tight insides such as constipation and high blood pressure. After awhile he is no longer aware of the anger as such but only of the pain in his insides. He can then truthfully say he doesn't get angry. Only his gall bladder is "acting up." What happened is that his feelings have gone underground. They are still operating, but are doing so out of his range of awareness.

Some people don't go this far, but instead develop a storage tank for anger that fills up and explodes periodically at small things.

So many children are taught that fighting is bad, that it is "bad" to hurt other people. Anger causes fighting, therefore anger is bad. The philosophy with far too many of us is "to make a child good, banish his anger." It is almost impossible to guess how much harm this kind of teaching can cause a child.

If you permit yourself to believe that anger is a natural human emotion in an emergency situation, then you can respect and honor it; admit it freely as a part of yourself, and learn the many ways of using it. If you face your angry feelings and communicate them clearly and honestly to the person involved, you will drain off much of the "steam" and the need to act destructively. You are the chooser and, as such, can feel a sense of managing yourself and, as a result, feel high pot. Family rules about anger are basic to whether or not you *grow* with your anger or allow it to make you die from it, a little at a time.

Now let's consider another really important area in family life: affection among family members, how it is expressed, and rules about affection.

I have found all too often that members of families cheat themselves in their affectional lives. Because they don't know how to make affection "safe," they develop rules against all affection. This is the kind of thing I mean. So often fathers feel that after their daughters reach the age of five, they are no longer supposed to cuddle them as it is sexually stimulating. The same holds true, although to a lesser degree, with mothers and their sons. Too, many fathers refuse to show overt affection to their sons because affection between males is taken as homosexual.

What we need to do is rethink our definitions between the sexes whatever ages or relationships are involved. The main problem lies in the confusion many people experience between physical affection and sex. If we don't make a distinction between the feeling and the action, then we have to inhibit the feeling. Let me put it bluntly. If you want hanky-panky going on in your family, play down affection and have lots of taboos about sex.

Displays of affection can have many, many meanings. For example, I have had hugs and other physical means of expression that have meant a lot of things. I've been hugged in such a way that I wanted to slug the hugger. Other times a hug is an invitation to sexual intercourse; still another hug could simply be an indication of being noticed and liked. Still another kind of hug might be a way of expressing tenderness, a seeking to give comfort.

I wonder how much of the truly satisfying, nurturing potential of affection among family members is not enjoyed because family rules about affection get mixed up with taboos about sex.

Let's talk about that. If you had seen as much pain as I have that clearly resulted from inhuman and repressive attitudes about sex, you would turn yourselves inside out immediately to change your whole attitude to one of open acceptance, pride, enjoyment, and appreciation of the spirituality of sex. Instead, I have found that most families employ the rule, *"Don't enjoy sex—yours or anyone else's—in any form."* The common beginning for this rule is the denial of the genitals except as necessary nasty objects. *"Keep them clean and out of sight and touch. Use them only when necessary and sparingly at that."*

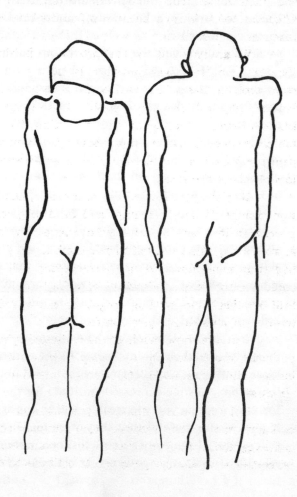

I can say that without exception any person I have seen with problems in sexual gratification in marriage, or who was homosexual, promiscuous, or who was arrested for any sexual crime grew up with these kinds of taboos against sex. I'll go further. Anyone whom I have seen with any kind of coping problem or emotional illness also grew up with taboos about sex.

Our genitals, our sex are integral parts of ourselves. Unless we openly acknowledge, understand, value, and enjoy our sexual side as well as that of the opposite sex, we are literally paving the way for serious personal pain.

This taboo also applies to nudity, masturbation, sexual intercourse, pregnancy, birth, menstruation, erection, prostitution, all forms of sexual practice, erotic art, and pornography.

I once headed up a program for family life education in a high school of about eight hundred students. Part of the program concerned itself with sex education. I had a box into which young people could put questions they felt they couldn't ask openly. The box was usually full. I would then discuss these questions during the class period. Nearly all the students explained that they would not have been able to ask their parents these questions for at least three common reasons: the parents would become angry and accuse them of bad conduct; they would feel humiliated and embarrassed and would probably lie; they simply wouldn't know. In reality the students were sparing themselves and their parents, but with the cost of remaining ignorant and seeking information somewhere else. All of these young people expressed gratitude for the course, and for my accepting, knowledgeable, and loving attitude. The kids were also grateful that they were feeling better about themselves. I remember two questions particularly—both asked by boys. An eighteen-year-old asked, "What does it mean if I have lumps in my semen?" Another question was from a fifteen-year-old boy: "How can I tell if my mother is in the menopause? She seems awfully irritable now. If she is, then I will treat her nicely; otherwise I'm going to tell her how mean she is. Should I tell my father?"

How would you, as parents, feel about being asked these questions? If asked, what would you say?

There was quite a nice follow-up to my course for the students. They asked me if I'd run a similar course for their parents, to which I agreed. About a quarter of the parents came to it. I had the same box, and I got very similar questions.

In short I think we can forgive ourselves for not always knowing the complexities of our sexual selves. We cannot forgive ourselves for going on in ignorance and covering up by a don't-talk-about-it attitude, implying that sexual knowledge is bad, criminal. *Society and the individuals who make it up pay heavily for this kind of ignorance.*

Fear on the part of family members has much to do with rules about taboos and secrets—even though the rules may be expressed by the adults as "protection for the kids."

This leads the way to a discussion of another kind of taboo that I find absolutely rampant in families—that is the adult mystique almost wholly invented by adults to "protect the children." The rule is usually expressed by, "You are too young to ——," the implication being that the adult world is too complicated, too terrifying, too big, too evil, too pleasureful for you—the mere child—to discover. The child gets to feeling there must be some kind of magic password to get in and that when he reaches twenty-one, he will automatically know it. I find people over twenty-one in droves who haven't discovered the password.

What makes the "you-are-too-young-to" pattern even worse is that the adult is implying at the same time that the child's world is bad. "You are just a child; what do you know." Or, "That is childish," they say. Since obviously there are gaps in what the individual child is ready to do and what he might like to do, I think the best way of preparation is to teach the child how to make bridges for these gaps, rather than denying him the opportunity of bridging the gaps at all.

Another aspect of this business of family taboos concerns *secrets*. Common examples of family secrets are as follows: a person was conceived before his parents were married, a mate conceived a child who was later adopted, a mate hospitalized or jailed. These kinds of secrets are usually heavily shrouded in shame.

Some of the biggest secrets have to do with parental behavior during their adolescent years, the rule being that, by definition, no parents "ever did anything wrong." It is only "you kids" who ever misbehave. This kind of thing has happened so many times that I consider it almost a formula. If I hear a parent getting hysterical about something his child is doing, I look immediately to what secret the child's behavior has stirred up in the parent's youth. The behavior of the child may not duplicate that of the parent, but it can come close. My job in this instance is to help the parent get rid of his shame so he doesn't have to lock part of himself away. Then he can deal rationally with his child.

There is also the whole category of present secrets, again, shrouded in shame. Many parents try to hide their "goings on" from their children ("to protect them"). Examples of such present secrets that I have run across are the father has a mistress, the mother a lover, either or both drink, they don't sleep together, and so on. Again, it is the case of, if it isn't talked about, it doesn't exist. This simply does not work, ever, unless everyone you are "protecting"

is deaf, dumb, and blind.

Now let's take a look at what you might have discovered about your rules for commenting in three areas in sequence.

There is the human-inhuman sequence, which means that you ask yourself to live by a rule which is nearly humanly impossible to keep. *"No matter what happens, look happy."*

Then there is the overt-covert sequence, which indicates which rules are out in the open, and which are hidden, yet obeyed. *"Don't talk about it. Treat it as though it didn't exist."*

Then there is the constructive-destructive sequence. An example of a constructive way of handling a situation is, *"We've got a problem about a money shortage this month. Let's talk about it."* An example of an obstructing or destructive way of handling the same situation is, *"Don't talk to* me *about your money problems—that's* your *problem."*

Let's summarize some of the things we've been discussing in this chapter. Any rule that prevents family members from commenting on what is and what has been is an excellent source for developing a restricted, ignorant, and uncreative person, and a family situation to match.

If, on the other hand, you are able to get in touch with all parts of your family life, your family life could change drastically and dramatically for the better. The family whose rules allow for freedom to comment on everything, whether it be painful, joyous, or sinful, has the best chance of being a nurturing family. I believe that anything that *is* can be talked about and understood in human terms.

Almost everyone has skeletons in the closet. Don't you have at least one? In nurturing families these are simply friendly reminders of human frailty, and they can be easily talked about and learned from. In other families they are hidden away and treated as gruesome reminders of the badness of human beings, which must never be talked about.

I hope we have seen that rules are a very real part of the structure of the family and its functioning. If the rules can be changed, the family operation can be changed. Check into the kinds of rules by which you are living. Can you understand more now what is happening to you in your family? Can you allow yourself to be challenged into making some changes? New awareness, new courage, and new hope on your part can enable you to put some new rules into operation.

The courage will come from your ability to let yourself accept new ideas. You can discard the old and unfitting ideas, and you can select from those that you have already found to be useful. This is just plain logical. Nothing remains eternally the same. Think of your pantry, the refrigerator, a tool shed. They always need rearranging, replacing, the discarding of the old and the adding of the new.

You've thought about your rules and examined them. Why not check your rule inventory out against the following questions?

What are your rules?

What are they accomplishing for you now?

What changes do you now see you need to make?

Which of your current rules fit?

Which have to be discarded?

What new ones do you have to make?

What do you think about your rules? Are they mostly overt, human, up-to-date? Or are they mostly covert, inhuman, and out-of-date? If your rules are mostly of the second variety, I think you realize you and your family have some important and necessary work to do. If your rules are of the first category, you are probably all having a ball.

8   Systems: Open or Closed?

In this chapter I want to discuss something that at first you might not think would have much to do with your family and peoplemaking. Stay with me. "System" may be borrowed from the world of industry and commerce, but it is also a vital and dynamic force in your day-to-day family life.

Any system consists of several individual parts that are essential and related to one another when a certain outcome is desired. There are actions and reactions and interactions among the parts that keep changing. Each part acts as a starter to all the other parts. It is this constant action, reaction, and interaction that form the most important part of my concept of system. A system has life only *now* when the component parts are there to give it.

Sound confusing? It isn't really. You put yeast, flour, water, and sugar together, and you have bread. The bread isn't like any one of its ingredients, yet it consists of all of them.

Steam isn't like any of its parts, but it consists of all of them.

An operating system consists of the following:

A purpose or goal. Why does this system exist in the first place? (In families the purpose is to grow new people and to further the growth of those already here);

Essential parts. (In families, adults and children, males and females);

An order to the parts' working. (In families, pot, rules, communication);

A means to start the system. (In families, the male and female getting together sexually);

Power or means of maintaining energy so the parts can work. (In families, food, shelter, air, water, activity, and beliefs about the emotional, intellectual, physical, social, and spiritual lives of the family members and how they work together);

Ways of dealing with changes from the outside. (In families, relating to the new and different).

Now, we hear a lot about "bucking the system" these days, which would seem to say that all systems are bad. Not so. Some are and some are not.

There are two kinds of systems—closed and open. The main difference between them is the specific reaction to *change* from the outside. An open system provides for change; a closed one provides for very little or for no change at all.

An open system offers choices and depends on successfully meeting reality for its continuing life.

A closed system depends on edict and law and order and operates through force, both physically and psychologically.

If one were to deliberately design a closed system, his first step would be to separate it as completely as possible from outside interference.

The fact is, I don't believe anyone would deliberately design a closed system. Closed systems evolve from certain sets of beliefs which are few, but powerful:

Man is basically evil and has to continually be controlled to be good.

Relationships have to be regulated by force.

There is one right way and the one with most power has it.

There is always someone who knows what is best for you.

In other words, *in closed systems:*

Self-worth is secondary to power and performance.

Actions are subject to the whims of the boss.

Change is resisted.

In open systems:

Self-worth is primary, with power and performance related to it.

Actions are the outcome of reality.

Change is welcomed and considered normal and desirable.

Communication, system, and rules all are related.

Most of our social systems are closed, or very nearly so. Of course there is always a little change allowed, and in my opinion the provision for even a little change is the reason we have been able to limp along as well as we have.

We're just beginning to see the implications of system to personal, family, and societal behavior.

Now we come to an important philosophical question. Do you believe that all human life deserves the highest priority? *I do believe this with all my being.* Therefore I unashamedly admit that I will do everything I can to change all closed systems into open ones.

I believe that human beings cannot flourish in a closed system; at best they can only exist. Human beings want more than that.

Right now you and I could point to countless examples of closed systems—of dictatorships in current society, schools, prisons, churches, and political groups. What about the system in your family? Is it open or closed? If your communication now is mostly growth-impeding, if your rules are inhuman, covert, and out-of-date, you probably have a closed one. If your communication is growth-producing and your rules are human, overt and up-to-date, you have an open one.

Let's return to an exercise we've done before and do it again with different goals in mind and different reasons for doing it. Ask your family members or any other five people to work with you. As before, ask them to take different names. They can be a family or a factory meeting or a board meeting. Ask them to take one of the forms of growth impeding communication (placating, blaming, computing, and distracting), and try planning something together for ten minutes. Notice how quickly the closed system begins to emerge. Before I was asking you to do this with three people to see what happened to you individually. This time you might begin to see how closed systems develop. You might begin to feel your back hurting, a headache forming, and you don't see and hear so well. You are experiencing going off center. You may also begin to feel how you are locked in. People begin to look like strangers or burdens. You may even notice that you are holding your breath.

Now try the same planning experiment with the leveling response and see if you can see the beginnings of an open system. In contrast to the experience in the closed system, you may feel more loose, more lucid, and your body is beginning to feel better. You are breathing easier.

The following diagram shows how the closed system applies to troubled families and the open system to nurturing families.

POT   low

COMMUNICATION   indirect, unclear, unspecific,
                        incongruent

                        blaming
                        placating
                        computing
                        distracting
                        (growth impeding)

RULES   covert, out-of-date, inhuman rules
                        remain fixed, change needs to con-
                        form to established rules

                        restrictions on commenting

OUTCOME   accidental, chaotic, inappropriate
                        destructive

Self-worth grows ever more doubtful and leans more and more heavily on the outside for support.

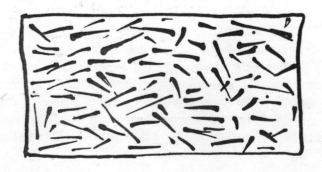

OPEN SYSTEM

POT	high
COMMUNICATION	direct, clear, specific, congruent, leveling (growth producing)
RULES	overt, up-to-date, human rules, rules change when need arises
	full freedom to comment on anything
OUTCOME	related to reality, appropriate, constructive

Self-worth grows even more reliable, confident and draws increasingly more from the self.

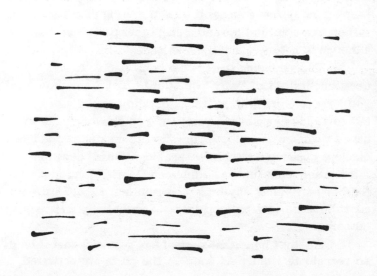

All right. When three or more people are related in any way and are joined in one common purpose, they will develop into a family system. Once it's established, the system becomes part of that family machinery, very much in operation, even when not in evidence. If it's a closed system, it will probably operate on a *life-death*, *right-wrong* basis. If open, it probably operates on a *growth-reality* and *intimacy* basis.

Put very simply, *your self-worth, your communication, together with your rules and your beliefs are the ingredients that make up your family system*. Leveling communication and human rules characterize an open system and make growth flourish for every person in that system. Crippling communication and inhuman rules make a closed system, retarding and distorting growth.

An awareness of the presence of a system in the family usually opens up the way for family members to become searchers and to stop berating themselves and others when things go wrong. This helps make it possible for everyone to know that he and everyone else are most significant factors in keeping the system going as it is. Discovering your part in the system at a point in time and seeing other parts is an exciting, although sometimes painful, experience.

Understanding the system helps people to ask "how" questions instead of "why" questions. You know how hard you have to work with a "why" question so it doesn't come out sounding like a blame question. You know how hard you have to work with a "how" question to make it sound like a blaming question. Generally speaking, "how" questions get information and understanding, and "whys" produce defensiveness. And anything contributing to defensiveness contributes to low pot and leads to potentially unsatisfying outcomes.

Another important part of any system is that it tends to perpetuate itself. As soon as the parts are activated, a

118

life develops that works toward self-perpetuation. Once started, a system will stay the same until it dies naturally or something happens to change it. This could be a breakdown of any one part from lack of care, defect, or a natural wearing out. Sometimes even a minor outside happening can overwhelm the system. This means that the designers of the system either overlooked or did not figure a means of coping with change. In a family this is flexibility. Obviously, a closed system would be more in jeopardy since it is usually man-made and is not designed to cope with change. The importance of system to family life can certainly be seen when you consider that the very life of the family depends upon its system to a very large degree.

Let's look at the family system in another way. Maybe another comparison would help at this point.

In a mobile all the pieces, no matter what size or shape, can be grouped together in balance by shortening or lengthening the strings attached, or rearranging the distance between the pieces. So it is with a family. None of the family members is identical to any other; they are all different and at different levels of growth. As in a mobile, you can't arrange one without thinking of the other.

Try this. Take objects—any objects—that are very different from one another and work out a balance for them. Take as many as there are different people in your family, and think of them as your family members.

If you settle for the first balance you achieve, you will be doing what so many people do: making the only way they know the "right way." All other ways to bring balance to your family are resisted because of fear of experimentation.

So you don't get in this bind, find at least two more ways to make the pieces balance. There are many more, but I will have made my point if you find three. You now have three options, and you need not be stuck with only one.

The more parts to your mobile, and the greater the differences among them, the more variety and interest you'll have.

Going back to your "family mobile" now, the trick of making a vital family system is to make it possible for all family members to have a truly individual place and to have fun in that place. The way to bring off this trick lies in your ability to change and to adjust the "strings." The strings are your pot feelings, rules, and communication patterns. Are they immovable or flexible?

While you are working on your mobile, think of the parts of a family. They can be divided into two major categories: adults and children, then males and females. Even the most casual glance at this array shows a great diversity in what poeple have to give each other in any point in time.

There is no established rule that says one person has to do all the giving and everyone else does the getting. Yet some families cripple themselves by appointing a specific person to be the giver, and nothing ever changes. The reality of ordinary life is such that even if someone agreed to do so, he couldn't always give without great cost. One time it may be only the husband who is able to give; another time it may be only the wife or one child. Many families have rules that dictate who may give to whom:

Boys always give to the girls.

Mother always gives to the children.

Husband always gives to the wife.

Eventually, everyone gets cheated.

I think we agree that the hoped for outcome of a family today is the growth of all members concerned. The family job, then, is how to make use of all of its parts so this growth occurs.

How can adults use themselves so the children can grow? How can the children use themselves so the adults can grow? How do the males make it possible for the females and the females for the males? How does everyone help everyone else—adult, child, male, and female alike? These are significant questions in families' efforts to become more nurturing.

I think the most important thing that happens is that each group has a world that members of the other group does not share. Sharing respective "worlds" and offering the variety and stimulation of those worlds not only adds interest, but also expands the whole reality aspect. No woman knows what it feels like to carry a penis around, and men don't know what it is like to carry babies. Far too many adults have forgotten how to enjoy the simple pleasures in life. Simple sharing among groups can help greatly in these areas.

All families are in balance. The question is, however, what is the cost to each family member to maintain that balance?

I think the stakes are high regarding the nature of your family system. The family is the one place in the world where all of us can expect nurturing to take place, and when I say nurturing, I am talking about soothing the bruised soul and inspiring and elevating self-worth—pot—as well as getting things done.

The family is obviously the place for learning this nurturing and growing. To achieve these goals and to become truly vital, there has to be continual observation and changing and reshaping in the family. This can only take place in an open system.

9 The Couple

Why did you get married? Why did you marry whom you did? Why did you marry when you did? The chances are pretty good that whatever you answer, your reasons for marrying probably represented an opportunity to add something to your life. Only the unusual person and for very unusual reasons would knowingly go into a marriage that he thought would make his life worse.

You had great hopes, I am sure, of how things would be much better for you after you married. It is when something happens to this hope that the stirrings for divorce begin to show, unless the individual involved has decided to resign himself to duty or death. My intention in this chapter is to talk about love and hope and the kinds of things that can happen in a marriage that can threaten or even destroy the couple.

In our western culture I believe most of us would say that we married for love, and we expected our lives would be enhanced by whatever we thought love would bring us (attention, sexual fulfillment, children, status, belongingness, being needed, material things, and so on).

I believe in love—in loving and in being loved. I think that heterosexual love is the most rewarding and fulfilling feeling any human being can experience. Without loving and being loved, the human soul and spirit curdle and die. But love cannot carry all the demands of life, as I hope we will discover in this chapter. Intelligence, information, awareness, and competence have to be added as well.

Love is a powerful feeling that releases the potential of one person to strive for his dreams without threat of judgment, to momentarily transcend his need for the need of another, to be patient and not lose his feeling of worth as the struggle to find meaning with the other person occurs, as bridges between individual differentnesses are built, and while he bears the loneliness that inevitably exists from time to time when each person must, in order to live his own integrity, take separate ways from the other. I would estimate that probably only 4 1/2 percent of young couples who marry are prepared to do this.

Everybody else has to learn how, and it's usually painful. Our divorce rate is a pretty clear indication of our failure.

Once more, our feelings of self-worth (our pot) have much to do with how we label what a love experience is and what we expect of it. I would go so far as to say that the higher our pot, the less we depend on continual concrete evidences from our spouse that we count. Conversely, the lower our pot, the more we tend to depend on continual evidence from our spouse that we count, all of which leads to mistaken notions about what love can do.

Truly loving means I put no strings on you, nor accept them from you. Each person's integrity is respected. I like the description of love and marriage as written by Gibran in *The Prophet:*

> But let there be spaces in your togetherness,
> And let the winds of the heavens dance between you.
> Love one another, but make not a bond of love:
> Let it rather be a moving sea between the shores of your souls.
> Fill each other's cup but drink not from one cup.
> Give one another of your bread but eat not from the same loaf.
> Sing and dance together and be joyous, but let each of you be alone,
> Even as the strings of a lute are alone though they quiver with the same music.
> Give your hearts, but not into each other's keeping.
> For only the hand of Life can contain your hearts.
> And stand together yet not too near together;

For the pillars of the temple stand apart,
And the oak tree and the cypress grow not in each
other's shadow. *

Go back in time and try to remember what you hoped would be better for you when you got married. What were *your* hopes?

Let me review some hopes people have shared with me over the years. Women's hopes centered around having a man who, of all people in the world, would love only them, who would respect and value them, and would talk to them in such a way as to make them glad to be women, who would stand by them, give them comfort, and be on their side in times of stress.

Men have said they hoped for women who would see that their needs were met, who enjoyed their strength, their bodies, regarded them as wise leaders and who would also be willing to help them when they expressed their needs. They spoke of having good food and good sex. As one man put it, he wanted someone "who is all for me. I want to feel needed useful, respected and loved—a king in my own house."

From THE PROPHET, by Kahlil Gibran. Copyright 1923 by Kahlil Gibran; renewal copyright 1951 by Administrators C.T.A. of Kahlil Gibran Estate and Mary G Gibran. Reprinted by permission of Alfred A. Knopf, Inc.

Neither men nor women, for the most part, had seen these kinds of things in their own parents. Nevertheless, these were the hopes and dreams of most people. Over the years I haven't noticed a great deal of difference in hopes between the sexes. In the early years of my career it was a constant puzzle why the hopes so many confided to me never came true. I've come to learn, sadly enough, that many of these dreams could come true, but fail because of gross ignorance and unrealistic expectations as to what love is all about.

I think many marry people whom they really don't know. The state of biological sexual attraction is just that. It contributes nothing to the reality of the context in which it is found, nor does it add anything about how the tastes and desires of one individual might fit in with those of the other individual. If a person is clearly a sexually developed, congruent person, he will be attracted to members of the other sex who are equally developed and congruent. That's part of being human. You can be physically attracted to someone without recognizing that your pot and your body are not in the same place.

By the way, I certainly do not believe that there is only one man in all the world who can be biologically attractive to a woman. There are many. In fact, I now believe many men can interest many women at a moment in time and vice versa. If one were to make his life choices on whom he was physically attracted to, and that's all, he could find himself in a peck of trouble. Being able to make a satisfying creative life with someone else requires compatibility in many, many additional areas. You spend relatively little of your total time in bed.

Lest I be misunderstood, I am saying that sexual responsiveness is basic to a satisfying heterosexual relationship. I am also saying that a day-to-day relationship requires much more.

I think that few children grow up with healthy, satisfying heterosexual models as far as their own parents are concerned. What you have seen going on between your parents as you were growing up perhaps doesn't come very close to the romantic ideal so highly publicized in our western culture. I have heard so many adults express wonder that their parents ever got together in the first place. It was hard for them to imagine their parents in bed together, much less ever having had a romance.

It's really sad that it's impossible for children to know their parents when they were younger—when they were loving, courting, and being nice to one another. All too often by the time children are old enough to observe, the evidences of romance have long since faded or gone underground.

For these and other reasons, people often want a different kind of marriage than that of their parents. But familiarity exerts a powerful pull. Most people will choose the familiar, even though uncomfortable, over the unfamiliar, even though it might be comfortable. Haven't you seen women whose fathers were cruel end up with cruel husbands? And haven't you also seen men who had nagging mothers end up with nagging wives? People often work out marriages similar to their own parents' not because of heredity; they are simply following a family pattern.

We're getting pretty close to talking about "parenting," and I want to reserve that very important subject for a later chapter. Right now our concern is with couples.

There are three parts to a couple: *you, me* and *us.** two people, three parts, each significant, each having a life of its own, and each making the other more possible. Thus, *I* make *you* more possible, *you* make *me* more possible, *I* make

*See Gerald Walker Smith and Alice J. Phillips, ME, YOU, AND US (New York: Peter Wyden, Inc., 1971) for a good discussion about coupling.

127

us more possible, *you* make *us* more possible, and *us* makes each of *me* and *you* more possible.

At this point I am convinced that whether or not the initial love between a couple flowers depends upon how the two people make the three parts work. How these three parts work is a part of what I call the *process*, which is crucially important in marriage. I'll deal with it in detail a little later.

I find that love can truly flourish only where there is room for all three of these parts, and no one part dominates. The single most crucial factor in understanding how an initial love relationship flourishes is the feeling of worth each has for himself, together with how he expresses it and what demands he makes of the other, and how each acts toward the other as a result.

Love is a feeling. It cannot be legislated. It either exists, or it doesn't. It comes without reason, but to continue and to grow, it has to be nourished. Love is like a seed that manages to germinate and poke its head above the ground. But if it doesn't get proper food, light, and moisture, it will die. The loving, caring feelings of courtship flower in marriage only if the couple understands that its love needs nurturing every single day. Successful nurturing is related to the process the couple works out between them. Process refers to the how of marriage. Process consists of the decisions the couple reach together, and the way in which they act on these decisions. I am referring in particular to the kinds of things the two of them have to do together that they once handled alone—such as money, food, fun, work, and religion. Love is the *feeling* that begins a marriage, but *process* is what makes it work.

All couples stumble and bumble at times in their marriages—all have some pain, disappointment, and misunderstanding. Whether or not they grow beyond this, again, depends upon the process that exists between them.

I have seen so many couples who started out with love feelings, but became mixed-up, angry, and helpless. When they were helped to understand their processes, love again became evident. On the other hand, there are some couples who have endured so much that they are literally dead to one another. Since I have not had much success in raising the dead, I think in these cases the best policy is to have a good funeral and start over.

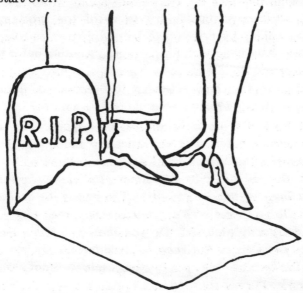

The chances of spouses doing at least some things different from one another are just about 100 percent, as neither was brought up in the same way. Likewise the chances are 100 percent that each will have to join the other on matters about which they feel different. As we'll see in detail in a later chapter, bringing up children highlights these kinds of differentnesses.

Making decisions is a major part of process. For many couples it becomes a battle, either quiet or noisy as to who has the right to tell whom what to do. Every time a decision has to be made, each feels worse about the other and himself. This kind of experience eventually develops into a feeling of tyranny and bondage in which the feeling of loving and being loved no longer exists. Each partner begins to feel lonely, isolated, victimized, angry, betrayed, and depressed. Each lays his self-worth on the table every time a decision is made. After enough battle experience, love and loving are gone.

Sometimes couples try to avoid the problems of decision-making by agreeing to let one partner be boss, and the other goes along with his decisions. Another out is to let a third person decide—an in-law, perhaps, or a child, or some trusted person from outside the family. Eventually all decisions get made. But how? And what happens as a result?

Let's pick up on some of the responses we talked about in the chapters on communication and apply them to how you and your spouse make decisons.

Do you do it by placating? Bullying? Lecturing? Distracting? Acting indifferent? Who makes the decisions? How? Do you meet each decision squarely, realistically, and using everybody's talents? Do you show you know the difference between competence in handling money and self-worth? (Writing a check is writing a check. It is not a way of showing love or not showing love.)

Go back over some of your recent and/or important decisions. Try acting them out with the communication responses and stances. Try to remember, then, exactly how the decision was reached in actuality. Were there any similarities?

Here is an example. Before marriage, John managed his money and Alice managed hers. Now they are married, and they need to handle it together. This calls for a big decision, probably the first big one they make after the wedding.

John says confidently, "Well, I am the man of the house, so I will handle the money. Besides, my father always did."

Alice's response is slightly sarcastic. "John, how could you? You're such a spendthrift! I naturally assumed I would do it. Besides, my mother always did it that way."

John's answer is very quiet. "Well, if you want it that way, I suppose it's all right. I naturally thought that since I'm your husband, and you love me, you would want me to handle the money. After all, it's a man's place."

Alice is a little frightened. "Oh, John! Of course I love you! I wouldn't want to hurt your feelings. Let's not talk about it anymore. Come on, give me a kiss."

What would you say about this decision-making process? Where do you think it will lead? Will it make for more or less love?

Five years later Alice says angrily to John, "The company is threatening to sue us! You didn't pay the bill! I am tired of dodging the bill collectors. I am going to take charge of the money, and I don't care what you think!"

John snaps, "The hell with you! Go ahead, and see if you can do any better!"

Can you see their problem? They can't differentiate between their feelings of self-worth and coping with their finances.

There is probably nothing so vital to maintaining and developing a love relationship (or killing it) as the decision-making process.

Let's go into something a little different now. Let's consider some of the basic differences between the courtship and the marriage, and some of the problems implicit in the differences.

In our system of courtship, the two prospective mates see each other by plan. They arrange their lives in such a way as to literally make time for one another. They know when they are together that the other has made definite plans for the meeting. This naturally gives each the feeling that the other sees him as a Very Important Person.

After marriage this feeling is subject to drastic changes. Work, family, friends, and special interests soon seem to become as important as just being together. Each partner feels he has become a Less Important Person in the other's eyes. In courtship it is easy to forget that the loved one has family, friends, work responsibilities, and other obligations of his own. All of these reappear and compete for his attention after the marriage, which helps pave the way to feelings of low pot. If one partner felt he was everything to the person he married and must now share him with a lot of outside influences, such comments as "I didn't know you were so attached to your mother," or "I didn't think you liked to play bridge so much" are bound to occur, and often lead to more serious disagreements.

Also, frequently a person marries only one facet of his spouse and then expects the rest of him to conform to that part. A man I know married a woman who always looked neat In contrast his mother always looked sloppy. When his wife later looked sloppy at times for one reason or another, he began treating her with his negative attitudes toward his mother.

Many couples bank on the illusion that since they love each other, all things will happen automatically. Let's compare this situation to someone who, say, wants to build a bridge. He isn't about to attempt this simply because he digs bridges. He has to know a good deal about how to build his bridge.

In the same way couples need to know the how (process) of marriage. Fortunately, many couples are realizing this today and are taking advantage of family life education classes, which are becoming much more common. We need love and process in family building. Neither works all by itself.

Let's carry our analogy a little further. The bridge builder who loves his work is going to endure the struggles and frustrations that are bound to occur as he learns his job much more than one who is indifferent to the task. Even so, the devoted engineer's job is by no means assured. If in the "how" process he feels he isn't progressing toward his goal he may stop loving bridges and stop learning as well. He may stay with it, but he will begin to shrivel.

So it is with couples. If the "how" in their marriage doesn't succeed in fulfilling their hopes and dreams, love goes. Many people are aware that their love is going, without being aware in the slightest degree that it is their process—the how in the marriage—that is shoving love out.

Do you remember the love feeling you had for your spouse when you got married? Can you remember how you thought your life would be different? Do you also remember that you thought the problems you knew about would be solved by loving? Can you share together what some of these were and what has happened about them?

We've seen that marriage reveals much more about each partner than did the courtship. Lots of times sweethearts don't let themselves know too much about one another's defects, perhaps feeling that if they did, the marriage might not go through. Nevertheless some defects are obvious. Some sweethearts have plans for changing them; others accept them as part of being human and live happily with them.

It's impossible to live in close contact with another person without those less desirable traits eventually showing up. This is the basis for cruel disappointment for many people. Disappointed mates often say to me, "You certainly never know a person till you marry him!"

The following are examples of the kind of faulty reasoning that can lead to these kinds of post-wedding disappointments.

A girl might say to herself, "He really drinks too much, but after we're married, I'll love him so much he won't drink." Or a man might say, "I really think she's a little stupid, but after we're married, she'll go to school to please me." A man I knew said, "I can't stand the way she chews gum, but I love her so much I'll tolerate it."

Two people living together as one unit is difficult at best. A successful job of it is very rewarding. An unsuccessful job can be dreadful. I often think of marriage as being similar to setting up a corporation. Whether the corporation succeeds or not depends upon the organization that gets built—the how of its organization, its process.

I know plenty of couples who loved each other very deeply, but couldn't make a marriage work because they couldn't get along with one another. Again, I might point out that your process will be dependent upon how you extend your pot when it's low, what you expect from marriage, and how you communicate about it.

One of the truly basic problems is that our society bases the marital relationship almost completely on love and then imposes demands on it that love can never solely fulfill.

"If you love me, you won't do anything without me."

"If you love me, you'll do what I say."

"If you love me, you'll give me what I want."

"If you love me, you'll know what I want before I ask."

These kinds of practices soon make love into a kind of blackmail, which I call "the clutch."

To be a bit more specific, if I do not feel that I count for very much and if you and I have a relationship that presumably is based on love, then I can easily depend on your compliments, your attention, your agreement, your money, and so on, to make me feel good. If you are not eternally showing me that you live for me, then I feel like nothing. This is a way of "talking love" but is actually black-mail. This practice can soon strangle the relationship.

Where are you now in your experience of loving and being loved? Facing this question squarely may help you to reshape what you are doing and may well extend the life of your love. If you put both your questions and answers into words, your partner can see what's happening with you.

Another way of "talking love" is practicing the *crystal ball* technique. In this one you assume that because someone "loves" you or you "love" him, he should know ahead of time what you need, want, feel, or think and act accordingly. Not doing so is the same as being unloved. The fact is that no matter how much you and I may love each other, that love doesn't tell me a thing about whether or not you like spinach or how you like it cooked.

I remember a couple who came to me because they felt very discontented in their marriage of about twenty years. As I talked with them, it became evident that both had tried to second-guess the other on the crystal ball theory: "If we truly love one another, we will always know what the other wants." And since this was the premise they had set up, they couldn't very well test it by checking through questions because that would cast aspersions on their love. This kind of guessing had proved all right in a few limited areas, as the husband reported no particular complaints.

Then as we began to work together, the couple realized it was safe to talk more openly. When we got to the part where I asked each of them to say openly what he resented about the other, the husband cried with a burst of emotion, "I wish you wouldn't always serve me that god-damned spinach!" After his wife recovered from the shock, she answered, "I loathe spinach, but I thought you liked it. I just wanted to please you!" This episode gave rise to a slogan that was used helpfully in other situations, namely "Remember the spinach!"

What had happened was that early in the marriage the wife had asked her husband what he liked to eat. He told her whatever she fixed would be fine. She did considerable private research to find out what pleased her husband. She once overheard her husband reprimand his young nephew for not eating his spinach, and interpreted this as a zest for spinach on his part.

This came out as we backtracked over the area. The husband didn't remember the incident, but did remember how sloppy he thought his sister-in-law was for not making her child eat right. Of course, I naturally brought up the question of how come the husband kept eating the spinach when he hated it, with no comment. He said he hadn't wanted to hurt her feelings. "Besides," he added, "she liked it. I didn't want to deprive her of it." He then turned to her. "But didn't you notice that I kept eating less and less?" "Oh," she said, "I thought you were reducing."

This is a prime example of the crystal ball approach. Probably no other couple in the world has had this particular spinach experience, but my guess is nearly all of you have had something pretty similar.

As one looks back on such an incident, and it becomes clear, it seems utterly absurd. And yet it happens again and again

Another myth that corrupts and destroys love is the ex-pectation that love means sameness. "You should think, feel, and act as I do all the time. If you don't, you don't love me."

Let's consider sameness and differentness a moment or two.

I believe that two people are first interested in each other because of their sameness, but they remain interested over the years because of their differences. To put it another way, if humans never find their sameness, they will never meet; if they never meet their differentness, they cannot be real or develop a truly human and zestful relationship with one another.

Differentness cannot be handled successfully until sameness is appreciated. Although each human is unique, there are certain qualities everyone has in common. Let's review them:

Each human being

came into this world concieved by intercourse and born from the body of a woman,

is encapsulated by skin which contains all the machinery for maintaining and growing,

has a predictable anatomy,

requires air, food, and water to survive,

has a brain capable of reason and the ability to talk and move (except those born incomplete),

is able to respond,

feels all his human life.

Now as to differentness—many fear it because they see it as the beginning of conflict, which is the beginning of a fight and is thus a threat and possibly even death to the relationship. Discovery of a difference doesn't have to mean a fight.

If you were brought up to think that fighting is bad, then the threat of a fight (real or imagined) could frighten you and fill you with guilt. But a good, healthy fight does not have to mean death—it can bring more closeness and trust. Yetta Bernhard and George Bach have done some excellent work on "clean fight training," which every couple needs to be able to do when the occasion demands it.* You notice I put the emphasis on *clean* fighting. We all know about dirty fighting, and that *is* scary and can end in death.

We have those attributes previously named in common. But we are all different from everyone else, and this is a natural consequence of being human. There are over three and one half billion people on this earth and every one of them can be positively identified by his fingerprints. There are no duplicate sets; every human being is unique. So any two human beings, no matter what their similarities, are going to find different-nesses. And *vive la difference!* Think how boring and sterile life would be if we were all the same! It is difference that brings us excitement, interest, and vitality. It also brings a few problems. The challenge then is to find a way to deal with our differences constructively. How can differences be used as opportunities for learning instead of excuses for separation?

The wise couple will strive to learn about its differences early. They will try to see how they can make their differences work for them rather than against them.

---

*Yetta Bernhard and George Bach, AGGRESSION LAB: THE FAIR FIGHT TRAINING MANUAL (Dubuque, Iowa: Kendal-Hunt, 1971).

If your pot is high, there are certain things you will have to come to know.

No two persons are exactly alike; everyone is unique.

No two persons are going to be timed exactly the same even in ways they are alike. Two people may like steak, but neither likes it fixed the same way, nor are they hungry for it at the same time.

A further important learning is that you won't die because you're alone. Periodic loneliness is a natural outcome of being a separate person.

As I come to the end of this chapter, I am aware that I have talked a great deal about the complexity and the potential pain involved in developing a satisfying, growing relationship between mates.

The ways of dealing with all this complexity, I have discovered, generally fall in the following directions.

The first has to do with the beliefs one has about what people are like. Realizing that perfection is something one can never know about ahead of time and that few people behave destructively by design should help you to see your mate as a person behaving like a human being.

The second direction has to do with becoming aware of yourself, getting in touch with yourself, and then being able to say where you are, so trust and confidence can be established.

The third has to do with knowing within one's bones that each person has to stand on his own two feet. No one else can stand on your feet for you. This means you come really face to face with whatever is in this point in time. This goes for the "nitty-gritty" as well as the "juicy." This means no one is carrying someone else on his back, thus making cripples of them both.

All of these ways culminate in a flow of opportunities for enjoying each other through the body, mind, feeling, and things. This is, after all, *where it really is at.*

When I first started working with entire families I was struck by the tremendous unrelated activity that went on in all directions—physically through bodily movement and also psychologically through double-level messages, un-finished sentences, and so on. More than anything else I was reminded of the can of angleworms my father used to take as bait on fishing trips. The worms were all entangled together, constantly writhing and moving. I couldn't tell where one ended and the other began. They really couldn't go anywhere except up, down, around, and sideways, but they certainly gave the impression of aliveness and purpose. It wasn't quite possible to talk to one of those worms to see how he felt, but it is my feeling that had I been able to, he would have told me the same kinds of things I have heard from family members over the years. *Where am I going? What am I doing? Who am I?*

The comparison between the way so many families conduct themselves and the purposeless, tangled writhing of the worms in the can seemed so apt to me that I termed the network that exists among family members a *can of worms.*

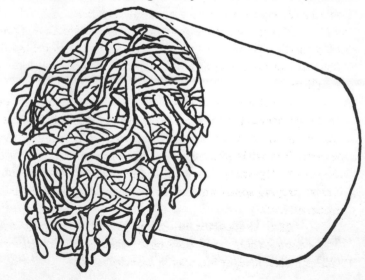

To show you what your family network is and how to map it will be the goal of this chapter. I think the best way to go about it is to take an imaginary family, the Lintons, and show you how their network works for and against them. No one can ever actually see this network, incidentally, but you can certainly feel it, as the exercises outlined in this and the following chapter will amply demonstrate to you.

All right. Here are the Lintons as individuals as their family is today.

THE LINTON FAMILY NOW

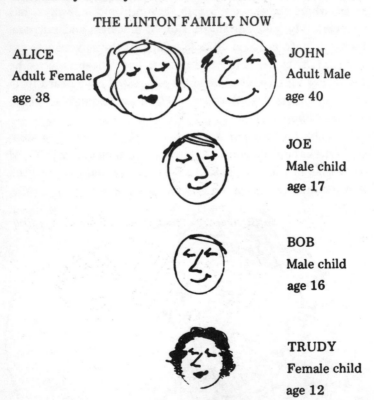

ALICE
Adult Female
age 38

JOHN
Adult Male
age 40

JOE
Male child
age 17

BOB
Male child
age 16

TRUDY
Female child
age 12

Take a large sheet of paper and tack it to the wall where all of you can see it clearly. Begin the map of your family by placing circles for each person, using a felt-tipped pen. *Your family may now include a grandparent or other person as part of your household. If so, add a circle for that person on the row with the other adults.*

If someone were once a part of your family, but is gone now, represent him with a filled-in circle. If your husband or father is dead, has deserted or divorced you and you have not remarried, your map would show it as follows:

If the woman has remarried it would be shown like this:

If the second child died or was institutionalized, your map would look this way:

I believe that anyone who has ever been part of a family leaves a definite impact. A departed person is often very much alive in the memories of those left behind. Frequently, too, these memories play an important role in what is going on in the present, and much of the time a negative one. This doesn't have to happen. If the departure has not been accepted, for whatever reason, the ghost is very much still around and often can "bug up" the current scene. If, on the other hand, the departure has been accepted, then the present is clear as far as the departed one is concerned.

Each person is an individual self (S). He can be described separately by name, by physical characteristics, by interests, tastes, habits, talents—all of the qualities that relate to him as an individual.

So far our map shows the family members as islands, but anyone who has lived in a family knows that no one can remain an island for long. The various family members are connected by a whole network of ties that link them together as a family. They may be invisible, but they are there, all right, as solid and firm as if they were woven of steel.

Let's add another strand to our network—pairs. Pairs have specific role names in a family. The illustration below shows the pairs in the Linton family with their *role names.*

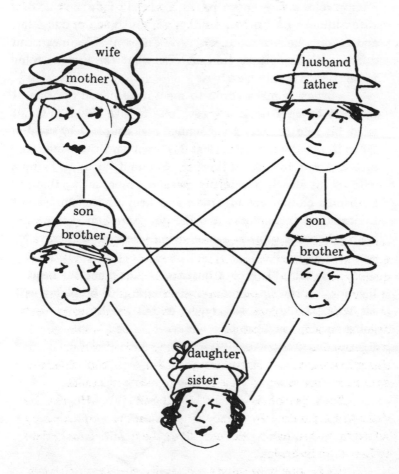

Roles in the family are of three major categories: marital, having the labels of husband and wife; parental-filial, having the labels of father-daughter, mother-daughter, father-son; and sibling, having the labels of brother-brother, sister-sister, and brother-sister. Each role has different expectations. Family roles always mean pairs. You can't take the role of a wife without a husband, nor father without a son or daughter, and so on. Beliefs about what the different roles mean can differ. It's important to find out what the various roles mean to each family member.

When families come to me a little mixed up, one of the first things I do is ask each one to give his ideas about what his role means. I remember one couple very vividly. When I asked each one what his own and the other role meant, I was told the following. She said, "I think being a wife means always having the meals on time, seeing that my husband's clothes are in order, and keeping the unpleasant things about the children and the day from him. I think the husband should provide a good living. He should not give his wife any trouble."

He said, "I think a husband means being the head of the house, providing income, and sharing his problems with his wife. I think a wife ought to tell her husband what's going on. She ought to be a 'pussycat' in bed."

You can see that each was practicing what he thought his role was, and the couple didn't know how far apart they actually were in these important areas. They'd never talked about it; they had just assumed that their views on their respective roles were the same. When they shared their ideas, some new understanding developed between them, and they achieved a much more satisfying relationship. I have seen this particular couple's experience repeated over and over again when troubled families have come to me for help.

What about your family and your respective role expectations and definitions? Why not all sit down and share what you think your role is, and that of your spouse and your offspring as well? I think you'll be in for some surprises.

Now let's examine another facet of this role business. Alice Linton is a person who lives and breathes and takes a certain dress size. She is also a wife when she is with John, a mother when she is with Joe, Bob, or Trudy.

It might be helpful if we think of her roles as different hats she puts on when the occasion demands, and only uses a particular hat when she is with the person who corresponds to the role-hat. She is constantly putting on and taking off hats as she goes through her day. If she or John were to wear all of their role-hats at once it would look like this, and it could get a little top-heavy. You never take off the self-hat; it's there all the time.

Go to your family map now, and add the network lines, linking every member with every other member. As you draw each line, think for a moment about that particular relationship. Imagine how each of the people involved feels about it. All of the family should share in this exercise, so each can try to feel what the different relationships are like.

So far I have presented the Lintons to you as selves and pairs—five selves and ten pairs. If this were all there were to the map, living in a family would be quite an easy matter. When Joe arrived, however, a triangle came into being. Here the plot begins to thicken, for the triangle is the trap in which most families get caught. I'll talk more about triangles later, but first let's add the network of triangles to the Linton family map.

Now the Linton's network looks like this. It's pretty hard to see any one part of it clearly, isn't it? You can see how the triangles literally begin to obscure and complicate things. And in families we don't live in pairs; we live in triangles.

In actuality when Joe was born, not one, but three triangles were formed, for a triangle is always a pair plus one. Since only two people can relate at one time, someone in the triangle is always odd man out. The whole nature of the triangle changes depending on who is odd man.

The three triangles above consist of John, Alice, and Joe, but each is different. In the first, John is odd man, watching the relationship of his wife and son. In the second, Alice watches her husband and son together. In the third, little Joe watches his father and mother together. How troublesome any particular triangle is may well depend on who is odd man at the moment and whether or not he feels bad about being left out.

There is truth to the old saying about "two's company, three's a crowd." The odd man in a triangle always has a choice among breaking the relationship between the other two, withdrawing from it, or supporting it by being an interested observer. His choice is crucial to the functioning of the whole family network.

All kinds of games go on among people in triangles. When a pair is talking, the third may interrupt or try to draw attention to himself. If the pair disagrees, one may invite the third to become his ally, thus changing the triangle and putting one of the original pair on the outside.

Can you remember a time recently when you were with just two other people? How did you handle the triangle? How did you feel? How are triangles handled in your family?

Families are full of triangles. In the Linton family of five there are forty-five triangles. For example:

John/his wife/his first son
John/his wife/his second son
John/his wife/his daughter
John/his first son/his second son
John/his first son/his daughter
John/his second son/his daughter

Then,

Alice/her husband/their first son

And so on.

Triangles are extremely important because the family's operation depends in a large part on how triangles are handled.

The first step toward making a triangle bearable is for each member of the triangle to understand very clearly that when three people are together, there cannot be equal attention to all at the same time. Maybe the best idea is to approach the inevitable triangle as people do Texas weather: stick around for awhile, and it will change. The second step when you are the odd man is to put your dilemma into words so that everyone can hear. The third step is to show by your own actions that it isn't a cause for anger or hurt or shame when you're odd man. Problems arise because some people feel that being on the outside means they are no good. Low pot!

To live comfortably in a triangle, it seems to me that certain feelings about oneself have to be in effect. The individual has to feel good about himself and be able to stand on his own two feet without having to lean on someone else. He can be temporarily odd man without feeling bad or rejected. He needs to be able to wait without feeling he is abused. He needs to be able to talk straight and clearly, and let the others know what he is feeling and thinking and not brood and store up his feelings.

If you glance again at the Linton's family map after the triangles were added to it, you can appreciate just how complex family networks really are. Probably the concept of the can of worms is more understandable to you, too.

Draw your family's can of worms by adding all the triangles to your family map. It may help to use a different colored pencil or ink to distinguish the triangles from the pairs. Again, as you draw, think of the real life relation that each line represents. Among any three people you will be drawing only one triangle, although three actually exist. Think of how that triangle looks from each person's point of view.

The Linton's network did not develop overnight. It took six years to gather the people now represented in the network—possibly eight years, if you consider the two years John and Alice courted.

Some families take fifteen or twenty years to assemble their casts—others take one or two years, and some never finish because the core (the male and female who are in charge) keeps changing.

Whenever the Lintons are all together, there are forty-two different units operating—five individuals, ten pairs, and twenty-seven triangles. There are similar living elements in your family. Each person has his own mental picture of what each of these units is like. John may look very different to his wife Alice than to his son Bob. Each person has his own picture of what each circle or line is like. Alice may see her relationship to Bob one way; Bob would see it differently. John's picture is probably quite different from either of theirs. All these varying pictures are supposed to fit together in the family, whether the individuals are aware of them or not. In nurturing families all of these elements and everyone's interpretation of them are out in the open and can easily be talked about. On the other hand, troubled families are either unaware of their family pictures or are unwilling or unable to talk about them.

Many times families have told me of their feelings of frustration, physical tightness, and discomfort when the whole family is assembled. Everyone feels constant movement as if he were being pulled in many directions. If family members could be made aware of the can of worms in which they are trying to function, they wouldn't be so puzzled and uncomfortable. When families see their network for the first time and fully realize how tremendously complicated family living really is, they have often told me of the great relief they feel. They realize it would be almost impossible to be on top of everything all the time. Who can keep track or control of forty-two units at once? Many have reported to me that when the whole family understood its network, the individual members had a much easier time together because they didn't feel the necessity to control things; they became more interested in observing what was happening and in planning creative ways to make the family function better.

The challenge in family living is to find ways each individual can participate or be an observer of others without feeling he doesn't count—being a victim of our old villain: low pot.

Let's consider for a moment what this push-pull in the can of worms does to the individual. Certainly it puts great demand on him. In some families it is difficult to be an individual at all. The larger the family, the more units to be dealt with, the more difficult it is for each family member to to get his share of the action. I certainly don't mean to imply that big families are always failures. On the contrary, some of the most nurturing families I know have large numbers of children.

Similarly, the more children that come into the family, the more pressure on the marital relationship. In a family of three there are only 9 self-pair-triangles. In a family of four, there are 22; in a family of five, there are 45, and in a family of ten, there are 376 units! Each time a new person is added, the limited time and other resources of the family have to be divided into smaller portions. A larger house and more money may be found, but the mother and father still have only two arms and two ears. And the air waves can still carry only one set of words at a time without total bedlam.

What often happens is that the pressure of parenting gets so overwhelming that very little of the self of either parent finds expression, and the marital relationship grows weak with neglect. At this point many couples break up, give up, and run away. They have starved as individuals, failed as mates, and probably aren't doing very well as parents, either. Frustrated, turned off, emotionally dying adults don't make very good family leaders.

Unless the marital relationship is protected and given a chance to flower and unless each individual in the partnership has his own chance for development, the family system becomes crooked, and the children are bound to be lopsided in their growth.

Being good, balanced parents is not impossible. It is just that parents must be particularly skillful and aware in family relations to maintain their selfhood and keep their marriage partnership alive when the can of worms is so full. Such parents will be in charge of nurturing families, and are living examples of the kind of family functioning I am talking about in this book—the kind of functioning that channels the pressures in the family network into creative, growth-producing directions.

11   The Can of Worms in Action

So far we've talked about the lines on the family map as if there were TV channels along which messages and feelings can pass. This is true, as far as it goes. But these lines are also in a very real sense family *ties.* These lines tie all the individuals together so that each one is affected by every other one. Obviously any one person can be in the middle of many pulls at the same time. And again, the problem is not how to avoid these pulls (because that's impossible), but instead how to live with the pulls creatively. That is precisely what I want to deal with in this chapter.

Incidentally, some of the exercises I am going to ask you to do in this chapter may seem silly, possibly too time-consuming, or too much bother. I urge you to undertake them anyway. What can be revealed to you in something as artless and simple as these games I think will absolutely astound you. Surely it is worth an investment of some of your time and effort when the reward could be much deeper understanding and a more fully functioning and creative family life.

We'll start with the Lintons. John comes home from work. Alice would like to have his company. Joe, Bob, and Trudy might also like to have his attention. If they all want to have his attention at once John will be in this position:

You can imagine how pulled he feels. You can do better than imagining by literally experiencing these kinds of pulls yourself.

Let's start with your "John." He should stand in the middle of the floor, straight and balanced. Then ask "Alice" to take his right hand. Ask your firstborn to take his left hand. The second born, your "Bob" to grasp him around the waist from the front; your "Trudy" should put her arms around his waist from the back. If you have a fourth, have him grasp the right knee, a fifth, the left knee. Just keep going until all members of the family have their hands on "John." Now, everyone pull gently, slowly, but firmly toward themselves until everyone feels the pull. Then freeze. After a very few seconds John will begin to feel stretched, uneasy, uncomfortable, and miserable. He may even fear he will lose his balance.

John's feelings in this exercise are very similar to what his actual feelings are when too many demands are made on him.

John cannot stay in this position forever. He has to do something. Several choices of action are open. He can decide to endure it and get increasingly more numb until he no longer feels anything. Once this numb he can wait indefinitely. Finally people will just let go, left with the feeling that "Daddy doesn't care." Or John can decide to "bull" his way out by using brute force. Some of the family members might accidentally get slugged or knocked over. Then as John looks at his family he can see he has hurt them. He may feel guilty and blame himself for not being able to do what they want, or he may blame them for putting burdens on him. The others are likely to feel that Daddy is mean, unloving, and hurtful.

Something else John can do is collapse when he feels the pressure. He literally drops to the floor, which represents his solution of becoming sick or helpless. When this happens, his family could feel they are bad because they have hurt Daddy. And he could feel angry at them for making him feel weak.

Another choice open to John is to start making deals by bribing and making promises he probably can't keep, but which provide a way out of his misery. In this case John asks each his price for letting go, and the sky's the limit. Whatever they ask for, John will have to say yes, but since the promises aren't real, they probably won't be kept. Distrust grows out of this maneuver, as well as all the other feelings one directs at a promise-breaker.

John has still another choice. At the point of his discomfort he can yell for help—to his mother, his therapist, his pastor, the neighbors, a visiting friend. "Come get me out of this mess!" And if the one he calls is skillful, powerful, or enticing enough, John can be freed. The entrance of an outside party, however, brings new chances for rifts. I think this is how many secret relationships develop outside the family—mistresses, lovers, and so on.

One more choice is open to John. He can be aware that he is an important person to all of those who are asking things of him. He realizes that all those pulling on him are not feeling the same as he is. He can tell all the other family members how he's feeling and have the confidence that he can ask *them* for relief, and ask for it directly—no hints.

John should now role-play all these ways of getting out of his bind. Then all members of the family can talk about how they felt as this was going on. I think all of you will learn something. Then go through the same procedure with each person having a turn in the center being pulled.

I would like to underscore the fact that any time you are in a group you subject yourself to getting into binds like this from time to time.

I know of only three ways to completely avoid these binds: (1) Become a hermit; (2) Plan your family contacts in such a way so that no one approaches anyone else without a previous plan and permission ("You can see me at 5:00 P.M. for five minutes on Tuesday"; (3) Simply don't care about anyone else. If there are other ways, I haven't found them.

None of these ways of avoiding binds is particularly satisfying. As a matter of fact when people practice them, they complain about them. The real skill, as mentioned, is not in avoiding binds, but in knowing how to resolve them. It is a fact, however, that most people use one of the approaches we had "John" enact in the last exercise: the martyr approach (enduring), bulling (fighting out), the poor-me (collapsing), the con artist (promises, promises), or passing the buck (calling for outside help). Darned few talk straight to the other family members and give them directions to help change the situation. And yet I have found very few people who refuse when asked directly and honestly for help.

Obviously there are times when one has to stand pain, when one has to battle, when one gets tired, and when one has to ask for help. There is nothing wrong with these states. It is when they are used solely as ways to avoid binds that they become destructive.

We've been talking about John, but the same situation holds true for all members of the family. Every wife and mother knows how Alice feels when John is waiting for his dinner, Joe has just cut his knee, Bob is late for his clarinet lesson, and Trudy is yelling, "Mama!" from the top of the stairs. And Alice has a headache.

Now Alice is the one in the bind. She has the same choices that John had. Which will she take? *Practice all of them to see how it feels.*

Joe is going out on his first date. Alice is giving him instructions on how to behave. John is warning him about staying out too late. Bob is teasing him about shaving, and Trudy is pouting because she'd hoped Joe would take her to the movies that night.

He, too, has the same choices. Which will he take? *Have your Joe practice the bind-breaking approaches his parents did.*

Bob has just cut his knee. Alice is scolding him for being careless. John is telling him to be brave, that "men don't cry." Joe is calling him clumsy. Trudy is crying. Bob, too, has the same choices. Which one will he take?

Trudy got two low marks on her report card. Alice is consoling her, John is scolding her, telling her she'll have to spend two hours doing homework every night until the next report card period, and under his supervision. Joe is winking at her, and Bob is calling her a dummy. Which of the same choices open to her will Trudy take?

You are in the center of this bind now. What kind of pressures are other family members putting on you? Try to feel them, then describe them to the people involved. Each of you take a turn. Then try to imagine what pressures you may be putting on the others.

As I said, you do break binds in these ways. But what is significant is what happens afterwards. The choice a person makes has after-effects, determines his reputation, and guides the ways the others treat him.

Now we're going to do a different kind of exercise. This one will succeed in literally making your family network come alive for you. It may seem like a lot of bother to you. but wholehearted participation can give you a good boost toward becoming a more vital and nurturing family, and that's worth it, isn't it?

Cut a piece of clothesline or heavy twine into twenty-foot lengths, four for each of you. In addition, cut five three-foot lengths, and tie one of the shorter lengths around each person's waist (some of you might prefer putting it around each other's necks, but I prefer the waistline). Next have each person tie his four longer ropes to his waistline rope. Now each of you literally has a line to each of your family members.

Now each of you hand your ropes to the person who belongs on the other end. For example, John, hand your husband rope to your wife. She will hand her wife rope to you. When everybody has another person at the end of each rope, you will be ready. And, you should excuse the expression, you have your hands full, don't you?

Tie the ropes you have received to your waist rope (many people do this immediately, almost without being aware of it). You'll look like the picture below.

Keep the lines tied while you do the following experiments.

Begin by having chairs placed in a circle no more than three feet from the center of the circle. Sit down. Now you'll hardly notice your lines. Everyone is in his own chair; you can talk to each other, read, or do other quiet activities.

All right. Now imagine that the telephone is ringing, and your oldest child jumps up to answer it. It's probably thirty feet away. See what happens to the rest of you. You're all shook up! Individuals may feel invaded, pushed, or may experience anger. You'll probably be aware that whatever your feelings are, they are feelings you have experienced before. ("Joe, why do you make so much noise?" "Why do you move so fast?") If the caller is a teen-aged pal of Joe's, settle in for at least ten minutes.

What is happening to the rest of you while Joe's talking? Maybe some of you will start to pull on Joe so you can be more comfortable. "Hurry up on the phone, Joe! You've got three minutes!" Joe starts to yell. "Leave me alone!" He may get breathless and raise his voice.

Let yourselves see and feel what happens to you as you live with this.

Now go back to your chairs, and we'll do another scene. Mother, it's your turn. You remember something cooking on the stove fifteen feet away, and it may be burning. See what happens to everybody else as you rush to the stove.

Then come back, get your balance, and this time, John, you are getting tired and maybe bored and you want to get up and take a walk. As you are headed for the door you feel tugs and pulls. "My God, can't a man even take a walk without everyone getting on his back?" What happens to all the rest of you? How do you feel about yourselves and your family members?

Now, Trudy, you are tired and want to go to bed. Go over and put your head on your mother's lap. See what happens now.

Bob, you decide you want to have a little fun with Joe and start wrestling with him. Now what happens to everyone?

All right. Come back and get your balance. This time let's make an extreme plot for our little play. Joe, you answer the telephone; Alice, see about the cooking; John, try to take a walk; Trudy, you're sleepy and head toward your mother's lap; Bob, you start something with Joe. Do this all at the same time.

Along about now you are probably all mixed up with one another and feeling angry and frustrated. Some of you have possibly tripped and are on the floor. The food is burning, the telephone still ringing, Bob is struggling with Joe who is still trying to get to the phone, Trudy caught her mother's foot as she turned and John, you didn't even have a chance, did you? (Won't it be nice to get back to work tomorrow?)

The feelings elicited by this experiment probably seemed familiar to you. Of course you don't run around every day with ropes attached to you, but I'm sure it often feels as if they were there. Perhaps next time you'll be aware of how easily family members can get in each other's way without meaning to.

Look on these lines as representing the love-care-comfort-duty relationships that exist among people in a family. It's easy to see how, without ever intending to, someone can upset the whole family applecart. What we should learn here is that we need to recognize each other's self-life, too.

Now let's try that last experiment again. Only this time when you feel the pull, say what you are feeling, and say what you are noticing. Then you'll have a chance to get your lines back from the others and to untie them so you are free.

This is straight, clear, and full communication to the rescue.

You may have noticed that there are only five people present, but there are twenty lines. A string pulled between husband and wife affects the lines between each parent and the offspring.

Here is another experiment you can do while you're still all tied up.

John, you and Alice start pulling against one another. See what happens to the others. If you pull quietly and lightly, maybe your children won't notice (after all, they shouldn't see you two fighting, should they?). If your pull is light enough, maybe neither of you will notice it either. But if you pull as if you mean it, the lines to the children get taut, which draws the attention of your children and starts the triangle moving.

Now, John, you and Alice draw close together and embrace. See what happens with the children; they'll have to move. Try the same thing with each pair becoming active and see what happens.

Ready for another experiment? The time comes when members of the family decide to leave it. This is Joe's wedding day. What happens to your ties now? Do you, John, give Joe your end of the rope and let him go? Do you just untie your end and tuck it in, symbolizing memories of fathering him? He's a grown man now. Joe, what do you do? It isn't enough for your parents to let go; you have to, too. Bob and Trudy have to do something about their ropes and Joe has to do something about his ropes to them. Joe needs to untie his old lines and prepare development of new ones as he prepares for the making of his own family.

For a final experiment, think of some important event about to occur in your family or perhaps some everyday situation that frequently causes problems. Act it out with your ropes, and see what happens to the ties among the

*various family members. Where is the pull? What might you
do to relieve it?*

Just as it is true for family rules, one of the very real
challenges of the family map is to keep it up-to-date. Compare
the Lintons of today to where they were twelve years ago,
when John was twenty-eight and Alice, twenty-six. Joe was
five, Bob, four, and Trudy, an infant. The only constant
from that point to the current one was the number in the
family. The needs, wishes, and literal form have changed
drastically. If the changes don't get "registered," it may be as
though you're taking a 1920 map of Chicago and trying to
locate a current address.

Perhaps Alice is still trying to treat Trudy as if she
were two. Is your map up-to-date? Are you still calling a
six-foot, four-inch son whose name is William, "Willikens," or
something equally absurd? "My baby," I hear a mother
describe her twenty-one-year-old daughter, and I notice the
daughter cringe.

Another common happening as families experience
changes is that several members are going through drastic
changes simultaneously, which creates what I call a normal
developmental crisis cluster. In short, things bunch up.

Let's take the Lintons one year from now. Joe will be eighteen and probably taking a big step on his own. Trudy might be starting her active dating life, Alice might be approaching menopause, and John might be reassessing his dreams. As they all go through these deep, yet normal crises, the stresses become greater. It is not uncommon for the wife-mother to be pregnant with her third child when the first child is just entering kindergarten, the second child barely talking, and the husband-father just recently returned from military service.

When there is a cluster of such crises, someone in the family falls on his face for awhile. When this happens, everyone feels squeezed, and the family can temporarily be as strangers, which is scary. I think this is fertile ground for developing the generation gap, as well as a marital gap.

For example, I know a young woman whose son, Joel, age six, became very interested in small garter snakes. For Joel the snakes were a source of interest and delight. For his mother they were frightening and horrid. In another instance, a man I'll call Josh one day announced to his wife that he had decided to have a vacation by himself. He wanted the chance to be totally outside any family demands. This fit *his* internal state, but to his wife it meant rejection. Suppose Alice Linton decided to take a job to add variety and interest to her life. This meant growth to her, but to John her move meant his wife was dissatisfied with his ability to provide. There are countless illustrations of this kind of thing.

Although these kinds of situations are generally the outgrowth of individual growth needs, they are often not understood that way. Always there is the dilemma of what action will be taken and what will be the consequences when family members' roles collide. Will Joel get to keep the snakes without giving his mother a nervous breakdown? Will

Josh be able to take his vacation alone without seriously rupturing his relationship to his wife? Will Alice get to keep her job without losing John?

I would like to briefly describe these major, natural, common steps a family undergoes as the individuals grow within the family. All of these steps mean crisis and temporary anxiety and require an adjustment period and a new integration.

The first crisis is the conception, pregnancy, and birth of a child.

The second crisis comes when the child starts to use intelligible speech. Few people realize how much adjustment this takes.

The third crisis comes when the child makes an official connection outside the home, namely, school. This brings the school world into the family, and brings in a foreign element for the parents and children alike. Teachers are generally parental extensions, and even if you welcome this, it requires adjustment.

The fourth crisis, which is a great big one, comes when the child goes into adolescence, with all this entails.

The fifth is when the child has grown to adulthood and is leaving home to seek his independence. There are often heavy loss feelings here.

The sixth crisis comes when the young adult marries, and the in-laws become foreign elements that have to be accepted in the family.

The seventh is the advent of menopause in the woman.

The eighth, called the climacteric for the male, is unpredictable. His crisis seems to be more connected to his feelings that he is losing his potency than anything physical.

The ninth comes, then, with grandparenting, which is chock full of privileges and traps.

Finally, the tenth comes when death comes to one of the spouses, and then to the other.

The family is the only social group I know of where so

many changing differentnesses have to be accommodated in so little space and in such a short time. When three or four of these crises are going on at once, life can get really intense and more "worriable" than usual. But the chances are good that if you understand what is happening you can relax a little so you can clearly see what directions to take to make changes. I do want to emphasize that these are normal, natural stresses, which are predictable for most people. Don't make the mistake of regarding them as abnormal.

There *is* a positive side to all this. No one has lived exactly the same number of years as anyone else. No one has had the exact kind of experience, and each has a wealth of experience to share with others. The Lintons, for example, have a total of 123 years of human experience from which to draw, and that is a whale of a lot of experience. Few families that I know of have looked at their accumulated ages in this way.

Change and differentnesses are constant, normal, healthy factors present in every family. If family members do not expect and prepare themselves for change and emerging differentnesses, they run the risk of falling on their faces; they expect homogeneity, when it doesn't exist. People get born, grow big, work, marry, become parents, grow old, and die. This is the human condition.

Becoming aware of one's family network helps to shed light on the squeezes and stresses in family life.

So does fully understanding roles in family life. Describing a family by its role names alone—husbands, wives, fathers, mothers, sons, daughters, sisters, and brothers—leaves out the human beings who live out these roles and give them life.

As far as I am concerned, a role indicates a name for a description of only one part of a relationship. Secondly, I think the role sets the boundaries for that relationship, and, thirdly, roles indicate the expectation that an affectional, positive tie exists between people who have compatible role names: the husband loves the wife, mother loves daughter/son, father loves son/daughter, children love parents, and so on.

If I say that my feeling toward you is as toward a father, I am saying that I feel you as protective and do not see you as a sexual partner. The same is true if I see you as a brother. I indicate a closeness, but am ruling you out as a sexual partner. The same goes if I see you as a son or a daughter, and vice versa if I were a male.

Two forms of what I call the role-function discrepancy appear frequently in families. One is where the son gets into a head-of-the-family role, commonly that of his father. This could be because the father is dead, divorced, has deserted, is incapacitated, incompetent, or neglectful. The other is where a daughter gets into the mother role, presumably because her mother is unavailable for similar reasons.

The child in this condition usually ends up with all the responsibilities and none of the privileges of the new role. To take on a new role, he leaves his real role behind, and this becomes a very lonely and unsure place to be.

For example, suppose Joe Linton at the age of eighteen now has become the main support of the family as his father has become chronically ill. As the wage-earner he could feel he has a right to decide how to spend the money, and therefore comes into contact with his mother as a husband might. His mother might turn to him as she would to a husband and ask him to help her discipline the younger children. He can't fully be a husband, son, *or* brother. I have found so often that first children seem to get into this bind more frequently. They are neither "fish nor fowl" as far as their family positions are concerned. The way a role is lived out in the family seriously affects the self-worth of the individuals involved— again, their pot.

I see nothing wrong with anybody doing whatever he can to help with whatever is necessary. The problem lies in the messages surrounding this behavior.

Look at your family map again. Are there any people who have one role name but really are performing another?

Because of the fact that so many men are literally or psychologically not functioning as fathers in their families, their sons carry impossible burdens. If the father is unavailable, it is a great temptation for a woman to begin to use a son as a substitute husband. This is usually quite to the detriment of the son.

Unfortunately, for a variety of reasons, many families have men who do not actively father. They're away because of work demands, they've been divorced, are incapacitated, or have emotionally resigned from fathering. As a result large numbers of families are run by the woman. We pay a heavy price for this. Have you ever heard a man say that raising a family is "woman's work?" That the "family doesn't need me; they get along all right."

If I have made it as clear to you as it is in my own head, then some things must have struck you about your family map. Let me briefly describe what strikes me.

Every family member has to have a place, simply because he is a human being and is present. For every family and for every family member, it is crucial that each person's place is fully recognized, accepted, and understood.

Every family member is related to every other family member. The importance here, again, is that these relationships be clearly understood.

Every family member affects and is affected by every other family member. Therefore, everyone matters and everyone contributes to what is going on with any one person and has a part in changing that person.

Every family member is potentially the focus of many pulls simply because he has so many relationships. It is normal and natural. What is crucial is not how to *avoid* the pull, but how to *deal with it comfortably*.

Since the family develops over time, it is always building on what it has already developed. We always stand on the top of what has been built before. Therefore, to understand what is going on in the present, one needs a perspective of the past. I would add that a past seen in terms of experience and the resultant learning therefrom will usually illuminate the present, and never mind about labeling it right or wrong.

Every family member wears at least three role-hats with which he lives and through which he lives. What is important is that you are wearing the role-hat that matches what you are saying and doing.

You need to develop a facility for being a quick-change artist so you can wear the right hat at the right time.

12 Special Families: One-Parented and Blended

Approximately 25 to 35 percent of the children today are being brought up by adults who were not the ones who brought them into the world. I refer mainly to families where the parents have divorced, one or both parents have died, the parents have never married, or parents can no longer take care of the children for whatever different reasons. When a new family is created for these children, they get the names of step, adopted, or foster. I call these reconstituted families *blended families*. When a family is not reconstituted, it is a *one-parent* family.

I would like to treat this chapter in two parts—first, the single-parent family, and secondly, the blended family.

All families are more alike than they are different. All the materials I have talked about so far apply to the blended and the one-parent families as well. These families just have additional aspects that sometimes make them seem quite different.

The one-parent family offers special challenges. At the present time these families are of three sorts—one in which one parent has left and the remaining parent does not remarry, the second is when there is one parent and a legally adopted child and the third is an unmarried woman who keeps her child. One-parent families, regardless of origin, are made up largely of a female parent and her children. The challenge is, how can a family made up of only one adult be a growth-producing one for the children? Here we can see the effect of the ghosts and shadows from the past. These have to do in part with answers to the question of why this is a one-parent family. For the most part, these answers have to do with how a male failed in some way. The big problem in this family is the presentation of a whole picture about males and females.

It is very easy for the remaining parent (usually a woman, as mentioned) to give negative messages about the departed male, particularly if the reason for the departure were divorce, desertion, an illegitimate pregnancy, or, in any case, was the cause of great pain for the woman. She will have to work pretty hard not to give messages to her children about the "badness" of the male. This, of course, has an effect on the male child who will find it hard to believe that maleness is good. If he can't feel that maleness is good, how can he feel that *he* is good? The female is handicapped in that it will be hard for her to see that the male is desirable, and therefore she often has a skewed picture of what males are like, thus building a foundation for unhappiness with males later on. Since the child in a one-parent family does not have the opportunity to experience an ongoing male and female relationship, he grows up without a model of what it is like.

There are a fair number of families, though relatively few in number, where the fathers become the sole parent. Many fathers feel quite inadequate to handle the intimacy and caring needs of their children. They usually have to bring another woman into the home to help care for the house and for the children. Does the housekeeper then care for these intimacy needs of the children? Much depends upon the personality of the housekeeper, the attitude of the father, and the kids themselves. The situation is anything but easy as the father many times feels he should have an emotional attachment for the woman when perhaps he doesn't really feel this way at all. It takes a great deal of patience and understanding on the part of everybody in this situation.

In one-parent families it is all too easy for the mother to pull an older son into the role of husband, thus skewing his own role of son with his mother and his sibling role with his brothers and sisters.

These problems are not insurmountable. It is quite possible for a woman to have a healthy, accepting attitude toward males and be mature enough so that she does not have to give these negative messages about males to her children. She can be willing to provide and encourage relationships between children and adult males she knows and admires.

These might be her own parents; they might be husbands of friends; they could be her own male friends. As far as putting one child on the spot by asking him to be a co-leader with her in the family, she can manage this by explaining the difference between competence at a given task and changing a full-time role. For instance, it is natural that if you are a boy and seventeen, you know more about putting up screen windows and are tall enough to do the job than if you were ten years old. Putting up screen windows or following through on any other job normally done by a father in the family doesn't mean you also have to take on the role of co-leader with your mother on a full-time basis.

Boys in a one-parent family probably face the greatest trap—being over-mothered, and/or getting the picture that the female is the dominant one in society, ending up with the feeling that the male is nothing. Very often the male's feeling of needing to nurture his mother's helplessness puts him into a position where he cannot himself take up his own independent life. Many boys react to this by either remaining with their mothers and just not acting on their own heterosexual interests, or they rebel and leave home, feeling that women are enemies and then alternately mistreat and worship women, all too often messing up the rest of their lives. A one-parent family is basically incomplete. If the adult female looks at this unit as basically incomplete, she will do all of the things she can to make the completeness possible. This might even consist of periodically having her children go to live with a whole family whom she trusts and loves—a kind of informal foster home arrangement.

The female child in a one-parent family can get dis torted learning about what male-female relationships are like. Her attitudes about being female can range all the way from being the servant girl—giving everything, receiving nothing—to feeling she has to do everything herself and be completely independent.

Now, let's turn to the blended family.

Much is said and written about preparing people for marriage who have never been married before. Indeed, I have done so in this book. But I feel that perhaps this kind of preparation is even more important for people who have been married before and are now making a second try. All blended families start out with great handicaps. I think that if these handicaps are understood, they can be overcome and used productively.

All blended families have certain things in common. They put together parts of previously existing families. There are basically three forms:

> 1. A woman with children who marries a man without children.
>
> 2. A woman without children who marries a man with children.
>
> 3. Both the woman and the man have children by previous marriages.

In the first case, the blended family consists of the wife, the wife's children, husband, and wife's ex-husband. In the second case, the unit is husband, husband's children, wife, and husband's ex-wife.

In the third case, the family consists of wife, wife's children, wife's ex-husband, husband, husband's children, and the husband's ex-wife.

Even though these groups may or may not (and probably don't!) all live under one roof, they are in each other's lives—for better or worse. Room has to be made for all of them. They are all significant to the growth and success of the blended family. Many people in blended families try to live as though these other people didn't exist.

All of these people have authority in one way or another. The problems arise when they do not openly find time to talk with one another, are in disagreement or in some cases, are avowed enemies.

Picture the child who has a mother and stepfather in the home, a father and stepmother living in another; all four of these adults taking some "responsibility" for him. Can you imagine what it would be like for that child to try to live in the atmosphere where each of them is in some way asking something different, especially if the adults are unaware of this and particularly if they are not on speaking terms with one another?

What is a child supposed to do in a situation wherein he gets two conflicting directions? (At times he may get as many different directions as there are parents.) For the child's sake, two things are necessary: first, the child needs to be encouraged by all concerned to tell what opposing directions he is getting. Second, all the adults concerned need to have periodic meetings with the child or children so they can discover what each of them is doing and how they agree or disagree. The chances are that if the respective adults are open about what they are doing, the child can at least choose and won't have to be a secret-keeper for the adults—a problem that often arises between divorced parents who still regard one another as enemies and use their children as spies.

I remember a sixteen-year-old girl who was acting alternately crazy and depressed. It developed that she lived with her mother and stepfather, went one weekend to her father and his fiancee, the next weekend with her father's previous wife and her new husband, the third weekend with her maternal grandparents, and the fourth weekend with her paternal grandparents. In each place she was asked to tell what went on in the other places, but was made to promise not to tell what went on"here." The sad part was that all these adults really liked the girl and wanted to help her, but they put the burden—innocently, I believe—on her for their jealousy, rivalries, and resentments toward one another. This same thing can go on in a natural family, with a husband and wife, if they can't be straight with each other. They inadvertently ask the child to deal with what they can't deal with themselves. Of course, the child cannot possibly do this in any constructive way, so the child often responds to this burden by becoming sick, bad, crazy, stupid or all of these things.

Needless to say, in the session with the family of the sixteen-year-old girl, there were a few stormy hours until all the truth got put on the table. Then some headway could be made so the girl no longer had to be crazy or depressed. This didn't happen overnight, for she had to slowly learn to trust again.

When all the adults around a child can be open with one another and take responsibility for what they think and feel, the child benefits from their honesty and is freer to choose because he can be honest, too. To be open with someone doesn't mean you have to love him. Former marital partners could hardly be expected to continue loving one another, but they can be open and not foist their problems with each other on the child.

It is not my belief that the fact that a family is blended is in and of itself any deterrent to developing a good family life. I have seen people develop blended families of all varieties very successfully. There are, however, many potential handicaps that can be used for growing, or they can be used for hurting.

Again, this leads us back to the process that goes on between people that is, I believe, the determining factor of what happens in families.

In a blended family, then, over and beyond all the difficulties that come up when two people live together, there are the problems that come from trying to make room for all the children involved in the new family, and the other people to whom they are connected. This usually means the ex-spouse. Many a potentially satisfactory new marital relationship has become painful because successful ways were not found to do this.

Let's examine some of the problems in detail. In the case of the divorced person who makes a new marriage, the experience of divorce itself is usually painful. Having to have a divorce involves disappointment, and the potential for developing mistrust is very much there, too. In a way, the second spouse has a harder row to hoe than the first one. There is often a subtle kind of psychology present that says, "You need to be better than the one before you." People who remarry after divorce have been burned once, and they don't forget easily.

This is why it is so important for people to work out for themselves the meaning of that divorce, understand it, and use whatever they discover in terms of mistakes they have made as a means of teaching them something. This is far preferable to bemoaning their fate, or carrying grudges or suffering extreme disappointment.

The woman with children who remarries is often inclined to treat her children as though they were her private property, thus introducing a handicap at the very beginning. She often believes that she does not want to impose on her new husband, feeling perhaps that he would not understand. Sometimes she feels a misplaced loyalty to her former husband. Any or all of these add up to the fact that her new husband doesn't have a well-defined role as a helper. A man coming into a family has the advantage of some new perspectives and new ways of doing things, which should be integrated in the new family.

One trap is that the woman may feel so much in need of a "man's firm hand" that she expects him to exert a power and an influence he has not had the chance to develop with the children. This is particularly true if she feels the children are "out of hand." This is a pretty big order. New husbands may be inclined to try to fulfill their wife's expectations and wishes, and often come off doing a poor job of it. Maybe he is the new head of the family, but as it is when chiefs in business or anywhere else are changed, they have to feel their way into the new situation. If a new husband takes charge prematurely, he may be in for unnecessary trouble from the children.

The question about including the stepfather comes up in other ways. Because the woman and her children have obviously had many years together, many times there are things like "in jokes," which can make a new husband feel left out. One of my suggestions when working with people who are preparing for a blended family life is that they constantly keep in mind the fact that each had a life before and much of what goes on in the present life will have a reference point in the past. If one hears something he doesn't understand, freely asking questions is the way out. Many stepparents, rather than asking, handle the situation by thinking "Well, maybe that's none of my business," or, "I shouldn't ask about it," or "Maybe I'm not supposed to know about it," or some such. This kind of message frequently gets translated directly into a low-pot message. Another frequent finding is, "If she wanted me to know, she would have told me."

There is another facet to this situation that has to do with previous possessions, previous friends, previous contacts, which, without anybody meaning it to, impinge on the present marriage. Something has to be done about it. We can't fall off the face of the earth, and destroy or get away from all that we had yesterday. There has to be room made for inclusion and new integration of the things that belong to yesterday. Among these, of course, are the in-laws or grandparents and relatives of the people getting the divorce. There are very few divorces in which the relatives don't have opinions and oftentimes have too much to say about what did happen, what could have happened, what should have happened. All of these things have to be taken into account. What is important is that everybody is clear about what has happened and straight about his way of communicating it. Sounds easy. I know it is not.

So far I have been, in general, talking about the woman who has been divorced and remarried, and some of the strains and difficulties she faces. I'd like to remind you that the husband, too, had a previous life and when there are children, the same kinds of problems are possible. When the husband also has children, they usually live apart from him in another household. This thrusts him into a situation where he has more time with his stepchildren than with his own kids just by proximity. Frequently this makes for a feeling of discomfort on his part, for he feels he is neglecting his own kids. Having his children come visit him in his new home can create a problem for his ex-wife, the children's mother, in that she shares parenting with another woman.

The parenting of both adults who remarry has to undergo drastic changes if they are to do a successful job. After all, it was the parents of the children who got divorced, not the children from the parents. How do parents manage parenting to their own children and stepparenting to their spouse's children without neglecting or cheating either set of children?

It is easy to see how really complicated the blended family situation is. If both divorced parents are mature, they can work things out together so that all the children involved gain instead of lose.

First, it is important to remember that the adults got married. The children are either willing or unwilling followers. They need to be allowed to keep a place for their original parents, and be helped to find a way to add another parent. This takes time and patience—especially at first, and I can hardly emphasize this point too strongly. The stepparent is a stranger. He could even be seen as an interloper. This has little or nothing to do with his goodness or his lovableness.

For the moment, let yourself look through the eyes of the child who is now part of the blended family. His questions will be, "How will I treat my new parent? What shall I call my new parent?"

Perhaps the single most serious problem faced by a child in a blended family is that he is not free to love whomever he wants to. If he loves someone other than whom he is permitted to love, he can get into trouble. He needs to be convinced that he has that freedom.

There are many who want to preserve the value of the divorced parent in the eyes of their children. This brings up a tough one. You are the wife. What do you say to your children when you have lived for many years with a man who was an alcoholic? He beat you and starved you, and now you're with a man who no longer does these things. Can you help your children to value their father and, at the same time, help them to receive the new man without somewhere sending out the message that the first one was no good?

Sometimes when the other parent has been sent to jail or to a mental hospital, or he has had a long history of irresponsibility—in any case, conditions that might make for a feeling of shame—the remaining parent tries to live as though the other person didn't exist. From where I sit, in the hundreds and hundreds of cases I have seen, any time a child is asked to turn his back on and denounce either of his biological parents, he runs a great risk of developing a big case of low pot. How can you say, "I am good," if you feel you came from bad stock?

I certainly am not saying that what one has to do is to say everything good about a parent, whether or not he is good. That isn't the point. The point is, really, the understanding of a person leads you to the awareness that people are made up of many parts, and when it comes to interrelationships among other people, sometimes the two negative parts get together and trouble starts. For example, a man who is violent doesn't get this way by himself. Very often, he is reacting to provocation from his wife, which triggers his lack of control, and eventually she gets a beating from him.

I have never found a human being who was all bad, incidentally. Such a violent man isn't all bad. It takes a good deal of maturity and understanding on the part of an adult to recognize this. For instance, the woman whose husband was violent toward her can gain something in her understanding of herself and her husband if she is able to see that her husband responded violently because of his low pot. She also needs to see that the interaction between the two of them served to trigger the kind of behavior of which he was capable. This helps to take away the blame message, which is one of the reasons so many parents ask their children to renounce the other parent.

As a stepparent in a blended family, you can take it easy and not push. You are an interloper and a stranger in the child's life. Give yourself a chance, too.

Make room in your own mind for the stepchild's other parent. He is there. You can't wish him away. Remember, again, you need to win the child's trust. Give him plenty of opportunities to let him know that you are not trying to replace his other parent. No one says you have to love him. You, can, however, give the child the status of a human being.

Important questions are always in what ways should the current spouse plan with the ex-spouse in relation to the child's welfare? How is the ex-spouse included in the current family?

This brings us to the questions of visitation and support, always difficult ones, particularly when minor children are involved. Answers to these are determined almost completely by the way each of the divorced partners has come to terms with the fact of the divorce. If there is still strain around the relationship, these questions are anything but easy to handle.

Shadows from the past are very real and must be dealt with by the new marital pair. The children are not exactly out of these shadows, either. They have been part of the old hurts; they often take sides. Their loyalties are torn. Frequently they are not living with the parent with whom they took sides. They lived in the troubled family; their problems don't necessarily disappear simply because there has been a change in who is at the head of the house.

Bringing together a group of children who do not know each other and who do not feel sure of their places can put a very great strain on the marriage. In fact, I would say that one of the biggest strains in a given blended family has to do with the fact that the children do not necessarily reflect the new joy of the spouses. The question is not *if* there will be strains, but what are they going to be and how will they be coped with? This is a great creative challenge to the new marital team. Time, patience, and the ability to stand not being loved (at least for a time) are terribly important. What reason is there, after all, for a child to automatically love his stepparent, any more than there is for the stepparent to automatically love the child?

There are also blended families containing "your children," "my children," and "our children." This situation only increases the potential for problems, and the process for coping is just the same.

One of the things I feel has helped many families in developing a way to deal with this is that the new husband and wife are quite clear that there are big handicaps, and they can be straight with each other and straight with the children. They don't ask the children to be phony with them, and they can be free to be honest. Again, I have to point out that this doesn't come easily. Also, just as with the husband and wife the first time out, life after marriage is very different from the courtship. There are often surprises. Life with your mama's boyfriend or your papa's girlfriend is just not the same as when this situation changes into a family unit.

I remember a ten-year-old boy whose father and

mother had been divorced when he was five. His mother remarried when he was eight. About a year after the second marriage, quite inadvertently the boy asked his mother a sudden question one day. "Hey, Ma. Whatever happened to Harold?" (Harold happened to have been a man who had come over fairly frequently for a period of time and stayed the night at his mother's home.) The stepfather immediately demanded, "Who's Harold?" Mother blushed and told her son to go to his room. He went, but was then privy to a quarrel in which the husband essentially accused the wife of keeping things from him and ended up by calling her a slut and a liar, and so on. Apparently she had created a kind of situation in which she had essentially said to her second husband that she had told him everything that had happened. It just so happened that Harold wasn't among those she had told him about.

Something else happens when the previous marriage has been a particularly hurtful one—especially as far as the mother is concerned, as she can begin to see her children as symbols of that hurt. Every time the mother gets into any kind of negative thing with the children, it brings back all the memories of the hurtful times and all her fears as well about the terrible effects she feared the children would inherit.

I know one woman, married the second time, and every time her four-year-old son would say, "no," she had visions of her husband always rebelling. Eventually he went to prison for assaulting someone. So when her young son said "no" to her, her image was of a person already in prison, and she beat him unmercifully to keep him from being a criminal. This is a clear illustration of how this woman's attitude created more problems. Her expectation of this child and what the "no" meant belonged to a different time, not with what was going on at that moment in time.

Almost every family develops some kinds of rituals or traditions or ways of doing things. These kinds of customs have to be recognized and understood by everybody, or they can be a real source of trouble.

Children have a lot of work to do to be able to be clear about a father who is now married to another woman with whom he has other children, when things aren't really straight between the children and their father. The situation can make for low-pot feelings, questions, jealousies, and so on. I have the impression that many of the children whose father has divorced their mother and remarried get deprived of their father more than is necessary because of the fact that the father and his second family aren't prepared to, nor do they really know how to, integrate those other children into the family.

The way that the current husband and his wife got together in the first place has a great deal to do with how things go on in the present. Suppose that the husband and wife were both previously married, met each other while still married, carried on a "courtship" while they were still married, divorced their respective mates, and made a new marriage of their own. Unless some very, very good and careful work has gone on, the one left "injured" can easily sway the feelings of the children against acknowledging this new relationship.

The children's ages have a good deal to do with the difficulties inherent in a second marriage. If the children are really young—perhaps under the age of two or three—the possibilities for interference from the past life are not so great as when the children are older. If the children are grown, then the new marriage becomes irrelevant to the children—it is a matter only for the new marital partners. This is true unless family matters are tied up with money, property, business, or something of that sort. I have known some cases where older children fought the idea of new marriages of their parents because of the trouble they expected about money.

For purposes of bringing home some of these points about new partners and children in blended families, let's examine another hypothetical family.

Jennifer and Jim are thirty-three and thirty-five years old respectively. After ten years of marriage, they divorce. Three years later Jennifer meets another man with whom she feels she can make a better marriage. She marries him. Jim and Jennifer have three children, and at the time of her remarriage, Tom is twelve, Diana, ten, and Bill is eight years old. Jim has moved to a new town about two hundred miles away. According to the divorce settlement, Jim was to see his children once a month. But because he had to start a new business, he didn't always get there that often. He was, however, continuing to pay alimony and child support. Before Jennifer's second marriage she lived with her mother who, together with her father, took on the parenting of Tom, Diana, and Bill. Jennifer's courtship with Jerry began about a year before they married. Because Jennifer, too, had to work, more and more of the parenting was turned over to her mother. Jennifer's job involved a lot of traveling—in fact, it was on one of her trips that she met Jerry. Much of the time she and Jerry were together was time not shared with her three children. Jerry had met them but only for short times. There had been nice feelings between him and the children, but in no way could Jerry feel he really knew them.

Jennifer and Jerry married. It was natural now that Jennifer would be setting up a home for the children, which meant taking them away from Grandmother and Grandfather, since Jennifer was now married and had a home. Jennifer and Jerry were very much in love. Without thinking too much about it, they just naturally expected they were going to be able to reconstitute the family very easily. Jerry, by the way, had also been married before and had a daughter, twelve, who lived with her mother in a city some seven hundred miles away. The divorce agreement allowed him to have his daughter, Theresa, stay with him for summer vacations. Generally speaking there was a good relationship between Theresa and her father.

All right. Let's consider some of the things that need to be looked at in order to develop this blended family.

First of all, there needs to be a clear recognition on everybody's part that when Jennifer's three children come together with their mother and her new husband, this will be a completely new unit. Even though Jim doesn't visit very often he does pay child support, and he is definitely part of the picture. The obvious question comes up immediately: what role will Jerry have with the children? His role name is stepfather. But what does that really mean? Ordinarily a wife hopes that her husband will participate with her in the bringing up of her children. And she may, without realizing it, rely on the fact that because her husband loves her and she loves him, that he will be in possession of facts pertaining to the children. He really doesn't have these facts and therefore should not expect to come into the lives of the children and be helpful immediately. Far too many stepparents expect this of themselves. Jerry is a stranger, and he will be a stranger to Jennifer's children for some time. Jim's shadow is still very much there, and to some extent, always will be. Sometimes people feel their self-worth rests on how much change can be made right away, when what is actually needed when coming into a new situation is time—all the time that is necessary in any situation to become fully acquainted.

Back to Jennifer and Jerry. What happened in the marriage between Jennifer and Jim may not have been totally acceptable to the children, which could form a barrier to their acceptance of their stepfather. Suppose the children are given very subtle messages that they must be on their mother's side against their father, and they must take her new husband as their father. Jennifer may still be feeling much pain, bitterness, and disappointment—a legacy from her first marriage. Many women feel this way and expect their children to feel the same, and the message is put over to the children in a variety of subtle yet very telling ways. Jennifer could say, with a very determined or blank look when the father calls or writes for them to visit, "Well, it's your decision. You do it if you want to." The message can be anything but subtle, too: "If you go to your father, just don't have anything more to do with me!" Subtle or direct, for Jennifer or anyone else in her place to expect her children to reflect her own feelings about her first husband is asking for trouble.

The legacy of pain from a first marriage is a source of trouble of another kind as well. The expectations from a second marriage can be monumental—close, sometimes, to expecting Nirvana. Many adults in blended families expect magic. Because they got rid of the troubling spouse and now have a better one, "all the problems are solved." They forget that people will still relate to people, that there will still be the arsenic hour (the time when the demands are far greater than any one person can meet), there will be the same pot-lowering kinds of things going on such as people being sassy with one another, or flip, angry, and/or stubborn.

It really comes down to the fact that people are people and will act like people whether in a natural family or a blended one.

For example, I remember a woman who had remarried when her oldest child was eleven. When he became fourteen he began giving his mother a lot of static. Her immediate conclusion was that it had been wrong for her to remarry, that if she hadn't remarried, her son wouldn't be the way he was. Certainly the communication that had gone on between her and the boy in relation to the stepfather had something to do with the situation, but it was as well the boy's experimenting with his mother and the fact that he felt on the outside of things. This could have occurred in a family where there was not a second marriage or a stepfather.

In short, anybody entering into marriage certainly expects his life to be better, and a second marriage is no exception. And further, it seems that the more you want out of life, the more you expect, and the greater your anticipation, the greater can be the disappointments when what is expected doesn't come about.

Another frequently found variation of a blended family is when two people make a second marriage where either one or both of the first spouses have died. There are different kinds of traps here. Suppose a woman was married fifteen years and her husband died. Relatively soon afterward she met a man who had never been married. Let us say that her first husband died a tragic, accidental death. Their marriage was fair—not too exciting, fairly on the dull side. But the impact of the death crowded out the memory of the boredom and the dullness of that marriage and left this woman with an exaggerated feeling of how good the marriage had been. Then she marries a man who could provide for her, whom she cares about, and who may be more exciting than her former husband. But at times when she feels disappointed or annoyed with her present husband she could put into words how much better life had been with her former husband, leaving it open for the second husband to be compared unfavorably with him. Of course, the same thing could happen with a man who marries again after his wife died. I take the view that people are not angels, and every relationship has its difficulties. Because of our peculiar attitude toward death, as we talked about earlier, we tend to elevate the departed one to the status of saint. And this is unreal. No human being can compete with a saint.

It is also important for both the husband and wife to accept the fact that somebody did live before, and that that person was a person in his own right, had a place, and, therefore, that place should be acknowledged. For instance, I know of several people who married after their spouses died, and the new spouse insists that no pictures or belongings of the former one be allowed, almost as if he were asking his mate to rid herself even of the memory of that other person. Again, this is a low-pot response, and it is almost as if the person is saying, "If you acknowledge your first marriage, then you can't possibly acknowledge the second." I consider this to be a rather emotionally underdeveloped attitude. In short— nonsense!

We talked before about the problems kids can have when adults either don't mention the person who has died or else deify him. It's pretty hard if not impossible for a child to try to relate to a ghost or a saint.

Another trap is when the new spouse coming in is sensitive to comment about how "things used to be." I've known some people, particularly, who have come into homes where a spouse has died and who really wanted to and were willing to do everything they could, but upset the whole household without meaning to because they asked people to behave quite differently from the way they did before. If such a person were to realize that he first has to build bridges to the children who are there, and in a gradual way make room for himself and for the new things he can bring into the house, I think things would be much different. Again, your pot level does not depend on how much change you can effect right away.

The foster family is another form of a blended family. The foster family may consist of one foster child and no other children; there may be one foster child and some "natural" children; then there may be one natural child and several foster children. The composition of the family makes a difference, at least in the kinds of handicaps that have to be overcome. Generally speaking, a child becomes a foster child when, for whatever reason, his own parents can't take care of him. This may be because the child's behavior is such that the people in his family cannot stand to continue living with him. Or a person in authority might decide that the family system is harmful to the child, and he would have a better chance if he went to another family. Frequently the parents in these cases were found to be seriously neglectful—parents whose behavior was so punitive, punishing, and hurtful that somebody came along and removed the child from the home. For example, the child has been badly beaten, or has had continued violence at home, and he is brought to a new place where he can have a better chance to live. Almost all foster children are placed in foster homes by reason of a court order, which brings another element into the picture—namely, the court. So the management of the child is now not only between the foster parents and the real parents, but also the court.

Sometimes both parents have died, leaving the child with no home. Relatives or guardians don't want to put him in an orphanage, so they look for a family to take him. For some reason he may not be adoptable, which means he will have no permanent status. Nonetheless, he will probably live in a foster home a long time. He is taken in, in a sense, as a boarder.

There are other instances where, for example, the mother has had to go to a mental hospital or jail. As far as the child was concerned, everything was fine up until the time his mother was taken away; (let's say the father is dead or divorced). Now there has to be a place for this child during the time when the mother is institutionalized. This kind of placement is more temporary.

In all these placements there is an implicit message about the kind of a place the child will have in his foster family. The message contains the answer to the question in the minds of the foster family members: "How come you can't stay in your own family?" The message is real and there is also a message about the message. This is what I mean: If the foster parents take a child who has been acting up at home, they might see themselves as being super strict to prevent the child from acting up again. If the child comes because his parents have beaten him, the foster parents would probably feel sorry for him and bend over backwards being super loving parents. There is nothing like abusive real parents to arouse the anger and protectiveness of foster parents. The trap here is that the foster parents might give negative feelings to the child about his own parents, in effect damaging his chances for developing an integrated self-concept. I can hardly express this thought too often: No one can feel good about himself if he feels he came from devils and bad people.

If the child has no living parents, foster parents have the job of feeling good about giving their "all" with someone who, after all, is not *their* child.

Running through a good deal of foster placements is the wariness on the part of foster parents not to get themselves too involved because, on the face of it, it is a temporary placement. The range of foster placement is from overnight to twenty-one years. One thing is certain—the child who comes into the foster home is having something done to him, for him, for his own good, and there is usually a strong message that somehow his own parents failed him in some way. Whether this becomes a real handicap to the child (the "bad seed" psychology) depends a great deal upon the emotional stability and development of the foster parents. If they can see themselves as really offering not only time, but a bridge for this child between himself and some new growth, and they can freely involve themselves with him in a true family, parent-child manner, there is a good chance that the foster family will be successful and produce a well-balanced human being with high pot.

Very often the natural parents of the foster child are allowed visiting privileges or some kind of contact while the child is in the foster home. Whether or not the child's natural parents can become an integrated part of the child's ongoing life and participate in his growth depends a great deal on how the foster parents view the natural parents. In some ways this situation is not too different from integrating the divorced parent into a child's life. I have known some foster families who were revolted at what they learned about the behavior of the real parents of their foster child and who found it very hard to treat the natural parents with any kind of acceptance when they visited.

This brings us to the question—how can foster parents treat the natural parents of a child as okay people if they know, for example, that the child has been badly beaten or burned by them? It is obviously destructive and irrational behavior for an adult to burn or beat a child. Again, being aware that this behavior comes from a person who has terribly low pot can help you to be more understanding and not just ready to damn the parents. I wish that for every foster child placed that there were someone who was trying to help the natural parents to grow and improve so that they could again become responsible, loving people who could do a good job of parenting. So often, if this happens at all, it comes about through the foster parents. I once saw a beautiful example of this. A pair of foster parents saw the parents of their three foster children as people who needed to grow. As opportunities presented themselves, they acted as parents to these parents in such a way as to help them get guidance with the result of their growing and ultimately feeling like okay people.

I want to say a word or two about another kind of family. This is the communal family, which seems to be becoming more and more widespread. There are variations, but in general, they are based upon a plan where a group of adults who have children live together in different ways, either in the same building or the same complex where they share common tasks and maybe even share common property. They also share parenting among the many children; some of them even share sexual life.

An advantage to this kind of family is that the child gets exposed to a variety of models. The one big problem, of course, is that there has to be a very good relationship among all of the adults so that the mutual parenting can really offer something. The kibbutzim are a model of a kind of communal living, except that here the major parenting goes on with an auxiliary parent, a woman. The biological parents are treated very much as visitors in the sense that they do not participate fully in the decision-making. They might have very little to do with the day-to-day living experience. Again, it is one thing to be told what happened and talk about what should happen from a distance, and another thing entirely to be involved face-to-face with what's going on at a given moment in time.

Because of household help—governesses or nurses who lived in the family—there have been many natural families where there was in reality an informal kind of foster family. Here are created some of the same problems of distance between the child and his actual parents as we have been discussing in this chapter.

Many children have had a great variety of experiences in blended families. A child, through the course of his life, may have been a member of a step-family, a one-parent, adoptive, and/or foster family. For example, it's possible for a child, between birth and maturity, to have his fathering done by five different males. He has, of course, a biological father. Maybe that father dies or leaves, and he spends time with his grandfather. Then the mother remarries, and he has a stepfather. It's possible that the stepfather may die, perhaps the mother remarries, and he has another stepfather. It is equally possible that the child has some kind of difficulty and then goes to a foster home where he remains until he is of age. This kind of thing happens frequently. The same is true, although to a lesser extent, for the person who fills the mother slot. There are many children who have had a number of different adults filling the role of mother.

One thread runs through all of these family variations: the adults are trying to lend their resources to help children grow. In the meantime, they are trying to manage their own growth and trying to work out some way so that the growth and the development of the children are compatible. All of the things I mentioned that happen in the variations of the foster families I've described can also happen in natural families. Husbands and wives can be jealous of each other, children can feel left out, or jealous of their sisters or brothers; they can all have experiences that make them feel isolated from other members of the family and feel low pot.

The point I want to make is that the form of the family is not the basic determinant for what happens in the family. Form presents different kinds of challenges that have to be met, but the process that goes on among the family members is what, in the end, determines how well the family gets along together, how well the adults grow, separately and with one another, and how well the children develop into creative, healthy human beings. For this, the *pot*, the *communication*, the *rules*, and the *system* are the chief means of making it work.

In this way, all special families are like natural families.

13 The Family Blueprint: Your Design for Peoplemaking

Adults are children grown big. The family is where it happens. Do you remember how you felt when you saw your first child for the first time and held him in your arms? Do you remember how you felt as you watched your spouse look at and hold this child? Do you remember your hopes, dreams, worries, and fears? My hunch is that a good many adults, faced with the job of making an acceptable adult out of the infant in front of them, quake at the prospect.

No one can look at any infant without realizing he will die unless some adult takes care of him. Every adult realizes he is farther along than the infant. Furthermore, since no baby comes equipped with a little bag of directions about how to grow and develop, someone has to make them up and deliver them—now, not ten years from now. These "someones" are you, the parents. And the little bag of directions becomes your blueprint, which is what this chapter and the following one are all about.

I believe most parents feel a heavy responsibility for doing the very best they can for their child. They may lack information, have mixed-up ideas or be insensitive, but I think their intentions, on the whole, are good.

Two big questions present themselves to every parent in one form or another: "What kind of a human being do I want my child to become?" and, "How am I going to use myself and my spouse to make that happen?"

Your answers, as parents, are the basis for your blueprint, your design for peoplemaking. Every parent has answers to these questions. They may be clear, vague, or uncertain, but they are there.

The job is anything but easy. Parents teach in the toughest school in the world—The School for Making People. You are the board of education, the principal, the classroom teacher, and the janitor, all rolled into two. You are expected to be experts on all subjects pertaining to life and living. The list keeps on growing as your family grows. Further, there are few schools to train you for your job, and there is no general agreement on the curriculum. You have to make it up yourself. Your school has no holidays, no vacations, no unions, no automatic promotions, or pay raises. You are on duty or at least on call 24 hours a day, 365 days a year, for at least 18 years for each child you have. Besides that, you have to contend with an administration that has two leaders or bosses, whichever the case may be—and you know the traps two bosses can get into with each other.

Within this context you carry on your peoplemaking. I regard this as the hardest, most complicated, anxiety-ridden, sweat and blood producing job in the world. It requires the ultimate in patience, common sense, commitment, humor, tact, love, wisdom, awareness, and knowledge. At the same time, it holds the possibility for the most rewarding, joyous experience of a lifetime. What parent has not had his juices flow when his child says with lights and twinkles in his eyes, "Gee, Mom—Dad—you're great!"

Peoplemaking has a large measure of trial-and-error experience. It is something you learn most about as you experience it "on the job."

I am reminded of the story of a psychologist who wrote his thesis on how to bring up children. At the time, he was unmarried, and his lecture read, "Twelve Requirements for How to Bring Up Children." Then he married, had one child, and his talk changed to, "Twelve Suggestions for How to Bring Up Children." He and his wife had another child, and his lecture title changed to "Twelve Hints on How to Bring Up Children." After the third child arrived, he stopped giving lectures.

I think the way most parents would describe the kind of person they want their child to become would turn out to be pretty much the same: honest, self-respecting, competent, ambitious, clean, strong, healthy, bright, kind, affectionate, and able to get along well with others and to be liked by others. "I want to be proud of him," a parent will say. Do these qualities fit into your picture of a desirable person? Read on!

My point is that I don't think the problem is only what parents want to achieve in their children—it is perhaps more a question of how to teach. Unfortunately we have been paying very little attention to the "how." I hope this book will be useful in shedding light on both subjects.

The combination of the "what" and the "how" is what I am including in this chapter and the next one. To go further, I also mean to deal with the set of goals and values parents hope their children have, and the directions they will go in order to achieve them. Every family has such a set. Blueprints vary from family to family. I believe there are some blueprints that result in nurturing families and some that result in troubled ones.

Perhaps as you read this you can let yourself be aware of what kind of a blueprint you are using. Maybe you can also look critically at how it's working for you and for the other members of your family at this point in time. You may also get some ideas about how you can change what isn't working well for you now. It might also be that you will find support for what you are doing in terms of your blueprint.

Since so many families are started by adults who are not mature themselves, many parents are in the position of not having learned the things themselves that they are expected to teach their children. For example, the parent who has not yet learned to control his temper cannot very well teach his children how to control theirs. There is nothing like the raising of a child to show up adult inadequacies. When this occurs, wise parents become students along with their children.

The best preparation for parenthood that I know of is in the maturity, openness, and awareness of the adults who undertake this monumental job. If adults enter into making a family before they have achieved their own maturity, the process is infinitely more complicated and hazardous—not necessarily impossible, just tough. Fortunately, changes can be made at any point in any family's life, if the family members see a need for change and find out how to do it.

Wherever you were in your own development when you became a parent, it is a fact that that was where you were at that point in time. There is no point in berating and blaming yourself now if you think with hindsight that you were not where you "should have been" when you got married, became a parent, and so on. The important questions are where are you now, what is happening now, and where can you go from here? Spending time on any kind of blame just lowers your pot, makes you ineffective as to what you can change. Blame is an expensive way to use your energy, believe me.

Most parents want their children to have at least as good as or better lives than they did, and they hope to be the means by which this happens. This makes them feel useful and hopeful. I know it's terribly disappointing when it doesn't turn out that way, especially when they have tried hard. They may not have been aware of how much of a part the experience that each person has in his own childhood plays and greatly influences the atmosphere in which they bring up their children. In fact, I would go so far as to say it is the main base against and around which most family blueprints are designed. It is easy to duplicate in your family the same things that happened in your growing up. This is true whether your family was a nurturing or a troubled one.

Picking your current model from your parental model is very natural, but it is full of traps into which couples can innocently fall. As with all traps, they can be avoided if you know they are there and you know how to avoid them.

If you liked the way your father and mother brought you up and felt good about the way they treated each other, they can be quite acceptable models for your blueprint. You say, "I will do it the way they did it."

If you didn't like what happened as you grew up, you'll probably want to change what you do. Unfortunately, deciding what not to do is not the whole story. You have to decide what you are going to do differently and how you are going to do it. This is where the trouble starts. In a way, you are in a kind of no-man's-land in the sense of having no models to follow. You have to make up a new one. Where will you find it? What will you put into it?

There are probably more people who want their parenting different from the way they were parented than those who do not. How many times do you hear, "I'm certainly going to bring up my kids different from the way I was brought up!" This could mean anything from being more strict to less strict, from being closer to less close, to doing more work, or less work, and so on.

Take a minute now and remind yourself about those parts of what you saw and experienced in your growing up that you wanted to avoid with your children. What have you tried to substitute? How well is it working? How much do you agree on what you want to avoid? Write down five experiences that you consider were helpful to you. See if you can figure out what was helpful about them. Then find five experiences you felt were destructive and analyze them the same way. Have your spouse do the same thing.

You might, for example, remember how helpful it was when your father told you directly and clearly what he wanted you to do. Maybe you remembered he looked directly at you, his hand gently placed on your shoulder, and he spoke in a clear tone and was firm and kind. "I want you to mow the lawn by five today." This might be in contrast to your mother who said in a shrill voice, "Why don't you ever do anything around here? You're going to get your allowance cut if you don't watch out!" Or the memories could be reversed.

You may remember that Grandma wasn't very helpful because she always said yes no matter what you asked. Somehow you got to feeling too obliged. It wasn't easy to be honest with Grandmother.

You may have decided that Dad was very helpful to you when you would take a problem to him. He would listen and then patiently help you struggle through finding a decision. This was in contrast to your uncle who always solved your problems for you. Your uncle delayed your learning for yourself and finding your own two feet to stand on.

You may have decided that neither parent was very helpful to you because whenever you interrupted them, they always stopped and put all their attention on you. This made you start to feel impossibly important, and you felt hurt and confused when everybody else didn't treat you the same way. You had not developed patience and an understanding that sometimes you have to wait for attention.

A destructive experience for you might have been when you said a "dirty word," and your mother washed out your mouth with soap and/or put you in the closet. Your body ached first, and then you plotted revenge. Later you cried because you felt unloved.

When you have made your list, go another step and decide how you can use this knowledge yourself.

Take your "destructive list" and try to figure out what your parent may have been trying to teach you. Now with your adult eyes you might be able to see what you couldn't see then. The chances are pretty good that you will have to deal with teaching your child the same thing, only now you should be able to find a more constructive way. For instance, is there a better way to respond to a child's use of a dirty word than washing his mouth out with soap or sticking him in a closet? Can you find it?

You may discover that some of the things your parents taught you turned out to be wrong. All the parents in pre-Columbus time must have been teaching their kids that the world was flat. There are many, many other instances of this kind of thing. For example, you may have been taught that "masturbating will make you crazy." You know, there actually was a time when even physicians believed that masturbation led to insanity. Almost everyone knows today that this is not so. Thoughts about having masturbated could be disturbing, but the act itself is harmless. The important point is to become aware of these kinds of untruths and learn the current truth.

New parents have much that is new to learn. For instance, many adults are ignorant of how the body literally grows. Many people are unfamiliar with the whole psychology of emotions and how emotions affect behavior and intelligence. There may be some people who still don't believe in human emotions and their power, although it is hard for me to believe when we are surrounded by so much convincing evidence to the contrary.

Somehow or other we have been a long time seeing that knowledge is an important tool for peoplemaking. We see it in the raising of pigs, but not so much with people. In some ways we got the idea that raising families was all instinct and intent, and we behave as if anyone could be an effective parent simply because he wanted to be, or because he just happened to go through the acts of conception and birth. This is the most complicated job in the world and most of us act as if we can all be great parents simply by going through the motions and taking a label. I often think of the terrible burden so many parents carry. They are expected to be experts, and they are not, even though some may act like it (but are inwardly not sure at all). The need is for mass efforts to offer help for parent training. I really believe this is essential. There are special things one needs to know about building and guiding a person to full humanness. Some of these things change from time to time as we learn more about what a human being actually is, and how he develops. Can you imagine what would happen if a new parent thought first about what is presently known about the huge job ahead of him, and availed himself of that knowledge? I am appalled when I think how long we have taken for granted this tremendously complicated job!

Now let's examine the beginning of a family for a moment or two. The couple has a baby, and obviously there are three where there were once two. All too often at this point the parenting becomes so weighty and demanding that the couple-life dies. If this happens, the children are going to pay a heavy, heavy price. If the couple-life dies, it is a ripe time for marital partners to make a major emotional involvement with someone outside the marriage—particularly for men.

Stop a moment and take stock. Is this happening with you? With your spouse? What effect is this having on all the family members? How did it start? What can you do about it?

Many people get discouraged at this point because so much of what they have tried hasn't worked. Your willingness to frankly admit this could be a turning point for you. You *can* learn to do things differently, no matter how long things have been going wrong.

First, you have to find out what you have to learn, and then search for a way to learn it. Someone whose name I've forgotten said, "Life is your current view of things." Change your view, and maybe your life can change. I heard about a man who always complained that everywhere he went it was dark. This all changed one day when he lost his balance and in falling, his glasses fell off. Lo and behold, it was light! He hadn't been aware he'd been wearing dark glasses.

Well, that may be a bit of an exaggeration, but I think it makes a telling point. Many of us have to have the experience of falling or getting off balance in order to discover that we have been looking through blinders. This can be a significant discovery.

If you discover that something is going wrong in your family, treat it as you would when the red light goes on in your car indicating that the engine is overheating. It's a signal that things aren't working right. Stop—investigate—and see what you can do. If you can't change it, find someone you trust who can. Whatever you do, don't waste your time moaning about "poor me" and "bad you."

Do what we talked about in the chapter on systems. Turn the family into a research team instead of a blame society. Can you see how different things might be for your family if you see the negative, hurtful things that happen as signals for attention? There is no need to blame and tear your hair out. Keep your hair and be glad you finally got the signal, whatever it is. It may not be especially pleasant, but it is honest and real and something can be done about it.

I remember a family I treated once. The father came with his wife and 22-year-old son, who was quite ill psychologically. When the treatment was finished, the father, tears in his eyes, put his hand on the son's shoulder and said, "Thank you, son, for getting sick, so I could get well." I still get goose bumps when I think about that one.

I referred earlier to the traps that one gets into by using his own parenting as a guide to how he parents. One of these is the effort the parent goes through to give his child what he did not have as a child. This can come out very well, but it can also come out as a terrible disappointment.

I once saw a vivid example of that. It was just after Christmas when a young mother whom I will call Elaine came to see me. She was in a rage at her six-year-old daughter, Pam. It seems that Elaine had scrimped and saved many months to buy Pam a very fancy doll. Pam reacted with indifference to the doll her mother had worked so hard to get. Elaine felt very crushed and disappointed, inside. Outside she acted angry. With my help, within a short time, she realized that this doll really was the doll *she* had yearned for as a youngster and never had. She was giving her daughter what really was her own unfulfilled dream, and she expected Pam to react as she, Elaine, would have reacted when she was six. What she had overlooked was that her daughter already had several dolls.

Pam would much rather have had a sled so she could go sliding with her brothers. When this was clear, it became obvious that this doll was really Elaine's. I suggested that she claim her own doll, and experience her own fulfillment, which she did. This particular yearning from her childhood could now be satisfied directly, and she did not have to do it through her child.

Is there any good reason why an adult cannot fulfill for himself, openly, in his adulthood, some of the yearnings of his childhood instead of passing them off on his kids? Children rarely appreciate what is not for them unless they have learned how to be "yes" men. I have a hunch that this is why parents put so many strings on their gifts to their children. I am thinking of the situation where fathers buy trains for their sons, then play with them all the time, and set out strict conditions under which their sons can use them. How much more honest it would be for the father to buy the train for himself. It would be his train, which he then might or might not allow his son to play with.

Many parents start out with a dream about what they want their child to be. This dream often has to do with wanting the child to do what they personally could not do, like, "I want him to be a musician. I always loved music."

It is easy for parents, without knowing it, to make plans for their child to be what would fit them, but might not necessarily fit the child. I once heard the late Abraham Maslow say that having these kinds of hopes and plans for your children is like putting them into invisible straitjackets. This becomes a trap when the child doesn't share the same dream. I often hear adults complain that they are not happy in what they are doing. I see the results of this in adults who say they wanted to "be" something else, but didn't want to disappoint their parents and also did not know how to deal with the pressures of their parents. After all, it takes a lot of guts and a lot of know-how on the part of the child to defy his parents successfully. What lingers from the parents' individual past that has been unresolved or incomplete often becomes part of irrational parenting. I refer to this as *contaminating shadows of the past.*

If you are still tied to your own parents, you may not feel free to use yourself effectively for fear of being criticized, which might make you deal crookedly with your child. Some quite insidious situations can develop. I refer to this as *fettered parental hands.*

For instance, I know a thirty-four-year-old father who won't chastize his child directly because *his* father would take the child's side and then he and his father would argue. He is still afraid to argue with his father, because he considers arguing bad. The effect, of course, is that he deals crookedly and inappropiately with his child, which doesn't match the ideas in his blueprint. Were he to give a lecture on the best way to raise kids, his speech would be far different from what he practices.

Every once in awhile I have this fantasy about just how different people could be if, overnight, they were already doing all the things we know about creating high pot in human beings. So much of what we actually do has the opposite result. We have the Ten Commandments, the Golden Rule, and the Bill of Rights, and they have been around for a long time. As I look around, my guess is that we have the *ends*, all right, but we are just discovering the *means.*

It is true that we do have much information that is necessary to all, but it is in the hands of a few. Professional people are supposed to have the information, and many do The problem is that the professionals are used largely by people with really serious problems. I don't mean to minimize the work of family life educators, but their work, good as it is, reaches only a relative handful of people. We haven't given peoplemaking the very high priority it deserves, probably because we lack conviction, aren't sure enough of ourselves, and haven't found the way.

I want to talk about something I call the *parental cloak* now. As I use the term it means the part of the adult that he uses to live out his role as a parent. To my mind, it has a use only so long as the child is unable to do for himself, and he needs to be the child's guide. One of the problems is that the cloak never changes, and it never comes off. A major factor in your blueprint is the kind of parental cloak you wear, and whether or not you feel you have to wear it all the time.

I would say the parental cloak has three major linings— the "boss" lining, the "leader and guide" lining, and the "pal" lining. There is a fourth one in which the cloak has no lining at all—there is no evidence of any kind of parenting. I think there are far fewer of these than the other three.

The boss has three main faces—the *tyrant*, who flaunts his power, knows everything, and parades as a paragon of virtue. ("I am the authority; you do what I say.") He comes off as a blamer. The second is the *martyr*, who wants absolutely nothing for himself except to serve the others. He goes to great lengths to appear as nothing to be considered and comes off as a placater. ("Never mind me—just be happy.") The third is the *great stone face* who lectures incessantly, impassively, on all the right things. ("This is the right way.") This person comes off as a computer.

The pal is the playmate who indulges and excuses regardless of the consequences and usually comes off irrelevantly. ("I couldn't help it—I didn't mean to.") Children need pals for parents like they need the proverbial hole in their heads. Irresponsibility in children is a frequent outgrowth of this kind of parental cloak lining.

I think we pay a heavy price for the ways parents use their power—which is another way of describing their cloak lining. To me, the most destructive lining of all is that of the tyrant, who insists on creating "obedient" human beings. In every case I found that this behavior was primarily a result of the low pot of the adult who tried to fill his pot by getting immediate obedience from the child. His kinds of actions represented his shame, his ignorance, his burden, his lack of maturity, his own curdled soul, and shriveled self. The child was the unfortunate (sometimes fatal) victim of that adult's low self-esteem.

When I have had to deal with adults who have mistreated children, my first reaction is one of outrage. After the waves of outrage and nausea pass, then I see these adults as children grown big who are quite understandably reaching to their own growing up. Then I roll up my sleeves and go to work to help these adults as well as the children with their shame, their ignorance, and their burden.

They need help badly, and the most frequent form of treatment they get is punishment, which usually only makes matters worse. Someday we will learn that punishment doesn't teach anyone anything about becoming a better person—

whether it be child or adult. Fortunately, the adults who abuse children are relatively few in number. But there are enough so that all our jails, mental hospitals, various institutions, and clinics of all sorts are filled to overflowing. There are also enough to keep the newspapers selling with accounts of murder, assault, and other atrocious acts one human can perpetrate against another.

Many parents might occasionally entertain a momentary wish to knock in their kid's head, but few do it. Many children feel similarly, but only a few act.

It is rare that children who grow up on the "obedience frame" become anything else but tyrants, or very permissive people, unless there is some unusual intervention in their lives. It is beyond me how judgment can be taught through "obey me" techniques, and if there is any one thing we need in this world, it is people with judgment. The person who cannot use his own common sense is the person who feels he must do what somebody else wants him or expects him to do. The obedience theme very often comes out, "There is one right way to do anything. Naturally, it is my way."

I heard this so much that at one point I did something I called silly research. I investigated how many ways there were to wash dishes. I found 247, all of them going from the state of being dirty dishes to becoming clean dishes. The differences were related to the kind of equipment available, and so on. Do you know anybody who swears by a certain detergent? Or swears that dishes must always be rinsed before being washed? After you have been around a person who insists on his way all the time, you probably want to kill him. Maybe it's no accident that over 50 percent of all murders are family murders.

People who are around someone who says "You do it because I say so," or, "It is so because I say so," suffer personal insult constantly. It is as though the other person were saying, "You are a dummy. I know best," all the time. Such statements have long-range crippling effects on the victim's pot, particularly the children who are on the other end of it.

In none of these parental cloaks can a trusting atmosphere be developed. Effective learning cannot be done in an atmosphere of distrust, fear, or indifference. I get pretty strong on the subject of the boss face, but I mean every word of it.

My recommendation is that parents strive to be leaders, which means that they are kind, firm, inspiring, understanding people who direct from a position of reality rather than power.

People play such cruel tricks on themselves when they become parents. Suddenly now they must "do their duty," be serious, and give up lightness and joy. They can no longer indulge themselves or even have fun. I happen to believe just the opposite. I think normal, every day difficulties in families are seen in quite a different light by people who believe that family members can be enjoyed and, indeed, do enjoy one another. I have met so many adults who have never known what it feels like to be enjoyed by another person. So instead of enjoying people themselves, they try to please, to get approval, and to keep from getting disapproval.

I remember a pair of young parents who told me they made their first priority one of enjoying their child. They were already obviously enjoying each other. That was fifteen years ago. The enjoyment still goes on today. I feel good every time I am around this family. There are now two other children. Growth is obvious, and there is pride in accomplishment and good feelings about everything. These are not indulgent parents, incidentally, nor is the family without secure and clearly set down limits.

Part of the art of enjoyment is being able to be flexible, curious, and to have a sense of humor. An episode of a five-year-old spilling milk all over the table can be quite a different experience dependent upon what family he lives in and how such matters are approached.

My friends Laurie and Josh would probably say, "Whoops! You let your glass be your boss instead of your hand! You will have to talk with your hand. Let's skip out to the kitchen and get a sponge and soak it up." Literally, then, Laurie and Davis would skip out to the kitchen and maybe even sing a song on the way back.

I can hear Josh saying, "Gee, Davis, I remember when that happened to me. I felt I had done something awful, and I felt terrible. How do you feel?" To which Davis would answer, "I feel bad, too. Now Mommy has more work to do. I didn't mean to do it."

I can imagine the same episode with another set of parents, Al and Ethel. Ethel grabs Davis, shakes him, and demands that he leave the table, saying to Al as he leaves, "I don't know what I'm going to do with that kid. He's going to grow up to be a slob."

Another pair I know, Edith and Henry, would have still another scene with the same ingredients as before. When the milk is spilled, Henry looks at Edith, raises his eyebrows and goes on eating in stony silence. Edith quietly gets a sponge and wipes up the milk, giving Davis a reproving look when she catches his eye.

I believe the way Laurie and Josh approached things is a way in which everyone benefits. It is questionable in the other two examples. What do you think?

Do people in your family have times when they obviously enjoy each other as individuals? If you think not, see if you can find out how to change things. I don't see how people who can't enjoy each other can really love each other.

One of the values I see as enhancing the life of everybody is the enjoyment of people. How do you teach children to enjoy their parents, parents to enjoy their children, sisters to enjoy brothers, and brothers to enjoy sisters? An important step is to learn to like yourself. Can you enjoy yourself? Do you like your own company when you happen to be alone? Some people get mixed up in that they feel if they enjoy themselves they will probably be anti-social, as if to say, if you enjoy yourself you can't enjoy others. I see the opposite. If you haven't learned how to enjoy yourself, you could be worrying about how bad you are and what's wrong with you. You could probably be a drag on other people, too.

The beginning of the child's joy in himself starts with learning how to enjoy parts of his body, his hands, touching, the feel of his skin, the colors and sounds around him, and especially the sound of his own voice together with the pleasure of looking.

He can enjoy the product of himself, his splashes and his splatterings and his spillings. Seeing the adults around him enjoy him enjoying himself goes a long way toward helping the child get a feeling that a person is also someone to be enjoyed. Enjoyment is a matter of aesthetics. Relatively speaking, we do very little in the usual child rearing to help children to enjoy themselves. I see so many families where the whole idea of raising children and being parents is a grim experience full of labored work, hysteria, and burden. I've been very interested in the fact that when I've had just adults together and once made it possible for them to get rid of their blocks against enjoying themselves as people, a great deal of lightness comes about. I don't know if you are aware of how much heaviness and grimness there is among adults. I am not surprised to hear numbers of children tell me that they don't really want to grow up because being an adult is no fun.

I don't think having fun takes away from being competent. As a matter of fact, I don't think that one can be really competent unless at the same time he enjoys what he is doing and there is a feeling of lightness about it. I think that being able to laugh at yourself, to be able to see a joke on yourself is a very important attribute to develop. This, again, comes from the family. If everything that Father says and Mother says has to be taken as though it were the weight of wisdom and of power, there's little opportunity to develop the fun side of things. Let's face it, just because adults become husbands and fathers and wives and mothers doesn't mean that they have now become non-people. They're just people who have some new jobs to do. I've been in some homes where the grimness and the seriousness hung like a fog in the air—where politeness was so thick that I had the feeling that only ghosts lived there, not people. I have been in homes where everything was so clean and so orderly that I felt as if I were an especially sterilized towel from the laundry. I would not expect enjoyment of people to develop in this atmosphere. *What kind of an atmosphere do you have in your family?*

The family teaches its young about loving. Did you ever stop to realize what a feeling of loving is like? When it happens to me, my body feels light, my energy flow seems higher, I feel exhilarated, open, unafraid, trusting, and safe. I feel an increased sense of my own worth and desirability. I have a heightened awareness of the needs and wishes of the person toward whom I direct these feelings. My desires go toward a joining of those needs and wishes with my own. I don't want to injure or impose on the one I love. I want to join with him, to share ideas, to touch and be touched, to look and be looked at and to enjoy him and be enjoyed by him. I like the feeling of loving. I consider it the highest form of expressing my humanness.

Taking my experience as the idea of what the love feeling is, I find it a scarce commodity in many families. I hear much about the pain, frustration, disappointment, and anger that family members feel for one another. There is so much time spent on doing the right things and getting the work done that there is no time for loving and enjoying one another.

All right. We've talked about some of the woes of parenting. Before I get into some of the ways to help you draft a strong, vital blueprint for your family, I want to take a completely different tack.

I am reminded at this point of a classic Robert Benchley story. Benchley was a college student, and one of his final examinations was to write an essay on fish hatcheries. He hadn't cracked a book all semester. Undaunted, he started his final something like this: "Much wordage has been devoted to fish hatcheries. No one, however, has ever covered this subject from the point of view of the fish." And this he proceeded to do in what is probably the most entertaining final in Harvard's history.

So, having devoted all these pages to parenting, we are now going to take a look at the family situation from the point of view of the baby.

I was a baby once, but can't remember what it felt like except in snatches of memory here and there, perhaps like you. I have watched many babies and their interaction with their parents, just as you have done. I have had many interactions with babies and young children. I have also read much of the available research about what babies are like.

Modern research has revealed that babies have all their senses available to them within a few hours after birth. Fifty years ago, babies were more or less thought to be things, or at best, incomplete, partial human beings.* We know better now.

*C. Anderson Aldrich and Mary M. Aldrich, BABIES ARE HUMAN BEINGS: AN INTERPRETATION OF GROWTH(New York: Macmillan Co.,1947).

I am going to try to be inside of a baby called Joe, somewhere around the age of two weeks.

"I feel my body hurting me from time to time. My back hurts when I am tucked in too tight, and I have to lie too long in one position. My stomach gets tight when I am hungry or hurts when I get too full. When the light shines directly in my eyes it hurts them because I can't move my head yet to turn away. Sometimes I am in the sun, and I am burning. My skin is hot sometimes from too many clothes and sometimes cold from too few clothes. Sometimes my eyes ache, and I get bored from looking at a blank wall. My arm goes to sleep when it is tucked under my body too long. Sometimes my buttocks and my crotch get sore from being wet too long. Sometimes my stomach cramps when I am constipated. When I am in the wind too long, it makes my skin prickle.

"Sometimes everything is so still that my body feels dry and uncomfortable. My body hurts when my bath water is too cold or too hot.

"I get touched by many hands. I hurt if those hands are gripping tightly. I feel clutched and squeezed. Sometimes those hands feel like needles. Sometimes they feel so limp that I feel I am going to fall. These hands do all kinds of things; push me, pull me, support me. These hands feel very good when they seem to know what I feel like. They are strong, gentle.

"It is really painful when I get picked up by one arm, or when my ankles are held too tight together when my diaper is changed. Sometimes I feel that I am suffocating when I am held so close to another person that I can't breathe.

"One terrible thing is when someone comes to my crib and suddenly puts his big face over mine. I feel that a giant is going to stamp me out. All my muscles get tight, and I hurt. Whenever I hurt, I cry. That is all I have to let anyone know that I am hurting. People don't always know what I mean

"Sometimes the sounds around me make me feel good. Sometimes they hurt my ears and give me a headache. I cry then, too. Sometimes my nose smells such lovely things, and sometimes the smell makes me sick. That makes me cry, too.

"Much of the time my mother or father notice me when I cry. Lots of times, it seems, they know I am hurting. They think of pins sticking me, my stomach needs food, I am constipated or lonely. Sometimes I get the impression that they just want to shut me up and get on with something else. They joggle me for a short time as if I were a bag of groceries, and then leave me. I feel worse than before. I guess they have other things to do. Sometimes I guess I must annoy them.

"My body hurts seem to go away when people touch me as if they like me. They seem to feel good about themselves, and I know they are really trying to understand me. I try to help as much as I can. I try to make my cries sound different. It also feels good when the voice is full, soft, musical. It feels good when my mother really looks at me, especially into my eyes.

"I don't think that my mother knows when her hands are painful to me and her voice so harsh. I think if she knew, she would try to change. She seems so distracted at those times. When my mother's hands feel painful many times in a row and her voice stays unpleasant, I begin to get afraid of her. When she comes around, I stiffen and pull back. She then looks hurt or sometimes angry. She thinks I don't like her, but I am really afraid of her. Then she sends my father in. He is gentler and I feel warm and safe with him. I see how good my father feels, and I feel relaxed. Later I hear my mother and father quarrel. I am sure it is about me. Maybe I should not have cried. Sometimes it is the other way around.

"Sometimes I think my mother doesn't know that my body reacts just like hers. I wish I could tell her. Some of the things she says about me and the rest of the family when I am in my crib and she is with her friends, I don't think she would say if she remembered that I have perfectly good ears. I remember once hearing her say, 'Joe will probably be like Uncle Jim,' and she started to cry. There were other similar things that happened, and I began to feel that something terrible was wrong with me.

"Years later, I find out that Uncle Jim was my mother's favorite brother who must have been a great guy. I often hear my mother say how much I looked like him. She cried because he died in an automobile accident in which she was driving. That put a whole different light on things for me, but not until later. I think if she had told me about her love feelings for Jim and how bad she felt about his death, particularly since I seemed to be like him in ways, I would not have felt so bad! I would have understood that when she looked at me and started to cry she was remembering him. I would like to tell all adults who bring up children to be free with telling them, no matter how young or old, what they are thinking and feeling. It is so easy for a child to read the wrong message.

"After I was born, I spent most of my time on my back, so I got acquainted with people from that position. I knew almost more about my mother's and father's chins from underneath than almost anything else. When I was on my back, I saw things that were mostly up above me, and of course I saw them from underneath. I thought that was how things were.

"I was very surprised to see how much things had changed when I learned to sit up. When I began to crawl, I saw things underneath me, and I really got acquainted with feet and ankles. When I started to stand up, I began to know a lot about knees. When I first learned to stand up, I was only about two feet tall. When I looked up, I saw my mother's chin differently. Her hands looked so big. In fact, a lot of times when I stood up between my mother and father, they really seemed far away and sometimes very dangerous, and I felt very, very little.

"After I had learned to walk, I remember going to the grocery store with my mother. She was in a hurry. She had hold of one of my arms. She walked so fast that my feet hardly touched the ground. My arm began to hurt. I started to cry. She got angry with me. I don't think she ever knew why I was crying. Her arm was hanging down, and she was walking on two feet; my arm was pulled up, and I was hardly on one foot. I kept losing my balance.

"I remember how tired my arms used to get when I would walk with both my mother and father when each had hold of one arm. My father was taller than my mother. I had to reach higher for his hand. So I was kind of lopsided. Half the time I did not have my feet on the ground. The steps that my father took were very big. When my feet were on the ground, I tried to keep up with him. Finally, when I couldn't stand it anymore, I begged for my father to carry me. He did. I guess he thought I was just tired. He didn't know that I was contorted so badly that my breathing was even getting hard. There were very nice times, but somehow the bad times stayed with me longer.

"My mother and father must have gone to a seminar some place because they changed. Whenever they wanted to talk to me after that, they would always stoop down, touch me gently, and look at me at eye level. That was so much better." (I try to contact all children at eye level. That usually means that I have to squat.)

Since first impressions make such an impact, I've wondered whether that first picture that the infant has of the adult isn't one of giantness, which automatically means great power and strength. This can feel like a great comfort and and support and also like a great danger, compared to the littleness and helplessness of the child.

I've mentioned this before, but it's important enough to bear a little repetition. When the adult first gets acquainted with his child, the child is, indeed, little and helpless. This could account for the fact that the parents' image of their child is little and helpless, and this can continue far beyond the time when that condition exists. That is, the son or daughter even at eighteen is still "a child" in his parents' eyes, no matter how grown-up, powerful, and competent the child really is. In much the same way the child could hang onto the image of his parents as all powerful even when he becomes powerful in his own right.

I think parents who are aware of this possibility help their child as quickly as possible to discover his own power, and let him know they have limits to their own powers. They freely use themselves to show their child how to become powerful in his own right. Without this learning, the adults who come out of this kind of situation often seem either to be

220

parasites on other people, dominate them, and/or play god to them, benign or malevolent.

Once I realized that an infant has all the physical responses that adults do, and I found out that the senses are all in working order at the age of two hours (as long as it takes to clean out the orifices), then it made sense that the infant was capable of feeling everything I was. Once I realized that his brain was working to interpret what he was feeling, even though he couldn't tell me what sense he was making, I could much more easily treat him as a person.

The human brain is a marvelous computer, constantly working to put things together and to make sense of them. Like the computer, the brain "doesn't know what it doesn't know"; it can only use what is already there.

One of the things I do when I work with parents is the following exercise.

One adult is asked to become an infant in a crib, lying on his back, not yet old enough to speak. He is asked to react only with sounds and simple movements. I then ask another pair of adults to bend over him, doing the things that babies need done for them, trying to follow the baby's clues. I have each adult become the baby. After about five minutes in this role-playing situation, I ask each adult to tell the other two what he was feeling as this was going on. In the middle of one of these situations I announce some outside interference such as the telephone or doorbell ringing. I try to choose the time when the baby is obviously fussy, then I watch to see what happens. Things frequently change. I asked the people to tell each other what difference the interruption made to all of them. Try this yourself.

This is a simple way to help adults get some kind of appreciation for what a baby might experience and how he could use this experience to begin building his expectations and his ideas of others.

The touch of a human hand, the sound of a human voice, and the smells in his home are the first experiences a baby has to begin his learning of what the new world is all about. So how a parent touches his child and sounds to him form the beginning for what the child learns. He must unscramble all the touches, faces, voices, and smells of the grown-ups around him. The newborn's world must be a very confusing place.

I believe the child has already developed some pretty clear ideas about what to expect by the time he can feed himself, walk, talk, and control his bowels and bladder. After that he just develops variations.

The infant must gradually learn how to treat himself, how to treat others, and how to treat the world of things around him. This is where the blueprint becomes crucial—*what do you teach and how do you teach it?*

No learning is single-level. While the child is learning to use his legs in walking, he is also learning something about how he is perceived and what is expected of him. From this he learns something about what to expect from others and how to deal with them. He also learns something about the world he is exploring and how to act in that world. "No, no! Don't touch!"

In the first three years of life, the child must learn more major and different things than in all the rest of his life put together. Never again will he be faced with learning so much on so many fronts in so short a time.

The impact of all this learning is much deeper than most parents realize. If parents understood, they would better appreciate the link between what they have already accomplished and the tremendous job their child has to do and could look for the best ways to help him. Through ignorance many parents do not begin to treat their children as persons until they are of school age, and sometimes not until they leave home. (Treating a child as a full person is a new idea to many adults.)

Many of the problems of families are the result of parental ignorance and insensitivity and not intent. We have been focusing too much attention on disciplinary methods and not enough on understanding.

There are three other areas that complicate carrying out the blueprint. They aren't so easy to single out since they are in the "iceberg," below the perceivable functioning of the family.

The first is ignorance. You simply don't know. And further, you may not know that you don't know so you wouldn't be aware of the need to find out.

The second is that your communication may be ineffective, so you are giving out messages you don't know about, or you think you're giving messages that you're not, so all the goodies you have to offer don't get across.

Many parents are amazed at what their children have taken from apparently innocent statements or situations where they have tried to teach them. For example, I know a couple who wanted to teach their children racial tolerance. They invited a little Negro boy into their home. When he'd left, the mother said to her child, "What did you think of his very curly hair?" But she said it in such a way that she gave the message pointing out his differentness, thus forging a first ring around a distance between her little child and the little black child. If parents are alert to the possibility of this kind of thing happening, they can check to see what their child has picked up.

I am reminded of another story. A young mother went through a rather lengthy presentation of the facts of life to her six-year-old son, Alex. Several days later she noticed Alex looking at her very quizzically. When asked about it, Alex said, "Mommy, don't you get awfully tired of standing on your head?" His mother was completely baffled. When she asked him to explain, he said, "Well, you know, when Daddy puts the seed in." His mother had neglected to embellish on the process of intercourse, so Alex filled in his own picture.

The third area in the iceberg has to do with your values. If you are uncertain of your own values, you can't very well teach your child anything definite What are you supposed to teach if you don't know yourself? And if you feel you can't be straight about your problem, this situation could easily turn into "Do what I say rather than what I do," or, "It doesn't really matter," or, "Why ask me? Use your own judgment." Any of these responses could leave your child with feelings about your unjustness or phoniness.

As I said before, the main data that goes into the blueprint comes from the experience from our own families and those other families with whom there was intimate contact. All the people you called by a parental name, or whom you were obliged to treat as if they were parents supplied you with experience that you are using in some way in your own parenting. Some of this may have been helpful to you, and some not. All of it had its effect, however.

Now we're ready to go on to the next chapter where I will get into a lot more detail about blueprinting.

14 The Family Blueprint: Some Essential Ingredients

Every child born into this world literally comes into a different context and a different atmosphere from every other child, even if he is born to the same set of parents. These are what I call the *atmospheric influences*, and they refer to what is happening when the child is born, and to the attitudes prevalent as he grows up. These influences are highly significant in the family blueprint.

The actual experience of conception, pregnancy, and birth often leaves shadows, which get into the atmosphere surrounding a particular child. If conception came at the wrong time or under undesirable circumstances for you, you might feel angry, helpless, or frustrated about it. These feelings could get in the way of using your blueprint the way you might have done so otherwise. The baby may become a symbol of a burden. Also, if the experience of pregnancy were accompanied with an extended period of sickness and continuing discomfort, and there were serious complications for either the mother or the child or both at birth, similar inhibiting effects may follow. You might develop unnecessary fears, which keep you from reacting normally to your baby, thus he might become a symbol of hurt or pity.

Some babies are born prematurely; some are born with physical parts missing or unusable, and some are born with internal and intellectual handicaps. When this happens, what is missing or unusable can become related to and out of proportion to the rest of the child and, again, the blueprint is affected. Often the child is not treated as a person, but as some kind of a cripple, which, of course, affects how he reacts and how he is reacted to.

There are also substantial numbers of children born to women whose husbands are away and who continue to be away for long periods of time after the birth. These husbands may be in the service, in prison, or business ventures, or hospitalized. This creates a difference from the beginning and lays the groundwork for skewing the family relationship. When the father returns he sometimes has a hard time finding as significant a place with his child as his wife has. It's quite a different matter to meet your child at the age of two and expect to be on a par with the adult who got there two years ahead of you.

If the father has died, deserted, or divorced at the birth of a child, this can often result in an exaggerated relationship between the mother and child, which eventually could hurt both of them. None of these consequences has to follow, but one has to be actively alert and creative to avoid them.

There are other unpleasant kinds of circumstances that can affect how the infant gets started in the world such as death, illness, unemployment of the wage-earner, or serious trouble for some member of the family. The pressing nature of these kinds of problems frequently require that parental attention gets focused elsewhere, not on the newborn child, which make for neglect and indifference—something the parents never really intended at all.

For example, I know a woman who already had two children, aged twenty-one months and ten months respectively, when a third child came along. She asked herself, "Where will I get enough arms and legs to take care of this one when I already have two babies?" A woman in tight financial circumstances was saying, "How am I going to feed this new child? I already have eight!" Or, "Good heavens, another girl, and we have three girls already!" Or, "Good heavens, another boy, and we already have five!" Perhaps there hasn't been a child for fifteen years, and then along comes another one.

Each child comes into his parents' lives when many other things are going on. Let's not kid ourselves that all babies came into the world at the best time for the parents. Adults are not always able to control the timing of the birth of a child. I have never taken the statistics, but I don't believe too many of us arrived at the best time we might have. That, by the way, doesn't make us rejected children, even though many of us could make a case for being "unwanted children" if we so chose. The most important thing is that we got here.

Another possible atmospheric influence is the fact that there might be trouble in the marital relationship when the baby comes. Marriage may not have turned out to be the satisfying experience hoped for by the marital partners. Very often this leads to the parents having difficulty in being sensible and realistic with the child. I think there is a direct relationship between marital harmony and successful peoplemaking. If the personal life situation of one or both parents is not particularly happy, the pots of each will be low, and it would be hard to apply the blueprint enthusiastically and appropriately.

Bringing a first child into a family is a very big first. Existing circumstances are changed drastically for the couple. That first child is the means by which adults first find out what parenting is all about. The first child is always the testing ground. First children, by the very fact that they are first and born to people who are being parents for the first time, have different treatment from any succeeding children. In many ways the first child forms the context for the children to follow. He is truly a guinea pig, and I don't see how it could be otherwise.

I have described briefly the important factors that can affect the atmosphere in which the blueprint will be carried out. Briefly summarized, the atmospheric influences are: the actual experience of conception, pregnancy, and birth, individual circumstances in the family, the condition of the infant, the relationship of the marital pair, the relationship to the grandparents, the adults' level of knowledge, their ways of communicating, and their philosophy.

Now I want to introduce what seems to me to be the essential learnings that have to take place for every human being between birth and adulthood. They fall into four main categories which, when translated into family life, come out in the following questions:

What do I teach my child about himself?

What do I teach him about others?

What do I teach him about the world?

And what do I teach him about God?

Could you sit down at this moment and literally write out what the basic things you would like to be giving to your kids? How are you teaching these things? Ask yourself and ask your child what he has learned and see if it is what you thought you taught him.

The teaching process includes the following: a clear idea of what is to be taught, awareness that each parent has of what he is modeling, a knowledge of how to interest the other in following that model, and the communication to make it work.

In the ideal family, we have adults who clearly show their own uniqueness, who demonstrate their power, who clearly show their sexuality, who demonstrate their ability to share through understanding, kindness and affection, who use their common sense, who are realistic and responsible.

Have we said it's no disgrace not to be a perfect parent? There are no perfect parents! What's important is that you try to keep moving in that direction and to be honest about where you are. Admit it, and then learn together. Your children's trust in you will increase rather than decrease. It is an impossible job for a human to play God. Yet many parents saddle themselves with this terrible responsibility.

I have never known any perfect families, any perfect children, or for that matter, any perfect people. Nor do I ever expect to meet any. I believe it's a fruitless search.

So the key words are *unique, powerful, sexual, sharing, sensible, realistic* and *responsible*. Can you describe yourself as I have indicated? Are you trying to teach your children to be what you are not? If you are, this realization may hurt, but if you use it as a signal, you may make a start on changing things in your family.

Just remember, if you as adults do not possess all these qualities, it is not too late to learn them. Just, for goodness' sake, don't try to sell your kids a bill of goods by asking them to do what you can't do, and then criticize them for pointing out this fact to you.

If the goals of what I've called the essential learnings are achieved, then there are a whole set of other things that I believe will follow—honesty, sincerity, creativity, love, interest, zest, competence, and constructive problem-solving, all of which we as human beings prize highly. Within this frame, the necessary information that all children need in terms of the four categories can be more easily taught.

Once you as an adult grasp the notion that a human being at any age is a *person*, whether at birth, two weeks, fifteen years, thirty-five years, or eighty years, your job as a peoplemaker will be easier. You have more in common with your children than you thought. For example, the disappointment that a grown man experiences at losing a desired job is no more painful than that of a four-year-old who loses his favorite toy. The experience of disappointment is the same at any age. The feeling in a child who is the brunt of a tirade from an angry mother is no different from the women's feeling when she has been the brunt of a tirade from her angry husband, or vice versa.

There are very few things a child feels that the adult does not know something about from his own experience. Children seem to thrive on the knowledge that their world of hope, fear, mistakes, imperfection, and successes is a world also known and shared by their parents. What adult is without occasional, if not frequent, feelings of hope, fear, disappointment, poor judgment, and mistakes?

Yet many parents believe that their authority is undermined if they express these feelings. If you act on this, you come out looking phony to your children. If you do have that attitude, I hope you will experiment with changing it. Children have much more trust in humanness than they do in sainthood and perfection.

If you want to check this out, literally ask your children what they know about your feelings and hopes and disappointments. Ask them how they feel about talking to you about mistakes that you make. And perhaps you could do it the other way around and tell your children your feelings about hopes and disappointments and mistakes that they make. An awful lot can be cleared up in this way.

Once a child develops a feeling of distrust for his parents, the feeling extends into personal isolation and general feelings of unsureness, personal imbalance, and rebellion. When adults do not acknowledge and express their own humanness and do not acknowledge the child's humanness, it is very scary to the child.

Now, to get back to the essential learnings, I think it isn't necessary to explain what I mean by "sensible," "sharing," and "realistic." I use these words in the same way you do. But when it comes to *uniqueness, power,* and *sexuality,* I want to go into considerably more detail, not only because my use of the words may be different from yours, but also because understanding of these concepts is of primary importance in the family blueprint.

I believe that *uniqueness* is the key word to self-worth or high pot. As I discussed in the chapter on couples, we get together on the basis of our similarities, and we grow on the basis of our differences. We need both. It is this combination of sameness and differentness in a human being that I call uniqueness.

Very early you and your child are going to discover that he is different, in some ways, from you and other human beings and vice versa. A frequently found example comes to mind. I know two boys in a family; one is fourteen and the other is fifteen. The fifteen-year-old is interested in athletics and prefers to spend his time on that. The fourteen-year-old is more interested in the artistic side of life and prefers to devote his time to those kinds of interests. These boys are the same coloring, of the same intelligence, but they have different interests. This is a very basic example of the kinds of differentness I am talking about. Fortunately for these boys, they have parents who respect their differences and help each boy evolve in his own way.

You see, genetically, each child is different even if he comes from the same parents. What I'm trying to say here is that the equipment each child brings into the world, just from a genetic point of view, is going to be different from every other child's. Each child, then, presents an opportunity to his parents for unique adventure as he unfolds and develops.

Interestingly enough, parents don't stop unfolding just because they get married and have children. And by the same token, each husband and wife is different from one another. Helping the child to learn to appreciate the differences between his parents becomes an important part of his learning. If parents try to present a facade of sameness, they bypass

231

this very important opportunity. Mama likes to sleep late in the morning, and Papa likes to get up early, and that's okay. People don't have to be alike. Some differences make life a little more complicated, but most difference can be used constructively. If infants don't have the opportunity to be treated as unique from the beginning of their lives, it will become difficult to react to them as whole people. They will tend to react more as stereotypes of people, and can expect to be plagued with a variety of ills of a physical, emotional, social, and intellectual nature. I don't mean to say that they are cursed, but they will be handicapped until they learn new ways of becoming whole people.

So how are you going to teach your child about his differentness? How are you going to teach him to distinguish between negative and positive differences? How are you going to teach him to judge which differences in others he should support and which ones he should influence for change? How can you teach him that he doesn't have to destroy people associated with differences, nor does he have to worship the person associated with sameness. We all have the tendency to do that, you know.

Strangeness and difference are scary, but they contain the seeds for growth. Every time I come upon a new situation or a strange one (which is another way of describing differences), I have an opportunity to learn something I didn't know before. I don't expect all of it to be pleasant, but I can't help but learn something.

I've said this before, but it's important. Differentness can't be handled successfully unless sameness is appreciated. The samenesses of people are few in number, but are basic and fundamental, predictable and always present, although not always obvious. Each human being experiences feeling all his life, from the time he is born until he dies. He can feel anger, sorrow, joy, humiliation, fear, helplessness, hopelessness, and love. This is the basis on which we have a ready-made connection to all other human beings at any point in our lives or theirs.

Children feel.

Adults feel.

Men feel.

Women feel.

White, black, brown, yellow, and red people feel.

Rich feel.

Poor feel.

Catholics feel.

Protestants feel.

Jews feel.

People in power positions feel.

People in non-power situations feel.

Every human being feels. It may not always show, but it's there. And the faith that it is there even though you can't see it can make you act different from the way you would have if you reacted only to what shows. Being absolutely convinced of this is what makes parents and therapists successful.

Developing your sense of uniqueness, then, is basic to developing high pot. Without a sense of our own uniqueness, we are slaves, robots, computers, and despots—not human beings.

Now I think we're ready to talk about power. *Power is essential to every human being.* To be an effective person, everyone needs all his powers developed as fully as possible. *Power*, as defined by Webster, is "to be able . . . capacity to act . . . capability of performing or producing . . . vigor, force and strength . . . the ability to control others . . . authority . . . sway, influence, physical force, energy to regulate, restrain, curb."

Body power is the first power developed. Almost everyone greets the evidence of the infant's lung power at birth with relief. He is alive. Physical coordination as shown in turning, sitting, walking, holding things, and toilet training are also greeted with joy. The child is growing as expected. Simply speaking, he is learning the management of his body muscles, the end point of which is to be able to manage one's body muscles so that body responds to the demands of that self. Over the years I have noticed that parents will have endless patience teaching their child body power and become joyful at the manifestation of every new successful effort. I think this is also a suitable way to teach the other areas of power—to use patience and to respond to the expression of the child's newfound power with joy and approval. Body power is only one kind of power—there are other personal powers to be developed, namely, intellectual, emotional, social, material, and spiritual power.

A person shows his intellectual power (thinking) in learning, concentration, problem-solving, and innovating. This is more difficult to teach, but can be met with the same kind of joy a parent expresses when his child, say, takes his first step. He can beam, "I've got a smart kid!"

A person's emotional power is shown in his freedom to feel all his emotions openly and clearly express them and channel them into constructive action. This is oftentimes the scariest power to teach.

His material power is demonstrated by the way he makes use of his environment for his own needs, while at the same time considering the needs of others. Unfortunately, this is all too often limited to the ability to work.

An individual shows his social power by the way he connects with other people, how he shares with them and teams up with them for achieving joint goals, as well as how he can both lead and follow. Too often this can become just a dry, oft repeated recipe.

Spiritual power can be seen in a person's reverence for life—his and all others, including animals and nature, with a recognition of a universal life force referred to by many as God.

Incidentally, many people limit this part of their lives to an hour or so on Sunday. I think most of us know that all human beings have a spiritual side, a side that is involved with their souls, which needs appreciation. Right now we're having some pretty hard times with relationships among people of different races, different economic groups, and different generations. A great deal of this would be solved if we had a greater development of our spiritual power and were willing to put it into practice.

To meet life freely and openly, I think we need to develop our power in all of these areas, for these kinds of power give us what we need to cope with life.

I'm going to make adjectives out of the words Webster used to define power: vigorous, forceful, strong, influential, energetic, controlling, regulating, restraining, and curbing. These are the main faces of power. Violence is the destructive use of power. Few people would object to the first five adjectives, but the last four words might bring up confused and/or negative messages. These are the words that are related to control, which is connected with authority in most people's minds.

Control, *responsibility*, and *decision-making* are related to power.

The questions of how much control I have over myself, over you, over the situation I am in and how I use this control come up over and over again.

Now, if I want to understand how action takes place between two people at a given point in time, there are three places I can look.

The first place is the pot level of each person (how am I feeling about myself at this moment in time). The second place is the individual's response to the other person (how am I looking and sounding and what am I saying), and the third is a person's knowledge of the resources that are available to him at a given point in time (where am I, what time and what place is this, what is the situation I am in, who is here, what do I want to happen, and what possibilities are there in this reality).

Added together we come up with the following:
The pot level of person A and of person B.
The response of A to B and the response of B to A.
A's picture of what possibilities exist.
B's picture of what possibilities exist.

It's a good idea to separate those things over which you have control and those over which you have only influence.

I have *control* over the *choice* of whether or not to act and the course of action I take. For this, I can be held *responsible* to myself as well as to others. I can't be responsible for what is presented to me; only for my response to it. I cannot hold myself responsible for the rain that falls as I am walking; I am responsible only for how I respond to it.

I cannot hold myself responsible for your tears. I can only be responsible for how I respond to them. The kind of response I make will influence your experience of crying, but won't decide it. You have to do that. It may be that I exerted a powerful influence, to which you felt you had to respond by crying. Each of us, I think, bears the responsibility of being aware of what we give out to ask the other person to deal with. If I am twenty-eight and bear the relationship of mother to you, and you are three, my responses to you will undoubtedly have a stronger influence with you than if you were also twenty-eight and a fellow employee. Some situations and some responses have a greater influence than others, and it is up to me to know about that, too.

I think there is a lot of murkiness about what responsibility is and how it can be exercised. I would like to tell you where I am in my practice of being responsible.

First, I clearly own what comes out of me—my words, thoughts, body movement, and my deeds. I might have been influenced by you, but *I* made the decision to act on that influence so that part is *my show* completely. The same is true of you.

Whatever comes out of you is your show, and represents *your* decision to use whatever influence was around you. I become responsible when I fully acknowledge this. I can use you to influence me, but *only I* can decide to act on that influence. There are three exceptions to this: when a person is unconscious, when he is seriously physically ill, and when he is an infant.

If we do not know that we make the choices about how to use what influences us, then it is easy to feel insecure and to create relationships with others that are blaming and dissatisfying, leaving us helpless and even more insecure.

I want to point out here that an objective piece of reality doesn't necessarily change because of our choices. Let's take the objective reality of blindness. If your eyes don't see, they don't see—period. As long as you are busy blaming the world for your blindness, you will be spending your energies in hating the world and pitying yourself, and consequently shriveling as a human being. Of course, as long as you're doing this, you're not taking responsibility for acknowledging what *is*. The moment you do that, you can use your energies for creating and growing yourself.

Here is the same theme in a different example.

A husband swears at his wife at 5:30 P.M. "You damned fool!" he shouts at her. Whether or not he should have or wanted to or even whether or not he knew what he was saying is irrelevant to the fact that this is something the wife has to deal with at that point in time. She has choices, whether she knows it or not. It may not be any more pleasant than blindness, but she *does* have choices. You should remember the possibilities open to her from the chapter on communication.

"I'm sorry; you're right." (placating)

"Don't call me names, you idiot!" (blaming him back)

"I guess in marriage one has to expect times like this." (computing)

"Dr. Smith called and wants you to call him right back." (distracting)

"You sound all worn out." Or, "I felt hurt when you said that." Either of which would be leveling, in the first instance responding to his pain, and in the second, to her own.

Each one of these responses can influence her husband's response. Because they are different, there are apt to be different consequences, but what she said doesn't necessarily have to determine how he decides to respond.

In families, it is unfortunately true that control and authority are assumed to be the primary province of the parent. "I (the parent) control you (my child)." In this way the child doesn't get an appreciation for positive uses of power and could run into some sticky problems. There are only two words that seem to make a difference. Does the parent speak as a *leader* or as a *boss*? If he speaks as a leader, the chances are good that he can use control as a learning as well as an implementing tool, and his teaching of power grows. You know my feelings about bosses from the chapter where I practically mounted a soapbox. Let's just say here that bossing a child doesn't teach him much if anything about developing his power constructively, and the main result is that his pot is lowered and another example of the generation gap is well into the making.

Developing material power doesn't seem to scare parents too much. When a child shows what he can do, his parents are nearly always pleased. But there are traps, as I hinted earlier.

What are you going to teach your child about using his power to be productive, competent, and creative? Most of us realize that we can find joy as we learn how to do things. However, for many people, producing and being competent gets associated with work alone, with making a livelihood, and this too often gets to mean denial of fun. Our competence suffers as a result, as does our pot level and, certainly, our joy in living. Such a feeling can also seriously hamper our initiative to try out new things and to be creative.

What really scares parents, though, is the development of emotional power—the basic emotions of loneliness, hurt, love, joy, anger, fear, frustration, humiliation, and shame. "Don't be angry." "How can you love her; she's Catholic, Jewish, black, or white." "Big boys are not afraid." "Only babies complain." "If you did what you were told, you wouldn't be lonely." "You ought to be ashamed of yourself." "Don't wear your heart on your sleeve." "Keep a stiff upper lip," and so on. These are typical comments that I have heard that suggest the kind of teaching that goes on in families with regard to emotion.

Unfortunately, few parents have developed their own emotional power enough so they can tolerate it, much less develop it, in their children, In fact, it is apparently so scary that it is actively squelched. Much of this fear is based on ignorance.

My own feeling is that if adults knew more about how to use their own emotional power more constructively they would become more willing to plan ways to develop it for their children. What you have read so far, I hope, has shed a good bit of light on this subject for you.

This brings us to the essential learning about sexuality. The family teaches maleness and femaleness—*sex* in its broadest sense.

Babies can be clearly divided into two sexes at birth, simply by noting the difference in their genitals. But this says nothing about how each will grow up feeling about his sex, or whether or not he will find out how to live with what he has in common with the other sex. Men and women are different—nobody's going to argue about that. But *how* different? A great deal depends upon what answers a parent gives to this child when asked this and how he is observed while doing this. This will be reflected in how he tries to establish the sexuality of his children and will become a basic part of his blueprint.

Each parent represents one sex, and the child has a chance to have a sexual model of what he can become.

Did you know that it takes a male and female both to develop the sexual identification of any individual child? From all that we can find out, each sex contains aspects of both sexes. Every man has some female potentials, and every woman, some male potentials. I am convinced that the only real differences between men and women are physical and sexual. All other supposed differences are imposed by the culture and vary from culture to culture. Anyone acquainted with anthropology knows this is true.

No woman can say how it feels to be a man, and no man can say how it feels to be a woman. This is immediately obvious when you realize that no woman knows what it's like to have and use a penis, or to have hair growing all over her face. Likewise, no man knows how it feels to menstruate, be pregnant, and to give birth. In the normal course of the lives of most people, a union is made with the other sex, so this is important information to share. Each needs to teach the other what it is like to be his sex. The father teaches the little boy what it means to be a male and how a male views a female. Likewise with the mother and her little girl. Out of this teaching the child develops a picture of what a male is, and of what a female is, and how the two of them relate to one another. It is clear to see where confusion can set in if (1) the parents don't understand this, or (2) they don't value themselves as sexual people, or (3) they do not see each sex as having different but equal value.

If a child's father and mother do not have healthy ways of finding their differences enjoyable, that is, each finds joy in and appreciates the differentnesses of the other (including their bodies), he comes out with an unclear idea of how to appreciate himself as a male and how he can enjoy and appreciate a female. It takes two parents to make this possible.

What is so sad is that many fathers and mothers, as husbands and wives, haven't achieved this for themselves. So how could they teach it to their children, much less talk about it? Further, as we talked about in the chapter on rules, for so many years sexual organs were considered dirty and shameful, which made an additional handicap to dealing openly with the whole male-female question. You can't really talk freely about maleness and femaleness without including talk about the genitals.

To make sexual identification possible, one has to acquire a knowledge of the care, maintenance, and operation of the reproductive parts of a person and understand their relationship to the life of each person. Almost every day we hear stories of personal agony and misery in adults because of poor, distorted, or nonexistent teaching about their sexual lives. You will remember when I was talking about rules that I stated that the majority of sex abuses can be accounted for by the frankly bad teaching that goes on about sex in childhood. How many adults have had childhood experiences of masturbating, peeking, and sexual experimentation for which they were severely punished and from which they still bear scars?

I have run into case after case of young girls who were unprepared for menstruation, and believed they must have severely hurt themselves or were being punished for something. Likewise young boys who got erections or had nocturnal emissions and secretly stewed over whether something bad was happening to them, or they were bad. We can save our young people that kind of needless pain.

Much is shown the growing child about himself as a sexual being in his home by the way the parents treat each other and how openly and frankly they can deal with male and female sexual matters.

If you, as a woman, do not appreciate and find joy and pleasure in your husband's body, how can you teach your daughter an appreciation of men? The same is true for the father. Somehow this veil of secrecy has to be lifted from the whole sexual subject so that adults who emerge from families are more fully whole.

There is another kind of learning that must take place. That is how males and females fit together, how they bring their separate selves to make a kind of new union—sexual, social, intellectual, and emotional. In the past it was very easy to pit males and females against one another—the old "battle of the sexes." This is unnecessary and uncomfortable. Many families train females to be subservient to males. She is told she has been put on this earth to serve the male. Still other families teach that males must always be the servants of the females—they must protect them, take care of them, think and feel for them, and never cause them any pain. Some children are taught that males and females are alike in every respect and deny the fact of difference. Still others are taught that they are sexually different, but do have things in common and they can join together. To use a rather homely comparison, when a plumber makes joinings, one part has to be smaller than the other. No plumber ever wasted his time wondering whether one part is better than the other. He needs both of them in order to make a smooth fitting that will carry whatever needs to be carried. So it is with males and females. Can there be a flowing between the two as a result of their contact without worrying about who is on top?

I would like to make a few observations about sexual stereotypes that determine much of the male-female teaching in families. The female is supposed to be soft, yielding, and tender, but never tough and aggressive. The male is supposed to be tough and aggressive, but never yielding and tender. I believe tenderness and toughness are qualities everyone needs. Yet in many families these stereotypes are what are taught. How can a man relate to the woman's tenderness if he hasn't developed it himself? How can a female relate to his toughness if she's had no experience with it? With these stereotypes as models you can see how easy it is for men to regard women as weak, and for women to look at men as if they were cruel and beastly. How can anyone ever get together with anyone else on this basis?

I've noticed that men live shorter lives than women, which I think to a large extent is attributable to the fact that he strangles his soft feelings. He's not supposed to ever cry or be hurt. He has to become insensitive, and if he has rules against being violent, then he can't vent his aggressive feelings. Having to bottle up these feelings, then, they go underground and play havoc with his body, and he ultimately gets high blood pressure and heart attacks. I have personally witnessed dramatic changes in at least a thousand men who were able to get in touch with soft feelings. Almost all of them had said they had been afraid of their violence before, but having honored their soft feelings, their aggressive feelings went into building energy instead.

Similarly, if women feel they can only demonstrate soft feelings, they feel in constant danger of being trampled on. So they get men as protectors, feeling as if they are in straitjackets. In order to get any kind of a feeling of worth, they turn into schemers.

If all human beings are estranged from soft feelings, they can become dangerous robots. If they are estranged from their tough feelings, they become parasites. The family is the place where all this can be changed.

We've been doing a lot of talking about teaching, but let me say here and now that it is not possible to teach a child what to do in every situation he meets. There are too many of them, and each is different. Therefore the parent has to teach ways of approaching things involving questions like which way do you use here? Which way there? In other words—judgment.

I have a couple of stories that highlight this point.

Epaminondos was a little boy of five who lived in a village far away. One day his mother needed some butter. She decided to send Epaminondos to the store for it. Epaminondos was very glad to do something for his mother because he loved her very much and he knew she loved him. His mother's parting words were, "Mind how you bring the butter back."

Epaminondos skipped happily to the store, singing a tune as he went After he bought the butter, he remembered his mother's words. He wanted to be very careful. He had never carried butter home before. He thought and thought and finally decided to put it on his head under his hat. The sun was very warm. By the time he got home, the butter had melted and was running down his face. His mother exclaimed disapprovingly, "Epaminondos, you haven't the sense you were born with! You should have carefully cooled the butter in the running brook, put it in a sack, and run home with it." Epaminondos felt very sad. He had disappointed his mother.

The next day his mother sent him to the store for a little puppy. Epaminondos was very happy. He knew just what to do. Very carefully and thoroughly he cooled the puppy in the brook, and when it was cold and stiff, put it in a bag. His mother was horrified. In a much sharper way she said, "You don't have the sense you were born with. You should have tied a string around his neck and led him home." Epaminondos was very, very sad and puzzled. He loved his mother very much and she loved him, but this terrible thing was happening. Now he knew exactly what to do.

The next day his mother decided to give him another chance. This time she sent him for a loaf of bread. Epaminondos gleefully tied a string around the loaf of bread and dragged it home through the dust. His mother just looked sternly at him and said nothing.

The next day she said she would go to the store herself. She had just baked a cherry pie. Before she left she said,

"Mind how you step around that cherry pie." Epaminondos was very, very careful. He placed his foot right smack in the middle of that pie!

This story highlights the sad dilemma that frequently occurs between parents and children. It is judgment that is very tricky. Judgment is the use of selecting "what to do when." There is no recipe covering all situations.

I am reminded of a near tragic incident involving young parents, Bill and Harriet, and their four-year-old daughter, Alyce. Harriet was alternately rageful and frightened as she told me how Alyce had viciously attacked a mutual college friend of the parents who had come to visit. She had already whipped Alyce severely, mostly out of her embarrassment. Although Alyce had never behaved in this vicious manner before, it was so dramatically different that Harriet wondered if this represented beginning criminal tendencies or even psychosis. She remembered that her great uncle had been some kind of a criminal character. After exploring the relevent facts, this is the picture that emerged.

In anticipation of the friend, Ted's visit, the parents had sent him a recent picture of Alyce, but had somehow neglected to do the same for Alyce by introducing her to Ted via a picture. When Ted arrived, Alyce was playing on the lawn. He knew her, but she did not know him. He approached her in a rather lusty fashion and tried to pick her up, to which Alyce responded by kicking and screaming and biting. Harriet and Bill were much embarrassed by this behavior, and Ted was angry and hurt.

When I pointed out that Ted knew Alyce, but Alyce did not know Ted, some light began to dawn. The final illumination came when I asked what Harriet and Bill had taught Alyce about responding to strange men. There had been some child-molesting going on in the neighborhood, and Harriet and Bill had made a big point of teaching Alyce that if a strange man tried to touch her, she should fight with all her might. Bill had even had her practice with him. Bill got about half way through this part, stopped, and recoiled from his own words with shame and a terrible feeling in the pit of his stomach. Alyce had done exactly what she had been asked to do. I shiver very much at the thought of how many more times this kind of thing happens and is never corrected. To Harriet and Bill, Ted was a friend; to Alyce, he was the strange man who was trying to touch her.

Now I would like to turn to a part of the blueprint that is an essential part of life, but is rarely talked about. Death. Some teachings about death are absolutely ridiculous. Use this medicine or that perfume—think this way and not that way, and maybe you can even cheat death. Impossible!

I know it is a hard subject for most of us to even talk about, let alone talk frankly and openly about. Yet it seems to me that life is meaningless unless we see death as a natural, inevitable, and essential part of life Death is not a disease, or something that only happens to bad people. It happens to all of us.

I think a good goal would be to make it possible to prevent *premature* death, not death itself, and this is possible through better medical care, safety, better environmental conditions and better relationships among people. I happen to believe that life is extremely precious, and I would like to be productively alive as long as I can. I would like to help make this possible for other human beings as well, and I think the family is a good place to start.

What do your rules say about death? If you have valued a person and he dies, you suffer a loss and you grieve. For me, there is something extra. If the person died prematurely, I feel a great sense of helplessness because a part of me senses that it might have been avoidable, *if.* There are usually about a thousand *if*s.

There are real accidents, certainly, but I feel that many premature deaths could be avoided if the person really had feelings of worth about himself.

Do you realize how much secrecy surrounds death? I know of adults who still try to hide the evidence of death from their children. They prevent them from going to the funerals of their grandparents. Then they compound the problem by dismissing the death with a statement like, "Grandma went to heaven," and never speaking of it again. I realize many adults think they are doing their children a favor by "protecting" them in this way, but I think they're doing them real harm. Children who do not see evidence of their parent's death, and are not helped to grieve over the death and integrate it into their lives, can develop serious blocks.

I could fill this whole book with stories of adults who never really integrated their parents' deaths into their lives, particularly if the parents died when they were children. These people suffered in some psychological way until they died themselves.

Further more, *people* die, not saints and devils. So often the adults who are left use the death experience to elevate the departed one to some kind of saintly status, which completely skews the child's view of the one who died as a person.

I know of one youngster, Jim, who was ten when his father died. Every time Jim mentioned some negative experience with his dad, his mother sternly reprimanded him for speaking "ill of the dead." Eventually this led to Jim's closing off all memories of his father. Then he developed a saintly picture of his father, with whom he could neither relate nor use as a model. Jim developed some serious psychological symptoms.

I know another situation in which whenever the child did anything wrong or questionable, his mother would tell him that he needed to be careful because his father was looking down from heaven and would punish him. Since the child believed this, he soon developed some paranoid ideas. Can you imagine what a helpless feeling it is to believe that there is no privacy for you anywhere; that you can always be watched?

At one time I was a staff member in a residential treatment center for girls. I was struck by how many of the children who had dead parents and did not participate actively in their deaths were troubled with serious self-esteem problems. I was equally struck how this began to change when I made it possible to show them evidence of their deaths. I found obituary notices; I went sleuthing for people who had been present at the funeral, took them to cemeteries where their parents were buried. Then, with their help, I reconstructed their parents as people. Many times we role-played scenes from life before death, and the death itself. This has also happened many times in the continuous contact seminars I have had with adults in later years.

Death is an inevitable part of life for all of us. I think that the acceptance of death makes life a real and rewarding experience.

I have a hunch that until this is done, we mistake a lot of other things as though they were death and we mess up our lives. For instance, some people have so much fear of criticism that they avoid it at all costs. I don't think on the whole that criticism is pleasant, but it is necessary and often useful. To treat it as a death matter mixes it up. Did you ever know anyone who never tried anything for fear of getting criticized? The fear of making mistakes, fear of being wrong—any fear for that matter—can get tied up with death. I have heard it said that many people fear so much that they die a little every day, and the rest of the time they are trying to avoid dying so they really die before they have ever had a chance to live.

Death is death. It happens only once in a lifetime. There is no other thing in life like it. When you make this distinction, then everything except the act of death is life. To treat it any other way is a travesty on life.

The question of safety is related quite directly to death fears in the family. How are you going to teach a child how to be safe and at the same time allow him to take risks so he can expand his own growth? You don't want your child to die before his time, so you teach him to be careful.

Of course, nothing is 100 percent safe. I've met so many parents who, because of their fears, practically kept their kids chained to the front porch. I can understand wanting to protect the young. Yet we are still around, so we should relax a little bit and give our kids the same opportunity to struggle with life's dangers we've had. I don't propose that we send three-year-olds across town alone. I do propose that we look at what our children want to do, being real about the dangers rather than maximizing or minimizing them.

I know a twelve-year-old boy, Ralph, whose mother wouldn't let him ride his bike for three miles because he might get killed. Ralph was a good, careful bike rider and the bike was his only means of transportation. He felt his mother was unfair, so by skillful lying he worked out a deal with his friends so he could ride anyway. This was doubly bad because his wish to ride reflected his need to develop independence and self-reliance.

I would like to see a parent ask his child at the close of the day, "What danger did you meet today? How did you meet it?"

Many times I quaked in my own boots when my daughters were teen-agers, and I watched them meet dangers. When is our desire to protect them real, and when is it just a sneaky way to calm ourselves? Judging when a child is ready to take on new dangers is anything but easy—but, as parents, we have to do it.

I remember when my second daughter took out the family car for the first time alone. She was only sixteen—just a baby, really, and my goodness, how was she going to manage in that heavy traffic? There were drunk drivers out there. She could be killed. Besides, we had only one car, and what if she wrecked it? What if I wasn't there to guide her? By the time I got through with my fantasy, the car was totaled and she was already stretched out in the morgue.

Yet in another part of my reasoning I knew that she had had good driver training. I had ridden with her, and she was a good driver. We had insurance, and I trusted her. Nonetheless none of these realizations kept me from sweating as I watched her go out the door. I wasn't going to bug her with my fears, so I managed to say, weakly, "How do you feel about going off by yourself?" She smiled and said, "Don't worry, Mother. I will be all right."

And of course, she was. Later we had a chance to compare our "insides." She told me she knew I was worried, and that she was too. She said she was glad I hadn't burdened her with my fears as they would have made her own worse.

Now, I don't want to end this chapter on such somber subjects as death and risk-taking. I want to go back to something I touched on in the Couples chapter—namely, dreams. Dreams and what we do about them are essential parts of our blueprint, too.

In fact, I think a big part of the blueprint has to do with encouraging and keeping personal dreams alive. The dream about what one will become is a big part of the lives of children. I think the dream stands as a beacon beckoning us to greater growth and greater accomplishments.

Your dream is your hope for yourself. When this dream is gone, "vegetablitis" sets in, with accompanying attitudes of indifference and resignation. You run the risk of becoming a robot.

Sad but true, the family is often the place where dreams die. We learned this when discussing the couple—too often individual hopes die in the family because hopes that were present in the courtship fall flat. Family members can give each other a great deal of inspiration and support for keeping their dreams alive. "Tell me your dream, and I'll tell you mine. Maybe then we can help each other achieve what we both want."

I recommend that families sit down and talk openly about their dreams. This can be so important for children. How much better it is to say, "How can we all work together to make your dream come true?" than to say something like, "Let me tell you why that isn't practical." Believe me, some exciting things can happen.

Don't take my word for it. Sit down with your family

and openly discuss your dreams and their dreams. Find out about some of this excitement yourselves, first hand.

I remember a family who tried this. One of the parents asked one of the children, "What do you want to be when you grow up?" Tom, a four-year-old, said he wanted to be a fireman. After several interested questions, it turned out that Tom liked to put out fires; he also liked to light them. He enjoyed the bright, shiny red fire trucks and liked the looks of the sturdy men who rode on them. The family decided that Tommy didn't have to wait until he was grown up to become a fireman. He was given special instructions in laying and lighting fires in the fireplace. His dad took him to the fire station, where he had a chance to talk "man-to-man" with the firemen. They showed him different ways to put out fires.

Everyone in the family got something out of helping Tom with his dream. Tom began to play a role in his father's dream of setting up a chemistry lab in his home. Could you do a similar thing?

What can you do to keep alive a spirit of curiosity and imagination, to stimulate a search for making new meaning, to find new uses for things already known, and to probe into the unknown for things not yet known? This is what makes for zest in life. The world is filled with much to wonder about, to be awestruck about, and to explore.

Dreams occur in the present. Chances are pretty good that some part of almost any dream can be realized *now*. I recommend that people live out their current dreams as much as possible. Sometimes it takes help from other people, but the other people have to know about the dream before they can help. Test out your dreams for appropriateness; look at them realistically; Realizing little dreams helps to have faith in having big dreams. The family is where it can happen.

In my lifetime alone, I have gone from crystal sets to

color television, from a Ford crank-it-yourself car to the slick comfortable cars that practically drive themselves, from walking three miles to a little country school to jetting all over the world in a few short hours, from cranking a telephone on the wall where you called someone named "Central" to a pretty colored Princess phone where all you have to do is press some buttons and lights come on. All this in a little over fifty years. During all of this, I was continually expanding my knowledge of the world and continued to find new things that awed, educated, and excited me. All of these things came out of someone's being willing to follow his dreams. Unfortunately, we haven't yet had dreamers who know how to bring along the world of people at the same rate. My dream is to make families a place where adults with high self-esteem can develop. I think we have reached a point where if we don't get busy on dreams of this sort, our end is in sight. We need a world that is as good for human beings as it is for technology. We have good tools. All we have to do is to "dream up" effective ways to use them.

I feel so sad about the number of adults that I meet in families that have turned their backs on their dreams. They are indifferent and resigned. "What difference does it make?" "It doesn't really matter," are frequently made statements.

I know some adults who out of interest for their children's development undertook to help them with their dreams and became interested in reviving or developing their own. We, as human beings, use so little of our potential. I hope you don't let your dreams die. If you have, see if you can rekindle past cherished dreams or invent new ones. See what you can do to realize them by literally sitting and talking and sharing them with your family members and asking for their help.

15 Family Engineering

Things don't just happen by themselves—in a family, or anywhere else. Some guidance is necessary. So in this chapter we're going to talk about family engineering. It isn't too different from engineering anywhere else in that a family, like a business, has time, space, equipment, and people to get its work done. With any kind of engineering, you find out what you have, match it with what you need, and figure out the best way to use it. You also find out what you don't have and figure out a way to get it.

Each family member at a point in time has his time, his space, his body, his ability to think, feel, and talk, his arms and legs and ability to move, his physical and emotional energy, his talent, his competence, his past experience, and his material possessions. These are the raw materials that families have to meet the mechanical problems of living. Planning how to use these resources is what I am calling family engineering.

One of the most frequent complaints I hear is that family members have too many things to do, too many demands, and too little time to do anything.

Maybe some of this burden is related to inefficient ways of carrying out your family engineering.

All right. In order to make the most of what everyone possesses, first you have to know what is there. Asking the question, "What are you now capable of?" (asked in a leveling way) will usually give you the answer. Many people guess at this and never check. Some go by age. If you are seven, you can help Daddy in the garage. If you are five, you're too young to help. Maybe Johnny, who is five, is really more capable than Harry, who is seven. Some families decide what they have by sex: "If you are a woman, you couldn't possibly . . . " or, "If you are a man, you would never . . . "

I feel that so many of the abilities of family members—especially children—are wasted. Children are not supposed "to be able to" so their abilities are never really discovered.

There would be far fewer harried mothers and fathers if children were allowed and encouraged to use themselves more fully in the family and at an earlier age. One of the most rewarding individual experiences for any human being is to be productive. You'll never find out how productive your kids are or can be unless you ask them and give them a chance to show what they can do.

How do you use four-year-old Johnny's ability to move fast? Maybe you can use him as an errand boy when you are working in the tool shed. How do you use seven-year-old Alice's ability at quick addition? Why not let her help you keep the household accounts straight?

We all know that families live in different kinds of settings. Some live in big houses, some in little, some with lots of equipment, others with very little. Incomes can range from $100 a month to $50,000 a month, and the number of family members can vary from three to as high as seventeen or eighteen.

Given the same house, number of family members, income, and the same labor-saving devices, some people will feel their needs are met and some will not. Using one's resources at a moment in time is also related to what one knows about his resources, how he feels about himself and about the ones he lives with. Put another way, the fate of the engineering department depends as much on the pot of the individuals, the family rules, the communication, and family system as it does on the engineering plans and the things to be engineered.

Let's take a literal look at the job situation first. Family jobs are frequently thought of as chores. Although necessary, these jobs are often thought of as negative, the "somebody has to do it" kind of thing. It is still true that these chores form a major part of the family business.

I would like to have you do something now that is similar to what you did in the Rules chapter. All of you sit down and make a list of all the jobs that your family has to do to make your family function. Appoint a secretary, as before. In your list you will include such things as clothes washing, ironing, cooking, shopping, cleaning, keeping accounts, paying bills, working at outside jobs, and so on. If you have pets or a garden or lawn, you will need to include these, too. If a family member needs special care, you will have to include that. These are the kinds of basic jobs that have to be undertaken regularly, if not every day.

Now consult your list and see how these tasks are now being carried out in your family. You will learn something about your whole job as you do this. Perhaps you have never sat down and looked at your family picture in this way.

Are you finding out that not all the necessary tasks are getting done? Maybe you'll discover that they are done poorly or that too many tasks fall on one person and too few on others. If any of these things are true, someone in your family is being cheated and/or feeling frustrated.

I find that this simple exercise done about every three months helps to keep a perspective in the family's engineering department. In business, this is where the efficiency expert comes in. Your list and what you do about it can become your guide to your own family efficiency.

It's not as easy as it sounds, however. Once you arrive at what needs to be done, choosing the best plan and the best person to get the job done is the next step and often the most difficult one.

How do you decide who should or can do what and when?

Most families find that different methods have to be used at different times.

There is what I call the edict method, where a parent

finds he has to use his authority as the leader and simply order what is to be done. "This is how it will be, and that is that!"

Sometimes it is more fitting to use the voting method, the democratic way, in which the majority reaches the decision. "How many want to do this?"

Other times, what I call the adventure method works out the best. In this rather freewheeling method everyone states his views, and these are all tested against reality to see what's really possible.

Still other times seem to require the expediency method. We all know this one. Whoever is available gets stuck.

All these methods fit some situations. What is important is to choose the method that best fits the particular situation, which in turn requires flexibility and freedom.

The word to watch out for is *always*. Too many families *always* use edict, *always* vote, and so on. And if *always* is lurking around your family engineering, somebody's getting strangled, and you will also find yourselves in the well-known unenviable rut.

Parents have to be able to say "yes" or "no" firmly about permissions to do things, at times. They also need the skill to ask, at times, "Well, what do you want to do?" Sometimes they'll need the insight to recognize a situation where they'll say, "This is something you'll have to figure out for yourself."

I know some families, for instance, where the parents never decide anything—it's always "for the children." Still other families have no leadership at all. They sit for long hours in judgment on everything—even as to whether or not Father should wear white shirts to the office. Other families are ruled solely by parental edict. Again, we have to fall back on judgment—knowing when to do what. Nothing about any of this is easy.

Families really ask for trouble when they always assign the same job to the same person. John always carries out the trash. Teresa always washes the dishes. Mother always does the shopping. Varying job assignments can do a lot toward minimizing the "chore" aspect of family functioning.

Another trap is that a plan, once made, is expected to stay in force forever. An example of this is a child is "supposed" to be in bed by 8:30 no matter what—or whether he is four or fourteen. This also exemplifies an out-of-date rule as far as the fourteen-year-old is concerned.

It's necessary to recognize that as a family grows, the resources of both children and parents also grow. Families go through phases. When it is young with, say, all of the children under five, the engineering in terms of using resources of everyone is different from when the children are five and twelve or twelve and sixteen or sixteen and twenty. It is very hard to make decisions, I know, and I also know how tempting it is to look hard for the "one right way" and then use that forever. I believe that well worked out plans should have a specific life, say, one week, one month, one year, until 3:30 today, when Mother gets back, or when you are three inches taller.

When a family is very young and the child is not yet old enough to walk, some adult has to be his legs and pack him around. As soon as he can use his own legs, he can walk there by himself, and should. The wise parent takes advantage of using each evidence of growth in the child. The child can then do things by himself and help with other tasks. One of the problems is to not let this evidence of growth get lopsided. When a child firsts starts to walk, he may walk slower than the parent is willing to put up with. The adult might be tempted to pick him up and stride off when the kid could really do it alone.

Here's another example. By the time you reach ten (and very possibly before) you could probably easily iron your own clothes. You certainly can help with the washing. With the washing machines of today, a child of six could probably run the machine. The creative family makes use of all of these hands and arms and legs and brains, as soon as they are available, in the interests of both themselves and of the family.

Many children have told me that they think there is some kind of a plot by the adults to shove all the dirty jobs on them and keep all the pleasant jobs for themselves. Maybe there is something to this. No matter who is stuck with the drudge jobs, there can be creative, humorous, light ways to make fun out of work. If not, you can at least feel a sense of accomplishment. Whoever has the dull jobs just shouldn't be asked to look happy while doing them.

Over and over again I make the plea for flexibility and variation. The engineering in a family goes a long way toward providing each family member with some concrete evidence of his value. Every person needs a feeling of *mattering*, of *counting*, as well as a feeling of contributing to what is going on. A little child, who can see himself as someone who matters, gets it from feeling that someone is requiring some of his contributions and that his contributions are honestly heard, are being considered, and are really being tried out.

Now I think we need to talk about *family time* for a bit. We all have twenty-four sixty-minute clock-hours available to us every day. But we work, we go to school, and we have many other activities that take this literal time from the family. How much family time does your family have? How much of it do you use for family chores?

Some families use so much of their time for family *business* that they have no time left to enjoy one another. When this happens, family members can get to feeling that the family is a place where they are burdened and the engineering begins to deteriorate. Here's a way to avoid this.

Go over your job list and ask yourself two questions. Is this job really necessary? If it is, could it be done more efficiently?

You may find that when you ruthlessly look at *why* you are doing your present job, you'll just find that it was "always done," and it really serves no purpose whatsoever.

This brings us to *priorities*. If the problem in your family is that family business squeezes out time for family members to enjoy one another, then I think you need to look carefully at your priorities.

I recommend that you start with the bare bones of what is necessary. Select those jobs that make the difference between life and death—the survival needs. Then, as time permits, other less pressing jobs can get done. Of course, this requires that you feel free to change your priorities. To bring that into focus I'm asking you to divide your family business into two categories: now *and* later. *Obviously, the essential* now *category has the highest priority. How many family items of business do you have in this category? If there are more than five items, there are too many. You may find that each day differs in terms of what may be in the specific categories.*

The second category, "It would be nice and could be done later," can be woven in as the situation permits.

Now let's take a look at how you spend the rest of your family time.

How much time is available in your family for contact with individual family members? Of the time spent in this contact, how much of it is pleasant and leads to enjoyment? When a large amount of contact becomes unpleasant, there is trouble. My experience is that in many families, by the time people get their "work" done, the actual time spent with each member of the family that yields any enjoyment is very little, all of which makes it much easier to look on your family members as burdensome and uncaring.

Every person needs time to be alone. One of the anguished cries I hear from family members is the cry to have some time for oneself. In families, mothers particularly get to feeling guilty if they wish to have time alone. They feel as if they are taking something away from the family.

This family time needs to be divided into three parts: Time for each person to be alone (self time); Time for each person to be with each other person (pair time); Time when everyone is together (group time).

It would be great if every family member could have some of each of these kinds of time every day. Making this possible first requires being aware that it is necessary, and second, finding ways to do it.

There are some extra special factors that influence the use of family time in certain families.

Some have to break down their time in terms of the way they make their livings. Firemen or policemen are examples. Firemen are on twenty-four hours, and off twenty-four hours. Policemen change shifts regularly. There are people who work on night shifts, such as in transportaion facilities, where airline tickets agents have to work around the clock.

Most of our society is related to business going on between approximately eight in the morning and six in the evening. Most families are geared this way, too. This means that people who work at odd hours have to invent new ways to participate in their share of family planning and family business.

There are many families where the father travels for long periods of time. There are whole hosts of men who leave home on Sunday and return on Friday. This arrangement puts a great strain on the family unit, unless a superb system of communication is worked out, and the greatest contact use is made of the time when the man is at home. Otherwise this arrangement throws extraordinary weight on the one left at home, decreasing her opportunity for self time, and sometimes leading to "balm" in alcohol, extramarital affairs, overindulgence or overstrictness with the children.

Naturally, the size of the family makes a difference. The bigger the family, the more complicated the engineering becomes.

In an effort to help families take a look at this particular aspect of engineering, I have done what I call a time presence inventory (*where* are you *when?*). I ask each person to keep track for one day where he is at certain points in time. Choose two days, one a weekday, and one a weekend day.

Take a sheet of paper for each family member, and divide it up according to the hours in the day, starting when the first person gets out of bed and going on until the hour that the last person goes to bed.

If the first person gets up at 5:30 A.M. and the last one goes to bed at 12:00 A.M., your sheets would be divided as follows:

5:30 A.M.	12:30 P.M.	7:30 P.M.
6:30 A.M.	1:30 P.M.	8:30 P.M.
7:30 A.M.	2:30 P.M.	9:30 P.M.
8:30 A.M.	3:30 P.M.	10:30 P.M.
9:30 A.M.	4:30 P.M.	11:30 P.M.
10:30 A.M.	5:30 P.M.	12:00 A.M.
11:30 A.M.	6:30 P.M.	

Each member fills this out according to where he was at the different times of his day. At the end of the day, one person puts these all together, showing very dramatically what opportunities each person had for self time, pair time, or group time.

I remember one woman saying after we had done her inventory, "My God, no wonder I feel lonely! I never see anyone but the cat!" (She had a very active family.)

I found that it was indeed unusual to find more than twenty minutes a day when all the family members were together in group time. Twenty minutes to an hour a week was more like it. This means that all the burden of transacting family business would have to be done in twenty minutes, usually during meal time. That means that in twenty minutes everybody has to eat, transact whatever past or future business has to be done with one another, and take care of what comes up during that time, such as phone calls, people dropping in, or Junior falling off his chair. That's a big load to put on twenty minutes, and an even bigger load for people to expect themselves to grow in their knowledge, awareness, and enjoyment of one another in that tiny segment of time. Of course, people in families are transacting business all the time, whether they are together or not.

You can probably readily see that if a family transacts family business without all members present, chances for misunderstanding are greatly multiplied. From time to time, of course, this does happen, However, when it does, problems are minimized if someone is responsible for carefully noting what is going on so that a clear report can be given to the absent member. For example, "Last night when you were babysitting, Mother told us she is now going to work full time. We wanted you to know so you could start thinking about how this will affect you."

Once family members realize how important it is for all family members to be kept informed about all family business, then they make a practice of seeing who is absent when they are talking about important business, and then work out ways for the information to be given to the absent member. There are different ways to do this. Nominate a reporter. Someone can write a note. This kind of thing goes a long way toward filling in the "I didn't know," and cutting down on the "They do things behind my back." You have to remember that this is only a substitute for being there in person. But it does help. If trust among family members has slipped badly, it will be better to try to transact business only when all members are present, at least until new trust has been built up.

If the family habitually transacts business without all members present, and also has little pair time, then family members get to know each other through a third person. I call it *acquaintanceship by rumor*. The problem is that most people forget about the rumor part and treat whatever it is as fact.

For instance, husbands often learn from their wives how their children are, and vice versa. One child may tell a parent how another child is. In a family, regardless of whether or not one actually experiences the other or not, everyone thinks he knows the others. How many children know their fathers through their own experiences with them? How many children get to know their fathers through their mother's eyes? You can see what a dangerous practice this could be. It becomes something like that old parlor game, "Gossip," where someone whispers something in the ear of the person next to him, and it gets passed all around a circle of people. When the last person reports what he heard, it is nearly always totally different from what was originally said.

Yet this is the kind of communication that often goes on in families—*communication by rumor*. When families do not provide group time to transact family business, this is the best that can happen, if nothing else is done. In troubled families, this kind of communication is very frequent. There is no substitute for checking out your own perceptions and facts for yourself and hearing and seeing for yourself.

This has an effect on how well the engineering is working. For instance, a wife announces to her husband that their son, John, who is not present, did not cut the lawn today. "Do something about it. You are the father." He may feel called upon to discipline to make his wife feel better. He will probably, unless he is very aware, discipline without information.

Having group time, of course, is no guarantee that family business will be effectively transacted. When you are together as a group, what happens? What do you talk about? Does most of what you talk about concern faults of other persons, lectures by one or more members to other members on how things should be? Is the time taken up with long recitals of aches and pains of one person? Is there silence? No talking? Are people perched on their chairs waiting for a chance to get out?

One of the best ways to find out about this is to make a tape recording (video tape is even better, but I know that it is hardly standard equipment in most homes) of your family and then listen to it. If you don't have a tape recorder, ask each family member to take a turn, observe what goes on and report back. Another way to do this is to ask a trusted friend to take over this duty. This can be an extremely revealing exercise, and will point out to you how easy it is for us to be unaware of how our family process is taking place.

Do you find that you use this time to get reacquainted with your family members, getting in touch with what life is like for each now and maybe what is was like this day? Is this a time when the individual joys and puzzles as well as the failures, pains, and hurts can come out and they can be listened to? Is this used to talk about new plans, present crises, and so on? Few families realize that every day they, as a group, go through a splitting up and a reconciliation process. They leave each other and come back together. While they are apart, life goes on for them. Getting together at the end of the day provides an opportunity for sharing what happened in the world "out there" and renewing their contact with each other. Dinner time could be this time.

A typical kind of day in many families could be something like this.

The father gets up at, say, 6:30. He shaves and showers and then comes to the kitchen, where his wife had put out the coffee the night before. He may grab some cereal, and when he's ready to leave the house, he awakens his wife who then gets up about 7:15 because she has to make some breakfast for the six-year-old who has to leave on the 8:00 bus. In the meantime, the fourteen-year-old boy got up early and is out doing some running practice around the block. He will leave for school at 8:30. Between 7:15, when Mother gets up, and 8:30, when the oldest son leaves, the middle child, who is a girl, age twelve, spends the time in the bathroom getting herself ready. She pops in just as her little brother starts his breakfast at the far end of the table. She hasn't quite finished her homework from the night before, so she sits at the other end of the table. They both take the same bus. She's quiet, and he's busy thinking about what's going to happen in school that day. Mother is busy in the kitchen urging the children to eat because she's watching the clock and is afraid that the children will be late. Finally, the girl gets off, giving her mother a little peck on the cheek, and the son says, "Good bye, Ma." Each sits with his special friend on the bus. Maybe a few minutes after this, Mother leaves for her part-time job. Everyone has gone now.

In a few hours, the family members will start returning. The six-year-old will come home at 2:30 in the afternoon, when he will go over to the neighbor's as Mother isn't home until 3:00. Mother comes home at 3:00 and calls the neighbor who tells her her son is there. Then she gets busy with some laundry that she knew had to be done. After all, her husband needs some more shirts, and the children need underwear. The twelve-year-old girl is going to be at a Girl Scout meeting that day; the fourteen-year-old is going to have some kind of athletic practice. At 6:00 when the husband comes home, the six-year-old is back from play, the twelve-year-old is out with the Girl Scouts, the fourteen-year-old will come in later at 7:30. Wife, husband, and six-year-old all have dinner with the time hurried and most of the conversation spent on talk about which bill should be paid first. Then Father has his poker night that night, and he goes out. Then the fourteen-year-old comes home before his father and is alseep when he comes in. Father goes for a whole day without seeing his children. This could add up to several days. Although he is busy, he is interested in his children and might ask his wife how the children were. Of course she doesn't really know too much about it either—she's seen them here and there. Depending upon how she feels, she'll tell him what she thinks. What she says might depend more upon her pot than her experiences or her observation. Many, many days can go on like this.

Such days form a continual parade of half contacts. It is easy to lose track of people and the relationships. The separation is rather continual and prolonged. The reconciliation never comes about.

I have worked with families where there was no reconciliation until they all came together as a family in my office.

It is wise to get together at least once a day for every-once to touch base with each other. In the busy lives that most of us lead, *this kind of meeting needs to be planned.* It cannot be left to chance.

It is also very easy for the engineering to get overwhelming in this case. Families in this spot know that they live together in one house, but they really do not have much real experience with one another.

After seeing many thousands of these family time inventories, I believe that the idea that families live together is more illusion than reality. This helped me a great deal to understand much of the pain I encountered in families. This kind of living paves the way for all kinds of distortions about how things really are in the family. Making the time presence inventory is a first step to making clear how much of your idea of your family is an illusion and how much is real. I made up another saying: "That what you don't know is reality, and what you make up is fantasy." By a little planning, once one knows what the problem is, one can make the opportunities to really contact the members of his family. Maybe you can make some changes here, too.

There is another aspect to time that plays a big part in how well the engineering works. This has to do with how each person experiences time as well as how he experiences time differently in terms of what is happening. For instance, if you're excited about something that's coming up and you're anticipating it, the time seems often to drag. When you are busy and involved with something you particularly like, the time flies by. There is by no means a direct relationship of the experience of clock time to the experience of self time. Five minutes can seem like an hour, or it can seem like a minute. How different family members experience time has a relationship to how things get done.

Experiencing time is an important part of predicting time. Predicting time is basic to carrying out commitments and directions. I know many people who get into all kinds of difficulties with each other because one is late. The immediate assumption that the late one just wanted to bug the other isn't necessarily the case.

Little attention is paid to the individual's experience and his management of time as part of the problem. "If you loved me, you would be on time. If you were not so stupid, you would be ready." We've talked about blackmail before, and this is one form of it.

Children are constantly being criticized for being late. And a lot of families try to deal with this tardiness in their children by punishment rather than teaching.

When you come into the world, you know nothing about how to predict your time. This is something that is learned slowly over a long period. I think that learning about and using time is one of the most complicated kinds of learning in existence. Many adults still have difficulty with it. For a moment, just think of all the factors that have to be considered by anyone who at 8:00 A.M. says, "at 5:30 to-night I will be at such and such a place," which might be twenty-five miles away. There is a constant process of select-ing, rejecting, and managing all through the day with whatever comes up so that he can be on time. How can he finish the demands of his day on time? Can he gauge the transportation circumstances? What allowances have been made for inter-ruptions? Handling himself so that he can know enough about how this day can go or will go, so that at 8:00 A.M. he can assure you and himself that he can arrive there at 5:30 P.M. is really quite a miracle, if you think about it.

Think about yourself and your relation to time. Go back and look at your family's time inventory. If the com-plexity of the use of time were more widely understood, there would be more understanding and less blame. I would be willing to wager that in a great many families, children are asked to handle time in a way that the adults can't do.

Many homemakers get in trouble here. They agree to have the dinner ready at 5:30 P.M. As they go through the day, somebody calls up, or somebody comes to visit. They see some-thing that needs cleaning, they get engrossed in a book. Sud-denly they realize it is 5:30, and they are not ready—no supper. This creates situations that cause irritation. This woman might also be called bad names like "lazy" and "irresponsible."

The way that each person experiences time is related to his awareness, his motivation, his knowledge, and his interests; it is an aspect of his uniqueness. Getting ac-quainted with how each person uses time is an important factor in every relationship—no two people use it in exactly the same way.

If time schedules can be used more as desirable guides rather than as evidences of good character we might come a little closer to eliminating some of the problems that come out of it. After traveling over a million and a half air miles I find that even the airplane that is scheduled to depart at 3:47 sometimes doesn't leave until 8:10 A.M. or P.M. I have developed a guide for myself, which goes like this: I will use the best judgment I have in making a time commitment. Then I will do the best I can to meet it. If it turns out that things don't work out so I can keep it and I can't change them, I don't bug myself. I was brought up on the sacredness of *being on time*. If I were not, I would be punished, so no matter what, I *had* to be on time. The result was, of course, that I was frequently late. Now with my current guide, things flow. I am rarely late. I don't fight with me anymore.

Without our knowing it, the clock runs many of our lives. Instead of it's being our aid, it becomes our master. Our attitudes about time greatly influence our effectiveness in getting the job done.

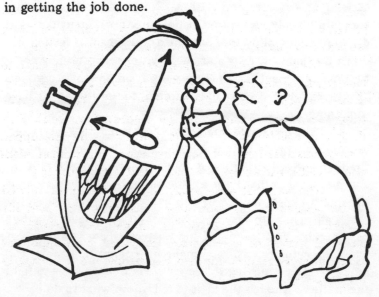

For instance, many people follow a plan of rigid eating times. That means that at a certain clock time, everybody is expected to be at the table, the cook is expected to manage in such a way so that the food is there. It may be that at that time everyone may not be hungry. It might cause difficulties if the person who cooked feels that unless people eat heartily of her food at that moment, they don't love her. I know that happens frequently. So, in order not to offend the cook, the person eats and grows fat or vomits when he can. Not eating has nothing to do with loving the cook, but has to do with where that person is in terms of his stomach. I am not necessarily making a plea for people to eat or not eat. What is important to me is that people do what fits for them—if they're not very hungry, then they don't have to eat very much. If they're hungry, they can eat more. Clock time and self time do not always coincide.

It's rare that any two people are at exactly the same point at the same time. This goes for sex as well as food, and certainly for desires and wishes. I have noticed that when people are really aware that people are in different places at different times, allowances are made. Instead of feeling put down by this fact, they start negotiations, and usually come to some agreement. This may not always represent everyone's "druthers," but a chance is offered for everyone to have something.

I know a couple where the wife is sometimes interested in going shopping in the evening. Her husband might be tired, and would rather not go out. She tells him of her wish, and he responds that he is a little tired, but he'd go along if she didn't expect him to be too exciting. If she replies that that's all right with her, then later the two of them might go to a movie. His feeling of having participated in terms of where he actually was, may make his energy flow more, and he can end up enjoying the movie. He doesn't have to fight the battle of who has the right to tell whom what to do.

The idea that *you* are to be where *I* am is a very costly one. In contrast, if this gal said to her husband, "I want to go shopping, and you'd better take me because you're my husband." He, in order to avoid a quarrel, goes but will feel very stiff and will not be a good companion. Then she can feel "put upon," and the battle is on. If we waited for everybody to be exactly at the same point in time as everyone else, we might wait forever. If we require that other people be where we are, we run the danger of developing interpersonal difficulty. If we ask where people are and tell them where we are and then enter into some kind of negotiations accepting what really is the current reality, something better can evolve.

The question then becomes, how can each person let the other one know, and how can they then find a place for each other so that both benefit?

Every member of the family needs to count on some space and some place that he can call his own, where he is free of invasion from anybody else, whether it is little or big doesn't matter, just so it is his own. It is easier to respect and value your place, if I have one, and it is respected and valued by you. To be able to feel I have a place, literally a place that's assured, has the meaning of "I count." Not having this assurance often leads to the attitude, "I don't care. So what. What difference does it make? I clean up the kitchen, and you mess it all up."

How many times, for instance, have you heard bitter comment from one child about how another child has taken some of his things or has invaded his space? Or have you heard a father (perhaps yours) yelling because a tool was taken out of his place for it?

The same is true for a woman working in the kitchen, who is looking for something somebody else took and didn't put back. I've heard similar complaints from older brothers and sisters. Just let yourself imagine how you feel if you worry about someone stealing your things.

This leads to having places where clothes are put and kept. Being able to count on managing your own things and participating in the decision about how and when your things will be used by others is a very important aspect for a person to feel that he counts. This makes it more possible to feel that he can count on others. Material possessions are not always easy to come by. They need care. The use of things often reflects the feeling of self-worth; I care about myself, and I care about my things; I care about you; I care about your things. There needs to be a clear message of ownership which, I believe, is related to privacy and to caring about belongings.

I think that a clear reliable experience in ownership paves the way for eventual sharing because it is a message of self-worth and removes the fears about sharing. I think that a child needs to know crystal clearly, "This is mine and I can do what I want with it." Some parents buy one child a toy, for instance, with the expectation that he will share his toy with another child. Then they get upset because the sharing doesn't work. If the toy is to be a house toy—a shared toy—then it should be so designated. Very often the failure comes because the assurance of privacy and ownership has not been established. I believe sharing is a good thing to teach. Sharing is another one of those complicated learnings that take a long time to fully grasp. Sharing can only be done if there is trust. I think that parents often ask children to share before they know how to, and then punish them for bad results. In these same families, I often see no evidence that the adults have learned to share successfully.

Sharing, to me, is the decision by one person to let another person in to his belongings, to his time, to his thoughts, to his space.

By the way, I have nothing against shared toys, but I think it should be clear which are "house toys" and what are individual toys that *can* be shared. How many times have these shared toys been strewn all over the living room, and when the parent calls, "Pickup time!" every kid says, "That's not *my* toy." I think there is something to be learned here. Why not make it a house toy, and loan it out for the day? For that day, you have the pleasure of it and the responsibility for it. Many people try to teach sharing without the trust and feeling of worth that go with it.

Perhaps at this point, you may now have done the necessary work that has enabled you to have a crystal clear, firm list of the jobs it takes to make your family run.

You may have come to some new awareness about your priorities. There would be no engineering necessary if there weren't people. Engineering is necessary only because it can make the lives of people better. If it makes the lives worse, then you need new engineering.

Through what I have asked you to focus on in this chapter, you may now have more ideas about how you can be less burdened and more hopeful.

What ties the whole engineering aspect together is an efficient, well-understood information system, which operates in a context of trust and humanness.

16 The Extended Family

Everybody has heard the old saw, "You can pick your friends, but you're stuck with your relatives." Yet relatives—in-laws, grandparents, aunts, uncles, nieces, nephews—are all people who are related legally and by blood to one another. They are *there* by the nature of things, and no amount of wishing will make them go away.

What I think is so sad is that most of us are introduced to our relatives when we're babies, and so we never get to know them *as people*. We feel we are simply "stuck" with them, and we don't allow ourselves to enjoy them.

Do you enjoy your in-laws, grandparents, grandchildren, nieces, or nephews? If you do, then you can treat them as real people, sharing criticisms, doubt, pain, and your love. Maybe it is the other way around, too: if you treat your relatives as real people, then maybe you can enjoy them.

There are some parts of all people that can be enjoyed at a given point in time. Who on earth ever said that all parts of every person are enjoyable all the time?

If, in this chapter, I can get over to you the importance and possible joys of getting to know your relatives and in-laws *as people*, then I will have achieved my goal.

What happens many times is that we meet our relatives after we have been conditioned by someone else's opinions. It is common, for example, for husbands and wives to have conversations such as the following:

"Your father is a tightwad."

"Your father is just wishy-washy. He does everything your mother tells him to do."

"Your mother is never going to baby-sit my children."

"My mother just loves *her* grandchildren."

There may be even direct comments such as:

"Be careful of your language when your grandmother is around."

It is easy to see how children get stereotyped ideas of

their relatives. Before ever trying to get to know them, they are presented as saints, devils, burdens, or nothings. Each child begins seeing his grandparents through the eyes of his parents, and this presents some pretty serious handicaps in ever trying to see them as human beings.

Heaven only knows there are plenty of traps that exist among relatives. In some cases there is virtual war, in other cases, simply avoidance. Some try to handle an existing problem by estranging themselves. I hear people say, "I wish my children could know their grandparents. I feel bad about that sometimes. But it is so painful to go visit them."

Or, "My mother is always spoiling the kids, and I don't want them spoiled."

Or, "My father shows partiality to my son and ignores my daughter." Or vice versa.

You have probably heard these and undoubtedly many more like them. When I hear these kinds of things, I hear them as extensions of what hasn't been worked out in terms of the person's feelings about himself. Also, he not only doesn't consider the adults in his family as people, but he has the person confused with the role. This is a very common failing.

Husbands and wives do this kind of thing to their parents, too, by labeling them "the old people." Once you hang a label on someone ("old," "auntie," "grandpa," whatever), you stop thinking of him as a person. Such labels form a large part of the atmosphere in which the extended family finds itself. The generation gap, then, exists as much between parents and grandparents as it does between parents and children. I define the generation gap as an area of strangeness that has not yet been bridged.

On the other hand, if the spouses have become peers to their parents, then all of them can be people together, with each treated as a unique, valued person. Each has respect for one another's privacy, with the ability to enjoy what is enjoyable about one another and the capability of trying to change a part of life that may not be so enjoyable. These people take the *people* point of view instead of the *role* point of view. The husbands and wives of today are the grandparents of twenty years from now. The children of today are the husbands and wives of tomorrow, and the grandparents thirty or forty years in the future. They grow older and take on other roles as they mature. But throughout all this it is *Jane* who is a wife, *Jane* who is a mother, and *Jane* who is a grandmother. What I am trying to say is that husband-wife, parent-child, grandparent-grandchild are names of roles that people assume at different points as they go through life. The roles have two parts: the description of who is related to whom, and how this particular role is lived out. Essie Hawkins is my *grandmother* on my *father's* side, or Essie Hawkins says that Jane Sutter is her *grandchild*, the *daughter* of her *son*, Harry. When Essie and Jane meet, who are they meeting? People or roles? Roles are sterile and awesome; people are exciting.

I am trying to say something that, once realized, is pretty obvious, yet so many, many of us miss it. Underneath every role name is a personal, given name—Alice or Henry or Mary Bell or Wadsworth. Roles are like different clothes or hats one wears, depending on who is around at a moment in time.

Let me illustrate: Here is Alice Sweetworth, forty-six, who is married to Guy Sweetworth, forty-seven. They have been married twenty-six years. Alice and Guy have three children: Margaret, twenty-five, Bruce, twenty-three, and Allan, seventeen. Margaret is married to Hans, thirty. Margaret and Hans have three children. Bruce is married to Anita, also twenty-three years old, and they have one child. Let's take Guy as an example.

When he is with Alice, he calls himself husband because Alice is his wife, and they do marital things together. When he is around Margaret, Bruce, or Allan, he wears his father hat, assuming that he is doing something that fits into his idea of what fathering is all about. When he is with Hans and Anita, he is a father-in-law, doing whatever that role asks of him. When he is with Margaret's kids, he is a grandfather. Now, suppose he is in the presence of all these people. He then can put on any one of these hats. Yet I know people who, by the time they get as far as Guy in life, wear only grandfather hats. Their father-in-law, father, husband, and self parts just somehow went away.

I remember a family who came in to see me once. Ethel, the wife in the family, brought her seventy-three-year-old mother, who was introduced to me as "Grandma." I looked at her when I took her hand, and I asked her what her name was. At first she looked at me blankly, and then finally, after a few moments, said very softly, "Anita." So I said to her, "Hello, Anita." At this point the tears streamed down her face. She said it was the first time she had heard her given name in almost twenty years. Somehow seeing Anita as a person, not just a grandmother, was a very important factor in this family's opening up to some new ideas about how they could work together as people. I would like to see new meanings put into role names. Instead of the emotion we usually read into roles, I would like to see the role name as merely descriptive. Why not let whatever two people have at a point in time *be* and never mind if they're Aunt Fanny, Uncle Pete, Cousin Ella, or Baby Jane. First and foremost, these are people. I don't know of any universal behavior that means mothering, fathering, husbanding, wifing, aunting, or uncling, and I've never found anybody who did.

An important adjunct to all this is the fact that people in families almost always think that they really know one another. You know this. What parent doesn't feel he knows his child up to the time he is fourteen or fifteen? What individual doesn't think he knows his mother and father? What is actually often the case, as I hope you're beginning to see by now, is what the person knows is the *role* of the other one. The cure for this gap is for each to get acquainted with the other as persons, who change from time to time, applying the same means to get to know one another as do any two people seeking to get acquainted. Let's face it—it's quite a bit harder to do this with people to whom you are legally or by blood related because of this pesky assumption that you already know them. I have found in my many contacts with families, that family members are the most likely to be strangers to one another.

What happens so often is that family members got literally stuck with one of their roles, and then that role takes over their whole self. I am convinced that a great many of the problems among older people and other members of the family is that the oldsters' feeling about themselves is tied up in grandparenting and that's all. I might say here that we have been victims of a good deal of mythology. The myth is that if you are between the ages of birth and twenty-one, you are too young to do most things; if you're between twenty-one and forty-five, you're presumably in your right place; between forty-five and death, you're too old to do anything. Now, the interesting thing about this is that if you spend the first twenty-one years of your life being "too young to," you're really not prepared when you get in your "right place," so you can't make proper use of it. Then while you're in your "right place," you have only to look forward to being in the "wrong place," so you can't fully enjoy yourself. In just this strange way many of us go through life never feeling we're exactly in the place we ought to be.

Once we allow ourselves to see that *no matter what*

our age, we are in our right place for where we are at that point in time, and we can freely develop our feelings of worth and take joy in this phase of our development. After all, how good can you feel if you are constantly told, "You're too young to do this," or, "You're too old to do that."

My feeling is that a person starts out at birth into a new area of growth that continues until he dies, and after that, I don't know. If we were to do what is possible for us as human beings to do, we would be constantly evolving. Certainly there is a great deal of evidence now to show that the body follows the feeling of worth about oneself—the skin, bones, muscles are more related to how one feels about himself than almost any other single factor, with the possible exception of nutrition. And I might say here that almost everybody knows that people who are more prone to illness have incomplete, distorted, and undesirable images of themselves.

I'd like to put something here on family ritual and traditions, which are oftentimes one of the most troublesome areas as far as the extended family is concerned. There are many ways to use ritual. An effective use of ritual is developing some ways of doing things that reflect a certain life-style of individual families. These rituals aren't "written in blood," and they can be changed from time to time, but they do serve as indications of what is significant in the family. In a family I know there is a ritual that when each child becomes fifteen he automatically gets a watch; when each reaches sixteen he can drive a car, and so on. Another use of the ritual is that it indicates a sense of belonging—a kind of clan symbol. Further, a ritual does not have to require that everybody has to be present. Some of the worst kinds of things that happen in families are mandatory demands that every member of the family be present, let us say, at the home of the older generation for the holidays. In this way the ritual frequently becomes a *duty* when it is accompanied by a *rule*. I know some young couples who absolutely ruin their holidays because they've got to spend Christmas with the husband's parents, and they also have to spend Christmas with the wife's parents. And so they busy themselves with eating two dinners, or some other wild thing like that, and they never have a chance to develop their own autonomy as a family. Perhaps if all family members were friends to one another and related as *people* to one another, they would cherish the opportunities of getting together. Their rituals would be flexible and available; they would be together when it was possible.

To be together because it is a family requirement can be a really odious experience for most people, and very little is accomplished toward bridging any possible gaps in this way.

The young couple who feels the pull of having to go to either set of parents, and also wanting to have something of their own, experiences a terrible frustration. It would perhaps be well for the rituals be become diluted once the children have developed their own families. We all tend to do this exaggeration of the rituals, I know. I once knew a young couple who, no matter what, believed that they had to go to his mother's home every Friday night or terrible things would happen—his mother, mother-in-law, or grandmother would get a heart attack, wouldn't ever speak to them again, or they would be cut out of someone's will, or something. That's a pretty heavy price to pay for "peace in the family."

The most hurtful thing I could find out about my daughter would be that she believed she *had* to come to my home for dinner on Christmas so my feelings wouldn't be hurt. I would feel I had failed miserably in developing her as an autonomous person as well as developing the kind of communication between us of what each could do to bring joy to the other.

I think it would be fair to say, at least from all I've seen, that a large portion of things that make for difficulty where grown-up adults now have their own families are caused by adults who haven't learned to let go of the parent-child relationship with their parents. What is needed is for them to enter into a peer relationship with each other, where each respected the privacy and autonomy of the other and came together on a joyful basis.

To turn this around, I have had many people in their sixties seek my help to get their grown-up kids off their backs. "They are always bossing me around and telling me what to do." It might be a new idea to some "grown-ups" in their thirties to realize that their ideas might not be that welcome to their parents!

Many binds occur from our awareness of the loneliness of others, which we try to alleviate by frustrating ourselves. This usually results in a duty, which can turn into a burdensome chore. That is, you are my mother and I see you as lonely; you don't have any friends, you don't do anything so I don't find much joy with you because you're always complaining. But I go over to see you and sit through the visit with clenched teeth, or else I bug you with telling you what you should do and then get frustrated because you won't do it. This is something that many people attempt and pay for with their own low feeling of self-worth. A person who is grown up has to be free to say *yes* and *no* realistically and, at the same time, be able to feel he has not lost something by standing up for himself.

This leads me to another point—helping. There are many older people who, because of reasons of illness, need the help of their children. How can two people give and receive help from one another and, at the same time, feel like equals? Sometimes the effort to help ends up in the familiar old blackmail (the "clutch"). That is, "You must help me because you are my sons; I can't do anything, I'm so little and feeble." Or, "You are my father or mother and you must let me help you." Again, this kind of thing represents two people who have not yet learned to stand on their own two feet. Anyone looking around at families today can see hundreds of examples of people blackmailing one another under the guise of helplessness and helpfulness, which, again, adds up to the clutch. For parents to feel valued, useful, cared about, liked but not clutched by their children, I think, spells success for them. I think it's the same thing for the children. If they feel their parents value them, find them useful, care about them, like them. and don't clutch at them, they, too, feel that the parents are successful and they are successful as people.

There are times, of course, when people need bona fide help. But the times "help" is used to clutch are far more numerous. I can just hear some of you as you read this. "Oh my God, how could I have contact with my daughter-in-law, my son-in-law, my mother-in-law, my father-in-law, my mother, my father, my daughter, my son, because the kind of thing you're describing could never happen between us because there has never been any joy between us. My mother-in-law never wanted me to marry her son anyway. My father doesn't like my husband. My mother didn't want me to marry my wife. My mother-in-law is always wanting my husband to do things for her." And on and on. Let me just say one thing. It doesn't happen overnight, and it is not easy. It is possible. All I can say to you is that there are no people who are 100 percent one way. Do some exploring and discovering with a fresh view.

I also want to comment that I think among people there are varying degrees of how much one can enjoy others. I'm certainly not saying that everybody can enjoy everybody else equally. However, there is much work that can be done in most families once the idea is implanted in the family members' bones that all people are made up of parts and no one *has* to love the unlovable parts. Furthermore, these parts do change from time to time. I think it's possible for people to have honest, real relationships with one another and that they can live in harmony with one another. As I've said before, it is simple, but it is *not* easy. This is an important point to remember because it's so easy for children to get caught in the middle between parents and grandparents. This is an almost overwhelming spot for a child. How can he go against a grandmother with whom he has a great deal of joy when his mother is telling him that Grandmother is no good? His experience with Grandmother hasn't shown him this—his mother was talking about her relationship to her mother-in-law. Or, take the example of the grandparent who tells the child that his father is no good, when the child's loyalty and maybe even his experiences do not validate what Grandmother is saying. It is all too easy to project onto another person some of your problems, and then ask someone else to go along with you to make what you did seem right. Lots of the problems in the extended family come about from this kind of thing.

I would like to make a few comments on the people

who are now grandparents, in-laws, and who are in the process of becoming auxiliary parts of the families of their grown-up children. Many grandparents like to babysit and freely offer to do so. I've known a number of others who were grandparents who would feel uncomfortable telling their children they would not sit for them. If this kind of a bind is present, there's going to be trouble. Sometimes the life needs or the life plans of the people who are grandparents don't allow for babysitting. Sometimes grown-up children who haven't worked out a feeling of peer relationship with their own parents exploit them, and then the parents, having settled for only a grandparenting role in life, respond by feeling resentful inwardly. And sometimes the women in the family—the current mother and grandmother—do not get along, and when Grandma still sits with the children, there is really apt to be difficulty.

I see nothing wrong in extending help to your family members if it is done as a result of two people coming together to decide about the helping freely, taking into consideration the life needs of each. To exploit, "You have to do this because you're my mother," or, "You have to let me do that because I am your daughter," is to me, then, changing the whole negotiation for help into one of control—the old clutch again. And unfortunately the children are the ones who get sacrificed. As mentioned, family members frequently blackmail each other in the name of love and relationships, and I think this is one of the reasons there is so much pain in families.

Actually, when we look at it, any family is actually composed of three generations, sometimes four, and all of these generations are relating somehow and affecting each of the other generations. When I think of a family, it's hard for me to think of it without the third generation—the people who are the parents or grandparents of the current husband and wife.

Something else very interesting can happen. The current husband and wife in the family often take parental roles toward their parents, whether they like it or not, deciding what's best for them, telling them what to do, and so on This kind of thing again brings us to the whole question of whether or not this is really being helpful. I can foresee the time when families will conduct themselves so that by the time the children are grown they will be peers with their own parents, self-reliant, and autonomous instead of remaining children to them or becoming parents to them. To me, this is the end point of the bringing up of children—that they become autonomous, independent, creative people who are now peers to the people who introduced them into the world.

17 The Family in the Larger Society

Put together all the current existing families and you have society. It is as simple as that. Whatever kind of training took place in the individual family will be reflected in the kind of society that is created. And institutions such as schools, churches, businesses, and government are, by and large, extensions of family forms to non-family forms.

So. Families and societies are small and large versions of one another. They are both made up of people who have to work together, whose destinies are tied up with one another. Each features the same components—relationship of leaders to the led, the young to the old, male to female; each is involved with the process of decision-making, use of authority, and the seeking of common goals.

Some families teach individual conformity, some teach individual rebellion, some teach group responsibility, some teach *laissez-faire* by default. Every family teaches something about how to deal with the outside world; how to get along, what to do about injustice and the ugly things in the world, and how to relate to all of it.

The *laissez-faire* attitude can easily be taught by building a cocoon around the children—by guiding their steps so they won't see ugliness and injustice. In short, the children are protected from seeing any part of the seamy side of life. The world then becomes only what they know; what they have been allowed to see. Television is making this kind of protection a little more difficult. It's pretty hard to stay in a cocoon when you can look at what is going on in the world through the window of TV. However, it is still possible to discount much of this because after all, if you don't know too much about the world and haven't experienced what is going on yourself, you can say it's foreign to you and forget it. Believe it or not, I still find people in the twelve-to-eighteen age bracket who have never seen a person of a race other than their own, have never seen a poor person or a rich person, have not taken a bath in an honest-to-goodness bathtub. Thus do children in the ghettos and "high rent districts" of the cities become isolated in their own neighborhoods and in their own economic levels.

To understand fully what is going on today in terms of families and society, I think a little historical perspective might help at this point. Once upon a time, the family was the only source for teaching its members what they needed to know to make it to adulthood. This meant learning how to care for and maintain themselves, how to care for and treat others, how to treat the world of things. The available knowledge was limited, and one person—perhaps two—could know it all.

Initially the content of this learning was probably very simple. Life then was much more a matter of simple survival—how to stay alive, how to get enough to eat, how to not freeze to death or be killed by wild animals, and so on. This was relatively simple learning. All one had to do was watch and then learn for himself. Obviously many of what we consider basic needs today would have been inappropriate and even irrelevant to ancient society. Why did early man need to read and write, study proper diet, or prepare for retirement? Many more secrets about life and mankind were still locked in the unknown. Man didn't know what he didn't know.

For example, it is probably quite hard to believe that at one time man did not know that babies were the result of sexual intercourse. Sexual intercourse took place, perhaps as a response to an instinct, which led to an awareness of pleasure, but was in no way associated with the development of the child. The large belly of the pregnant woman was connected with producing babies—that was a little easier to see. The explanation of how the baby got there was not related to intercourse, but instead may have been related to what a woman ate, some thoughts she had had, or a divine or evil intervention of some kind. Once the connection between sexual intercourse and pregnancy was made, the way was open for new discoveries. I cite this to show an example of the simplicity of information then and how far we have come since. We would have to agree that informing a girl today about the intricacies of pregnancy involves a great deal more than proper diet!

It is obvious that in the complexity of our society today no family could be expected to teach everything. We have developed specialists in special institutions to take on part of the teaching process for us. And by the very wealth of our technological advancement, we have been literally forced into an age of specialization. I'm trying not to get too bogged down in specific, obvious detail, and yet not over-simplify matters, either. Let's put it this way. Because we have had to parcel out learning experiences to institutions outside the family, together with our tremendous techno-logical progress, we have lost sight of the fact that our real wealth lies in our people. The family, as things have turned out, gets what's left over after business, school, church, and government get through. These institutions (which we created ourselves to help us in peoplemaking) are actually moving against the health of the family. Schools separate children from parents, business blithely expects men to be away from home much of the time, government extracts our young men from home to fight on foreign soil.

Of course, I would like to see all institutions relate themselves to the welfare of the family. And there is no reason on earth why this couldn't happen without forfeiting the goals of the institution.

But, I'm afraid we are a power- and thing-oriented society. And our families have become accustomed to going right along with this. We teach our children how to be grabbing and powerful in order to cope in the outside world. But what happens? After you win over someone else, where are you, really? You are left with the fear that if you don't watch out, someone will win over you, and you live out your life in insecurity, guardedness, caution, and fear. Suppose you retain your power and get all you want of material things? Can these things talk to you, have arms to comfort and support you? I've never seen possessions or money that were affectionate. Nor do I think for one minute that it is a matter of either-or. That is, either we have human values and we don't have power and material things, or we are powerful and have no human values. The whole question centers around the use of power; *use* is the key word. Too often we confuse the state of powerfulness with the person. ("I am powerful, I am something; I am powerless, I am nothing.") Compare that kind of thinking with, say, my using my power for my growth, and your growth. This kind of use of power doesn't exclude human values; it enhances them.

But let's not get too far off the subject of this chapter. What we need to do is examine and recognize the relationship between family training and the development of our institutions.

I could cite hundreds of examples, but for purposes of brevity and clarity, I think the point can be made by citing just one.

Most adults in families feel that they are the best authorities to teach youngsters about discipline, sex, ways of dealing with money, and so on. Then the kids are sent off to school where a different set of adults feel that they know best how to teach in these areas. What the parents and the teachers in school teach could be quite different. Then comes the interesting questions of how these two sources of information and learning get put together for the child, and what happens to the people involved because of these differences.

I am thinking of a boy whose father is an automobile mechanic. He goes to a trade school and then frequently runs into clashes with his dad about the right way to fix cars. This kind of conflict is not just a disagreement with a perhaps old-fashioned way of car repair and new fangled trade school ideas, but it is also a reflection of the almost universal belief that there is a universal right way to do whatever is required. Some of us may realize that this is faulty reasoning, yet a good many of us go right on using it.

Let's take another example. A precocious five-year-old in a local kindergarten could read, do simple arithmetic, and was a highly creative child. Kindergarten bored him and he said so at home. His mother sent a note to the school saying that school was too boring for her son, and the teacher should make kindergarten more interesting. This child happened to be one of forty kindergarteners, one the teacher noticed was "always disruptive." The teacher sent a note to the parents saying that if they didn't do something about Johnny, she would ask him to leave. These notes happened to cross each other in the mail. Incidentally, the teacher did not know that Johnny knew how to read; the parents didn't know that Johnny was disrupting the class. Both involved people who had incomplete information, and a fight and hurt feelings were in the making. Principals in the drama were "those permissive parents" from the teacher's view and "that incompetent teacher" from the view of the parents. Johnny was sure to lose as long as this kind of thing was going on. What was needed was a feedback system, which made it possible for information to be shared by all involved.

This kind of feedback paves the way for appropriate changes because it's a dead certain fact that no one can really know everything. I certainly cannot know the full effect of what I do to you unless you tell me. And what kind of a hope does a teacher have for changing parents she has already labeled permissive? How can a parent hope to reach, let alone change, a teacher he has already labeled incompetent? In this regard the attitude of "I know that I don't know everything" is very useful. Also, remember that whenever anything happens, there are many parts to the happening, not all of them readily apparent. Get a feedback system in any area—family, institutional, or areas where the two combine in some mutual goal. Without such feedback, attack, capitulation, and indifference inevitably follow.

These are insidious and hurtful ways to lower the pot and are true deterrants to any kind of problem-solving. What they really do is build walls around people, making the misunderstandings, voids, and gaps even greater. Thus human beings who feel misunderstood and violated suffer loss of the feeling of self-worth, which, in turn, cuts down on their productivity and their joy of living. And this happens whether or not the one who misunderstands and violates is a parent, teacher, pastor, business executive, congregation member, or whatever.

All right. At this point I think it would be useful to go back to the components that society and individual families hold in common as discussed earlier in the chapter. Each has to contend with relationships between leaders and led, young and established, male and female, together with the processes of making decisions, use of authority, and the achieving of common goals.

What is happening today is that these components are being challenged in families and institutions all over the world, particularly in this country. People are beginning to recognize the common thread basic to all relationships, and they are beginning to demand that our institutions recognize it, too. This basic thread is that every leader is a person, every youngster is a person, males and females are people. Decisions, use of authority, and goal-seeking are basically personal means of getting along together.

Finally, we must all recognize that life is run with people and that what goes on among people is the chief determinant of what happens to them and the environment around them. What people know, what they believe, how they handle their differences, all are begun in the family. At this point in time, the institutions reflect the family learnings. Further, we realize that some of these learnings have been deterrents to growth, and so the time has come when we need to change the basis upon which we operate. Put in very simple terms, it will not surprise you that all this has to do with self-worth (pot)—how it is manifested, how you communicate about it, what kind of group relationships follow as a result of people with high pot, who communicate in a leveling way, who know how to be intimate, who can openly trust.

I see a need for families to ask to become partners in any institution in which any of their members are involved and to be considered as part of that establishment. The family is *the* integral unit in society. Actually the family is one of the few units where numbers of pepole are small enough so that everyone can sit in one room and can be known.

The family is also the only unit where the geographical area is small enough so real communication can take place among all participants. Rare is the family numbering over fifteen. Fifteen is a recognized, good-sized, full group. So when a group is no larger than fifteen, on the same premises, everyone can expect (within a reasonable time) to be known, heard, and seen and to know, see and hear.

Remember the family meetings we talked about many chapters ago?

Sit down with your family for the express purpose of finding out where everyone is in relation to outside institutions—school, business, church, Camp Fire, Boy Scouts, the track team, whatever.

This family meeting would be the one place where lacks, oversights, injustices, rewards, and experience by individuals could be looked at in the frame of everyone's needs and the adjustments that might have to be made. This would provide you with the feedback system we mentioned before.

So what am I actually saying to you? Start with your family. You all know about pot, communication, process; now put these powerful forces to work in your family. And when they start to function in your family, making it a more nurturing one, these same kinds of forces will be applied in society. It could even be the beginning for a new kind of society. After all, the family unit is the synthesizing link to its parent—society as a whole.

18   The Family of the Future

Before discussing what the family of the future could be like, I'd like to review a few of the deeply ingrained ideas we have, which will have to change for the family of the future.

As it is now we have only one recognized, desirable norm. One man and woman of the same race, religion, and age, of sound mind and sound body, who marry during their early or middle twenties for life and are faithful to one another for life, have their own children, raise them, retire, and die. If one loses a partner by death, he is free to seek another. Other than this, anything else will carry some kind of stigma. You know what they are. Anyone who divorces is thought of as a failure. Children born out of wedlock are "illegitimate." Anyone wanting to live with someone of his own sex is a homosexual. The many-times-married are considered neurotic and so are people of different races who want to marry. Those who want group marriage are probably sex fiends.

What if all the practices that are now going on, which we have labeled as morally bad, were instead really evidence of the great variations in human beings? In the case of the many-times-married person, perhaps there are some people whose level of interest is short and so they choose one mate after another. Instead of considering this a shortcoming, what would happen if we treated this as a simple variation? Such people could enter a limited marriage contract, say from one to five years. If the contract were not renewed at its end, then the dissolution of the marriage could take place. Perhaps the married people who have heterosexual relationships outside the marriage are not simply "adulterers," but are people with a human need. After all, polyandry and polygamy were once respected forms of marriage. And why not have a group or communal marriage? When you think about it, marriage merely legalizes a relationship between a male and female adult that entitles them to certain property and a certain guarantee against exploitation. Why does it have to be limited to just one man and one woman? If we fully trusted one another and were truly responsible, we would not be exploitive and we could share fairly.

When people are fully developed, why would they have to marry at all? Maybe it would be useful to find out exactly what you feel at a moment in time, figure out what you could handle freely and responsibly, and find the plan that fits.

Very few of the ways I have described people living together are new. If we read the literature, we will see them all referred to from time to time. I think that in a more mature society, there would be an emphasis on having as many creative ways as possible for people to enjoy their lives and make them meaningful. Human beings could be given the opportunity of writing their own contracts and not be required to enter into a contract of someone else's dictation. I see more of this coming.

As I come to the last chapter of this book, I feel more than ever that what I hope for people is possible. Sometimes I think about what would happen if on a given night, by some miracle, everyone woke up in the morning knowing, feeling, and being able to use the leveling or flowing response. It is almost too much to imagine, yet it is really possible for each of us. At this moment, I am thinking of all the places in our society where people live—families, boarding schools, prisons, hospitals—and all the places where people work that would drastically change.

Well, such a miracle will not take place. This kind of change will have to be lived through by each of us. We have to start with where we are and go from there. If any of this book made sense to you, you probably could say the same things.

Of one fact there is absolutely no question. The adult of the present stands on the shoulders of the person he learned to be in his childhood. Childhood is the time when the foundations for life are laid, and they are laid by the adults who have charge of the bringing-up process. So today is the "childhood" of the future.

Will there be families in the future? As long as all people start out in this world as infants, there will be the challenge of rearing them. And as long as there is the need to rear children, we will have the problem of developing a set of beliefs and attitudes that go with whatever it is we believe a human being is. Obviously the beliefs held by the already-grown adults will shape that new human being.

At this point in the book you are familiar with what I think are good child rearing experiences.

If, as I hope, more people feel the possibility of what it can mean to be truly and fully human, and learn how to develop ways to make this happen, the future of the family looks bright and can bring about a world that has never yet been experienced on any kind of a big scale. There are growing numbers of people who know what it feels like to feel whole, real, to love and be loved, to be productive, and to feel that the world is a better place because they are here. But their number is small in comparison to what it could be. I have a real feeling of awe and wonder when I think of what people in the future would be like if they were brought up in nurturing families who live in nurturing contexts. All we really need to do is follow the leveling response with all that it entails.

Then we would be going toward a more human development of children, with some changes in beliefs and attitudes, and with a context that permits growth for the adults while at the same time, they are master-minding the growth of their kids, This would mean that right from the beginning, children would be seen as people and treated as people. This means that they would be regarded as whole people who felt, saw, and performed in terms of their growth. They would be seen as individuals, different in totality from from every other human being. The same would hold true for their parents.

These people would be forthright, strong, tender, healthy, vigorous, attractive people who could use their intelligence to make the changes necessary in their world to keep it up-to-date. They would be able to take initiative in a constructive way, not waiting for George to do it, and then blaming him for not doing it their way.

These would obviously be people who would have integrity and ingenuity. They would not cringe at the idea of being criticized, but would seek criticism and welcome it.

They would be people who valued their bodies, who understood the body's inner workings, and who therefore would not abuse their own body or anyone else's. They would really understand their sexuality and value it as an essential and beautiful part of themselves.

These would be people who would easily be in touch with their feelings, and they would know in their guts that feeling is the key to being human.

I can see that in the hands of people like these, that the real people-problems of the world such as poverty, ignorance, social and physical abuse could finally be solved.

The nurturing family would extend the small world around a single family so that there would be opportunities for everyone.

For instance, I see families that would take other

family's children and together form a kind of commune where they have common facilities. This comes about from knowing how to make more use of a group effort so that each individual within the group could be more fully enriched. Men could have more contacts with men, women with women, and children with one another. These are not the Utopias of the past where people made a "perfect" plan of how people should behave with one another. These would be people coming together, trying to make life richer for each other and at the same time for themselves, with the kind of understanding that variation is an important adjunct to the stimulation of life.

I am convinced that many families have unnecessary loneliness because there is only one of a kind. For example, in a single family, there is only one adult female. Can she really get all that she needs to experience herself as a fully functioning woman from her wifing and her mothering role? The same is true for the adult male. What about the children, who with the exception of twins, are only ones. Human beings are social beings. The fulfilling of selfhood in a single family is extremely difficult. I think it is this coming awareness that is making the appeals to many people who are experimenting with communes and different marital structures.

We have examples of children being brought up by all kinds of people—aunts, uncles, neighbors, governesses—and in almost every instance, the quality of bringing up did not relate to the label of the person involved but to the relationship that existed between the two and the relationship to other parenting figures, and also in a secondary way, the kind of sanction that was given to this. Human beings are remarkably flexible. The range of the belief that they are capable of having is infinite. The last fifty years have brought more widespread changes in things pertaining to the family than in all the years previous to that. If the next fifty years just equal the changes of the last fifty years, then by the year 2020, the family could look quite different.

We have a great deal more information about what the nature of the human being is like on a physiological basis and much on a psychological basis.

Over the years, there have been significant new attitudes toward specific family matters. Divorce is coming to mean more of a desirable social necessity and not a personal calamity. Contraception, greater freedom to abort, family planning, fathers present at a birth of a baby, retirement, the new notion of going into second careers, open talk about sex, premarital sex, the pill, more aggressive stances of women, increased women working, changes in reducing age of adulthood to eighteen (such as getting the vote), changes in education, extended life span, all have had their place in changing things.

This seems to be by way of saying that there are already new bases for giving more worth to the human being. These changes pave the way for more changes.

In light of this, what do we seem to be heading for? A more responsible human being who can make choices; who can plan according to his needs, and not according to someone else's plan for him; someone who will recognize that there are differences concerning people as well as predictable similarities.

I think we are in the beginning of another evolution in the history of man. Probably never before have so many people been so discouraged and dissatisfied with the state of the human condition as now. Everywhere, there are huge pockets of people demanding change. The main cry seems to be for greater feelings of individual self-esteem and loving, nurturing contexts that go with it.

I think we may be seeing the beginning of the end of people relating to people through force, dictatorship, obedience, and stereotypes. If the end is too long in coming, not enough of us may be around to make any difference. I used to feel that the atom bomb would get us, but now I feel, if anything does, it will be our distrusting, unloving, inhuman relationships with one another that divide us into "haves" and "have nots," the bosses and the bossed, and consequently into gross human indignity, which many seem to have decided they will die over rather than continue to endure.

Old, traditional, entrenched, familiar human attitudes die hard. It is a question of whether the old attitudes will die and new ones be born or that civilization dies out. I am working on the side of keeping civilization going with new values about human beings.

I hope that now you are, too.

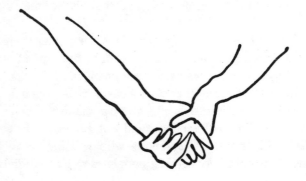